ENRIQUE'S JOURNEY

Sonia Nazario

RANDOM HOUSE
NEW YORK

B
ENRIQUE

Published in the United States by Random House, an imprint of
The Random House Publishing Group, a division of Random House, Inc.,
New York.

RANDOM HOUSE and colophon are registered trademarks of
Random House, Inc.

Portions of this work originally appeared, in different form, in the Pulitzer
Prize–winning series in the *Los Angeles Times* entitled "Enrique's Journey,"
published in 2002.

All of the photographs that appear in this work are by Pulitzer Prize–winning
photographer Don Bartletti and appeared in conjunction with the series in the
Los Angeles Times entitled "Enrique's Journey," copyright © 2002 by the *Los Angeles
Times,* and are reprinted here by permission of the *Los Angeles Times.* Don
Bartletti was awarded the Pulitzer Prize for these photographs in 2003.

Library of Congress Cataloging-in-Publication Data
Nazario, Sonia.
Enrique's journey/Sonia Nazario.
p. cm.
ISBN 1-4000-6205-5
1. Hondurans—United States—Biography.   2. Immigrant children—United
States—Biography.   3. Illegal aliens—United States—Biography.
4. Hondurans—United States—Social conditions—Case studies.   5. Immigrant
children—United States—Social conditions—Case studies.   6. Illegal aliens—
United States—Social conditions—Case studies.   7. Honduras—Emigration
and immigration—Case studies.   8. United States—Emigration and
immigration—Case studies.   I. Title.

E184.H66N397 2006
305.23'089'687283073—dc22
2005044347

Printed in the United States of America on acid-free paper

www.atrandom.com

246897531

First Edition

Book design by Lisa Sloane

To my husband, Bill

CONTENTS

MAP: ENRIQUE'S JOURNEY FROM
TEGUCIGALPA TO NUEVO LAREDO   vi

PROLOGUE   ix

1. THE BOY LEFT BEHIND   3

2. SEEKING MERCY   45

3. FACING THE BEAST   61

4. GIFTS AND FAITH   101

5. ON THE BORDER   137

6. A DARK RIVER, PERHAPS A NEW LIFE   179

7. THE GIRL LEFT BEHIND   197

AFTERWORD: WOMEN, CHILDREN,
AND THE IMMIGRATION DEBATE   241

NOTES   261

ACKNOWLEDGMENTS   289

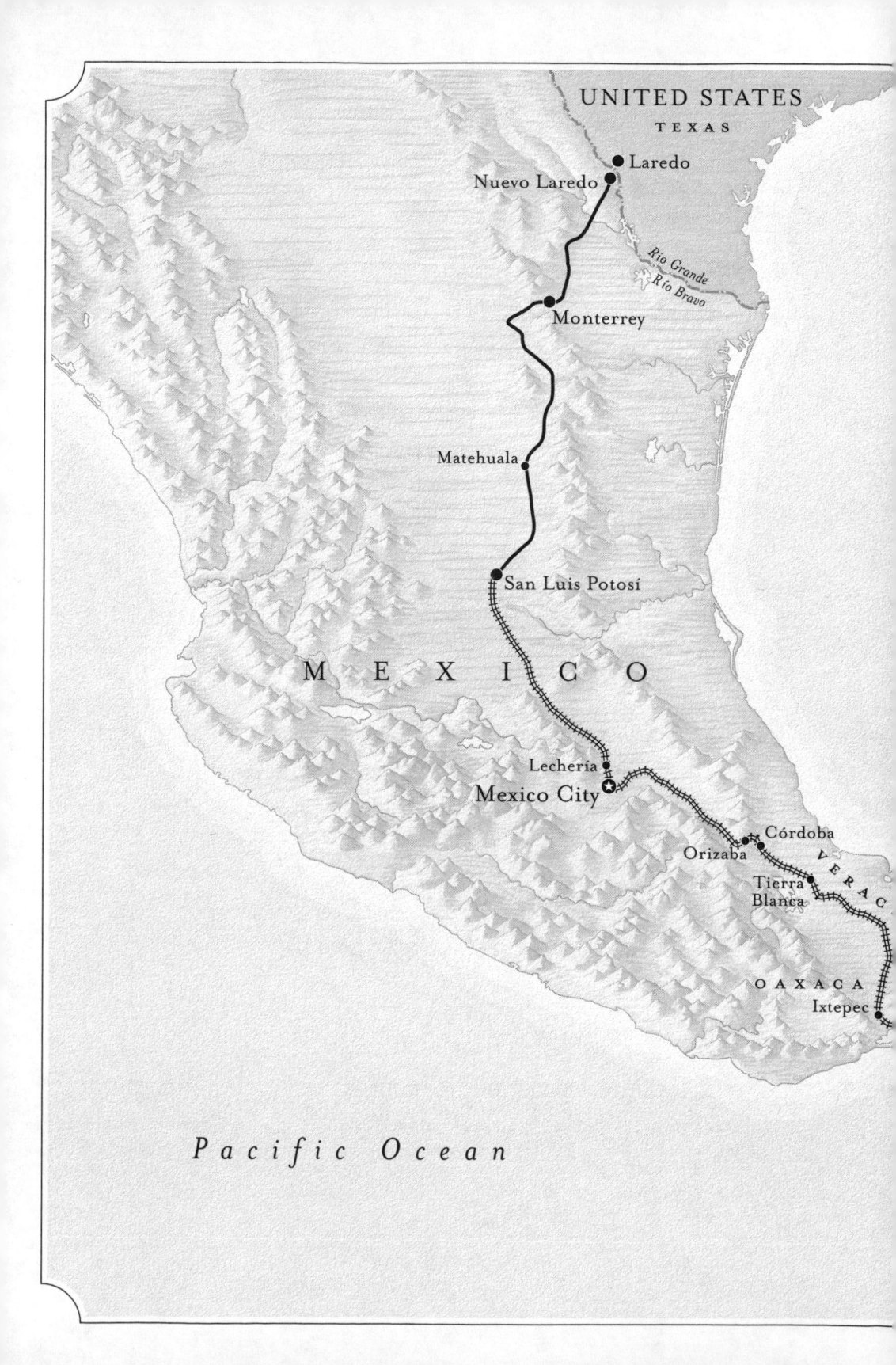

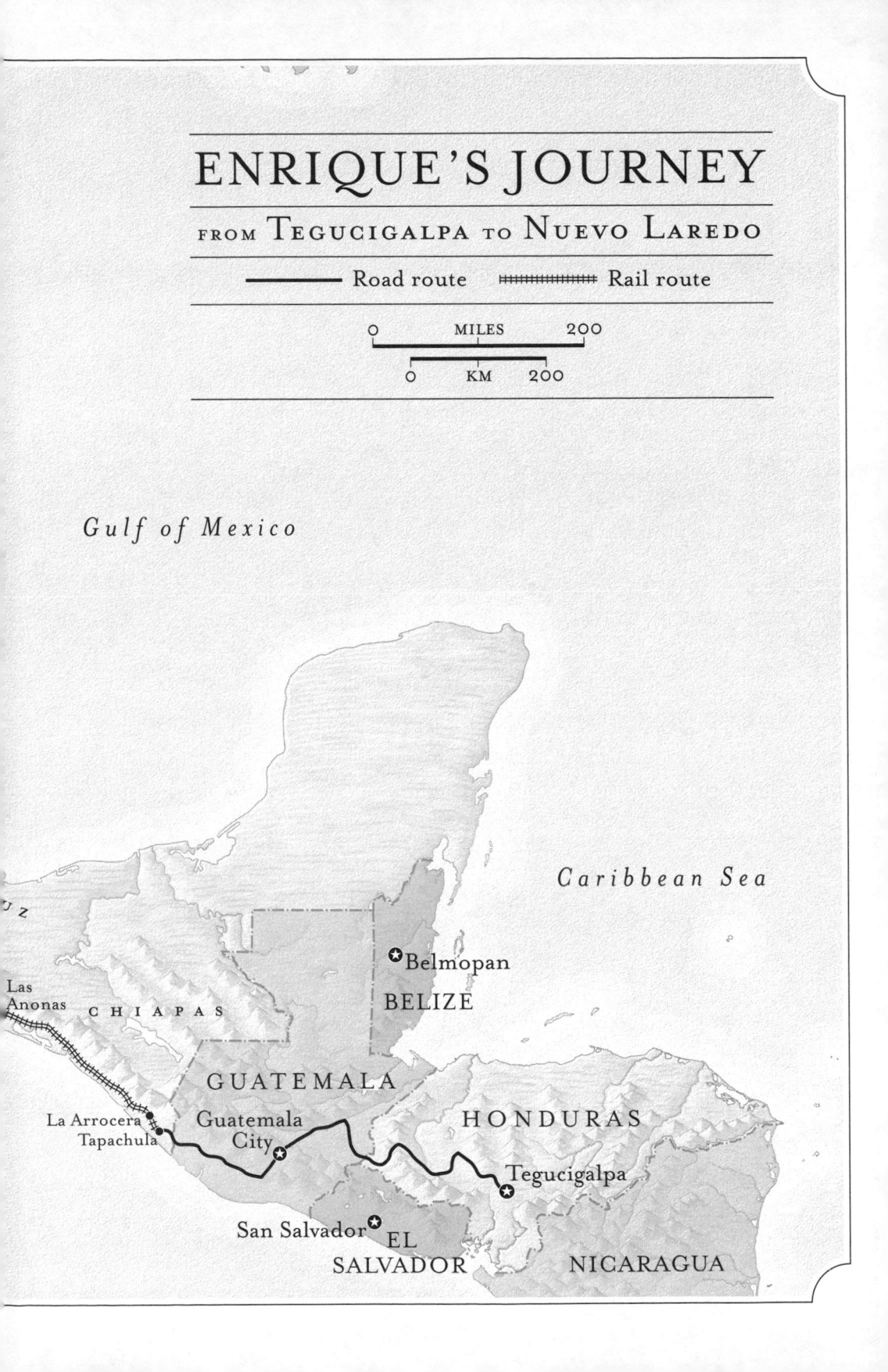

PROLOGUE

It is Friday morning, 8 A.M. I hear a key turn in the front-door lock of my Los Angeles home. María del Carmen Ferrez, who cleans my house every other week, opens the door. She walks into the kitchen.

Carmen is petite, intelligent, and works at lightning speed. At this early hour I am usually in a frenzy to get out the door and rush to my office. But on days when Carmen arrives, she and I shift gears. Carmen loiters in the kitchen, tidying things. I circle around her, picking up shoes, newspapers, socks—trying to give her a fighting chance at cleaning the floors. The ritual allows us to be in the same room and talk.

On this morning in 1997, I lean on one side of the kitchen island. Carmen leans on the other side. There is a question, she says, that she has been itching to ask. "Mrs. Sonia, are you ever going to have a baby?"

I'm not sure, I tell her. Carmen has a young son she some-times brings to watch television while she works. Does she want more children? I ask.

Carmen, always laughing and chatty, is suddenly silent. She stares awkwardly down at the kitchen counter. Then, quietly, she tells me about four other children I never knew existed. These children—two sons and two daughters—are far away, Carmen says, in Guatemala. She left them there when she ven-tured north as a single mother to work in the United States.

She has been separated from them for twelve years.

Her youngest daughter, Carmen says, was just a year old when she left. She has experienced her oldest boy, Minor, grow up by listening to the deepening timbre of his voice on the tele-phone. As Carmen unravels the story, she begins to sob.

Twelve years? I react with disbelief. How can a mother leave her children and travel more than two thousand miles away, not knowing when or if she will ever see them again? What drove her to do this?

Carmen dries her tears and explains. Her husband left her for another woman. She worked hard but didn't earn enough to feed four children. "They would ask me for food, and I didn't have it." Many nights, they went to bed without dinner. She lulled them to sleep with advice on how to quell their hunger pangs. "Sleep facedown so your stomach won't growl so much," Carmen said, gently coaxing them to turn over.

She left for the United States out of love. She hoped she could provide her children an escape from their grinding poverty, a chance to attend school beyond the sixth grade. Car-men brags about the clothes, money, and photos she sends her children.

She also acknowledges having made brutal trade-offs. She feels the distance, the lack of affection, when she talks with her children on the telephone. Day after day, as she misses mile-stones in their lives, her absence leaves deep wounds. When her oldest daughter has her first menstruation, she is frightened. She doesn't understand what is happening to her. Why, the girl asks Carmen, were you not here to explain?

Carmen hasn't been able to save enough for a smuggler to bring them to the United States. Besides, she refuses to subject her children to the dangerous journey. During her own 1985 trek north, Carmen was robbed by her smuggler, who left her without food for three days. Her daughters, she fears, will get raped along the way. Carmen balks at bringing her children into her poor, drug- and crime-infested Los Angeles neighbor-hood.

As she clicks the dishwasher on, Carmen, concerned that I might disapprove of her choice, tells me that many immigrant women in Los Angeles from Central America or Mexico are just like her—single mothers who left children behind in their home countries.

What's really incomprehensible, she adds, are middle-class or wealthy working mothers in the United States. These women, she says, could tighten their belts, stay at home, spend all their time with their children. Instead, they devote most of their waking hours and energy to careers, with little left for the children. Why, she asks, with disbelief on her face, would any-one do that?

The following year, in 1998, unannounced, Carmen's son Minor sets off to find his mother. Carmen left him when he was ten years old. He hitchhikes through Guatemala and Mexico. He begs for food along the way. He shows up on Carmen's doorstep.

He has missed his mother intensely. He could not stand an-other Christmas or birthday apart. He was tired of what he saw as his mother's excuses for why they could not be together. He had to know: Did she leave Guatemala because she never truly loved him? How else could he explain why she left?

Minor's friends in Guatemala envied the money and presents Carmen sent. "You have it all. Good clothes. Good tennis shoes," they said. Minor answered, "I'd trade it all for my mother. I never had someone to spoil me. To say: Do this, don't do that, have you eaten? You can never get the love of a mother from someone else."

Minor tells me about his perilous hitchhiking journey. He was threatened and robbed. Still, he says, he was lucky. Each year, thousands of other children going to find their mothers in the United States travel in a much more dangerous way. The children make the journey on top of Mexico's freight trains. They call it *El Tren de la Muerte*. The Train of Death.

A COMMON CHOICE

I was struck by the choice mothers face when they leave their children. How do they make such an impossible decision? Among Latinos, where family is all-important, where for women motherhood is valued far above all else, why are droves of mothers leaving their children? What would I do if I were in their shoes? Would I come to the United States, where I could earn much more money and send cash back to my children? This would mean my sons and daughters could eat more than sugar water for dinner. They could study past the third grade, maybe even finish high school, go on to university classes. Or I could stay by my children's side, relegating another generation to the same misery and poverty I knew so well.

I was also amazed by the dangerous journey these children make to try to be with their mothers. What kind of desperation, I wondered, pushes children as young as seven years old to set out, alone, through such a hostile landscape with nothing but their wits?

The United States is experiencing the largest wave of immigration in its history, a level of newcomers that is once again transforming the country. Each year, an estimated 700,000 immigrants enter the United States illegally. Since 2000, nearly a million additional immigrants annually, on average, have arrived legally, or become legal residents. This wave differs in one respect, at least, from the past. Before, when parents came to the United States and left children behind, it was typically the fathers, often Mexican guest workers called *braceros*, and they left their children with their mothers. In recent decades, the increase in divorce and family disintegration in Latin America has left many single mothers without the means to feed and raise their children. The growing ranks of single mothers paralleled a time when more and more American women began working outside the home. There is an insatiable need in the United States for cheap service and domestic workers. The single Latin American mothers began migrating in large numbers, leaving their children with grandparents, other relatives, or neighbors.

The first wave was in the 1960s and 1970s. Single mothers from a smattering of Caribbean countries—the West Indies, Jamaica, the Dominican Republic—headed to New York City, New England, and Florida to work as nannies and in nursing homes. Later, Central American women flocked to places with the greatest demand: the suburbs of Washington, D.C., Houston, and Los Angeles, where the number of private domestic workers doubled in the 1980s.

Carmen's experience is now common. In Los Angeles, a University of Southern California study showed, 82 percent of live-in nannies and one in four housecleaners are mothers who still have at least one child in their home country. A Harvard University study showed that 85 percent of all immigrant children who eventually end up in the United States spent at least some time separated from a parent in the course of migrating to the United States.

In much of the United States, legitimate concerns about immigration and anti-immigrant measures have had a corrosive side effect: immigrants have been dehumanized and demonized. Their presence in the United States is deemed good or bad, depending on the perspective. Immigrants have been reduced to cost-benefit ratios.

Perhaps by looking at one immigrant—his strengths, his courage, his flaws—his humanity might help illuminate what too often has been a black-and-white discussion. Perhaps, I start thinking, I could take readers on top of these trains and show them what this modern-day immigrant journey is like, especially for children. "This," a Los Angeles woman who helps immigrants told me, "is the adventure story of the twenty-first century."

FEAR AND FLEAS

For a good while, I sat on the idea. As a journalist, I love to get inside the action, watch it unfold, take people inside worlds they might never otherwise see. I wanted to smell, taste, hear, and feel what this journey is like. In order to give a vivid, nuanced account, I knew I would have to travel with child migrants through Mexico on top of freight trains.

I thought about starting in Central America and tagging

along as one boy tries to reach his mother in the United States. Carmen's son Minor had already explained enough about the trip for me to grasp that this was just shy of nutty. He'd told me about the gangsters who rule the train tops, the bandits along the tracks, the Mexican police who patrol the train stations and rape and rob, about the dangers of losing a leg getting onto and off of moving trains.

In short, I was afraid.

Then there was the issue of marital harmony: I'd just finished another project that involved hanging out in dark garages and shacks with speed, heroin, and crack addicts. My husband had spent months fretting about my safety. He'd had to ask politely that I strip in our garage each evening when I came home after hanging out in addicts' apartments. Apparently I'd been bringing home a healthy population of fleas. Talk of strapping myself to the top of a freight train, I figured, was not likely to be received with open ears. A year later, I hoped the memory of fleas had faded. I decided to move forward.

Cautiously.

First, I learned everything I could about the journey. What's the exact route? The best and worst things that happen at each step of the way? The places where migrants encounter the greatest cruelty? And the greatest kindness? Critical turning points in the journey? What are the favorite areas along the tracks where the gangs rob, where the bandits kill people? Where do Mexican immigration authorities stop the train?

I talked with dozens of children held by the U.S. Immigration and Naturalization Service in four jails and shelters in California and in Texas. Many had ridden the trains. So had students I had spoken with at a special Los Angeles high school for recent immigrants.

At a detention center in Los Fresnos, Texas, a talk with

fifteen-year-old twins José Enrique and José Luis Oliva Rosa forced me to shred my initial plan. I realized that my first choice—to follow one boy from the beginning of his journey in Central America to the end with his mother in the United States—wasn't doable. The twins had left Honduras to find their mother in Los Angeles. During the months they spent running for their lives in Mexico, they were separated from each other four times. Only sheer luck had allowed them to find each other. I can't run as fast as a fifteen-year-old. I also can't rely on that level of luck. I had to find a boy who had made it to northern Mexico and follow him to his mother in the United States. I would have to reconstruct the earlier part of his journey.

Children at the Texas center also brought home the dangers I would face making such a journey. At the Texas center was Eber Ismael Sandoval Andino, eleven, a petite boy with dark eyes and machete marks crisscrossing his legs. The marks were from working in the coffee farms of Honduras since he was six years old. On his train rides through Mexico, he told me, he had witnessed five separate incidents where migrants had been mutilated by the train. He'd seen a man lose half a foot getting on the train. He'd seen six gangsters draw their knives and throw a girl off the train to her death. Once, he'd fallen off the train and landed right next to the churning steel wheels. "I thought I was dead. I turned stone cold," he said.

The director of the Texas center told me I'd be an idiot to attempt this train journey, that I could get myself killed. These kids, he said, motioning to the children around him, don't really understand the dangers they will face. They go into it with their eyes closed. They don't know any better. I understood the exact risks. I would be doing it out of sheer stupidity.

I am not a brave person. I grew up, in part, in Argentina

during the genocidal "dirty war," when the military "disappeared" up to thirty thousand people. Often I walked to school with a friend, in case something should happen to one of us. My mother burned the family's books in a pile in the backyard to avoid trouble if the military ever came to search our Buenos Aires home. We kept the windows closed so neighbors could not hear any discussion that strayed from the mundane into anything vaguely political. Among the disappeared and murdered was a teenage friend, who we heard had been tortured, the bones in his face shattered. A relative was abducted by the military, tortured, and released many months later.

I avoid danger, if possible. If I need to do dangerous things to really understand something, I try to build in as many safety nets as possible.

I redoubled my efforts to reduce my exposure while making the journey. I lay down one rule: No getting onto and off of moving trains (a rule I broke only once).

A newspaper colleague plugged into the Mexican government helped me get a letter from the personal assistant to Mexico's president. The letter asked any Mexican authorities and police I encountered to cooperate with my reporting. The letter helped keep me out of jail three times. It also helped me convince an armed Mexican migrant rights group, Grupo Beta, to accompany me on the trains through the most dangerous leg of the journey, the Mexican state of Chiapas. At the time, the government's Grupo Beta agents, who are drawn from different police groups, carried shotguns and AK-47s. They had not patrolled the train tops for fourteen months. Even with that firepower, they explained, it was too dangerous; in 1999, their patrols had come under attack by gangsters four times. They agreed to make an exception.

The letter helped me obtain permission to ride atop the

trains of four companies that operate freight trains up the length of Mexico. That way, the conductor would know when I was on board. I would tell them to be on the lookout for my signal. I'd wear a red rain jacket strapped around my waist and wave it if I was in dire danger. I tried to have a source in each region I'd be in, including his or her cell phone number, so I could call for help if I was in trouble.

FINDING ENRIQUE

The average child the Border Patrol catches who comes alone over the U.S.-Mexico border is a fifteen-year-old boy. I wanted to find a boy who was coming for his mother and had traveled on the trains.

In May 2000, I scoped out a dozen shelters and churches in Mexico along the 2,000-mile-long U.S. border that help migrants, including minors. I visited a few. I told each priest or shelter director what I was after. I called each place day after day to see if such a child had arrived. Soon, a nun at one of the churches in Nuevo Laredo, the Parroquia de San José, said she had a couple of teenagers who had come in for a free meal: a seventeen-year-old boy and a fifteen-year-old girl. Both were headed north in search of their mothers. She put Enrique on the telephone. He was a little older than the INS average. But his story was typical—and just as harrowing as those I had heard from children in the INS jails.

A few days later, I traveled to Nuevo Laredo and spent two weeks shadowing Enrique along the Rio Grande. I talked to other children but decided to stick with Enrique. In Nuevo Laredo, most of the children I spoke with, including Enrique, had been robbed of their mothers' telephone numbers along the way. They hadn't thought to memorize the numbers. Unlike the others, Enrique recalled one telephone in Honduras he could call to try to get his mother's phone number in the United States. He still had a shot at continuing his journey and, perhaps, reaching his mother.

From Enrique, I gleaned every possible detail about his life and trip north. I noted every place he had gone, every experience, every person he recalled who had helped or hindered him along the way.

Then I began to retrace his steps, doing the journey exactly as he had done it a few weeks before. I wanted to see and experience things as he had with the hope of describing them more fully. I began in Honduras, interviewing his family, seeing his haunts. I took buses through Central America, just as Enrique had done. In Mexico's southernmost state, Chiapas, I boarded a freight train. I took the same path along the rails, traveling up the length of Mexico on top of seven freight trains. I got off where he did, in San Luis Potosí, then hitchhiked on an eighteen-wheeler from the same spot in the northern Mexican city of Matehuala, where Enrique had hitched a ride to the U.S. border. To follow Enrique's journey, I traversed thirteen of Mexico's thirty-one states. I traveled more than 1,600 miles—half of that on top of trains.

I found people who had helped Enrique and saw towns or crucial spots he had passed through or spent time in along the way. I showed people a photograph of Enrique to make sure we were talking about the same boy. I traveled on trains with other migrant children going to find their mothers, including a twelve-year-old boy in search of his mother, who had left for San Diego when he was one year old. From Tegucigalpa through Mexico, I interviewed dozens of migrants and other experts—medical workers, priests, nuns, police officers. All this added to the journey and helped corroborate Enrique's story. I returned to Enrique three times to ask if he had seen or heard some of the many things I had witnessed during my journey. In all, I spent more than six months traveling in Honduras, Mexico, and the United States. In 2003, to conduct additional research, I retraced much of the journey again, beginning in Tegucigalpa.

FOLLOWING A DANGEROUS PATH

For months, as I traveled in Enrique's footsteps, I lived with the near-constant danger of being beaten, robbed, or raped. Once, as I rode on top of a fuel car on a rainy night with lightning, a tree branch hit me squarely in the face. It sent me sprawling backward. I was able to grab a guardrail and keep from stumbling off the top of the train. On that same ride, I later learned, a child had been plucked off the fuel tanker car behind mine by a branch. His train companions did not know if he was dead or alive.

Even with the presence of the heavily armed Grupo Beta agents on trains as I rode through Chiapas, gangsters were robbing people at knifepoint at the end of our train. I constantly worried about gangsters on the trains. In Tierra Blanca in the Mexican state of Veracruz, during a brief train stop, I feverishly tried to get the local police to find and arrest a notoriously vicious gangster named Blackie, after learning he was aboard the train I was about to reboard. Nearby, a train derailed right in front of mine. Train engineers have described incidents where migrants have been crushed as trains derail and cars tip over.

At times, I came close to witnessing the worst the train had to offer. As I passed through the town of Encinar, Veracruz, I was riding between two hoppers with four other migrants. A teenage boy emerged from a railside food store to throw a roll of crackers to migrants on the train. A teenage migrant standing next to me was hungry. When the boy threw the roll toward the migrant beside me, it bounced off the train. As the migrant jumped off the hopper to run back for the crackers, he stumbled and fell backward. Both feet landed on the tracks. He had a split second to react. He yanked his feet back just before the wheels rolled over the track.

Things weren't much safer by the side of the rails. I walked along the river that flows by the town of Ixtepec, Oaxaca. It seemed tranquil, a very safe public spot. Above me was the main bridge that crosses the river, busy with trains and pedestrians. The next day, I interviewed Karen, a fifteen-year-old girl who had been raped by two gangsters she had seen on the trains. Karen told me she had been raped right under the river's bridge. I had been alone one day before the rape at the very spot where Karen had been assaulted.

In Chiapas, I hung out with Grupo Beta agents near the dangerous "El Manguito" immigration checkpoint. It is thick with bandits who target migrants. Suddenly we were on a high-speed chase on a two-lane road, trying to reach three bandits in a red Jeep Cherokee who had robbed a group of migrants and driven off with one of them, a twenty-two-year-old Honduran woman. I was in the bed of Grupo Beta's pickup. The pickup pulled up alongside the Cherokee, trying to force it to stop. A Grupo Beta agent stood in the pickup bed. He locked and loaded his shotgun and aimed at the bandits' vehicle. I was just feet from the Cherokee. I prayed that the bandits wouldn't open fire.

Farther north, human rights activist Raymundo Ramos Vásquez gave me a tour of the most isolated spots along the Rio Grande, places where migrants cross. We stumbled across a migrant preparing to swim north. He explained that the last time he had been here, municipal police officers had arrived. They had cuffed his hands behind his back, he said, and put his face in the river, threatening to drown him if he didn't disclose where he had his money. As the migrant described the abuse, two police officers walked down the dirt path toward us. Their guns were drawn—and cocked.

When I returned to the United States, I had a recurring nightmare: someone was racing after me on top of the freight trains, trying to rape me. It took months of therapy before I could sleep soundly again.

Often in Mexico I was tense. On the trains, I was filthy, unable to go to the bathroom for long stretches, excruciatingly hot or cold, pelted for hours by rain or hail.

Although I often felt exhausted and miserable, I knew I was experiencing only an iota of what migrant children go through. At the end of a long train ride, I would pull out my credit card, go to a motel, shower, eat, and sleep. These children typically spend several months making their way north. During that time, in between train rides, they sleep in trees or by the tracks, they drink from puddles, they beg for food. The journey gave me a glimmer of how hard this is for them.

TRAIN-TOP LESSONS

I thought I understood, to a great extent, the immigrant experience. My father, Mahafud, was born in Argentina after his Christian family fled religious persecution in Syria. My mother, Clara, born in Poland, emigrated to Argentina as a young child. Her family was fleeing poverty and the persecution of Jews. Many of her Polish relatives were gassed during World War II. My family emigrated to the United States in 1960. My father, a biochemistry professor working on genetic mapping, had greater resources and opportunities to conduct research here. He also wanted to leave behind a country controlled by the military, where academic expression was limited.

I understood the desire for opportunity, for freedom. I also understood, due to the death of my father when I was a teenager and the turbulent times my family experienced afterward, what it is like to struggle economically. Growing up as the child of Argentine immigrants in 1960s and 1970s Kansas, I have sometimes felt like an outsider. I know how difficult it is to straddle two countries, two worlds. On many levels, I relate to the experiences of immigrants and Latinos in this country. I have written about migrants, on and off, for two decades.

Still, my parents arrived in the United States on a jet airplane, not on top of a freight train. My family was never separated during the process of immigrating to the United States. Until my journey with migrant children, I had no true understanding of what people are willing to do to get here.

As I followed Enrique's footsteps, I learned the depths of desperation women face in countries such as Honduras. Most earn $40 to $120 a month working in a factory, cleaning houses, or providing child care. A hut with no bathroom or kitchen rents for nearly $30 a month. In rural areas of Honduras, some people live under a piece of tarp; they have no chairs or table and eat sitting on a dirt floor.

Children go to school in threadbare uniforms, often unable to afford pencil or paper or buy a decent lunch. A Tegucigalpa elementary school principal told me that many of his students were so malnourished that they didn't have the stamina to stand up for long at school rallies or to sing the national anthem. Many Honduran mothers pull their children out of school when they are as young as eight. They have them watch younger siblings while they work, or sell tortillas on a street corner. Seven-year-olds sell bags of water on public buses or wait at taxi stands to make change for cabdrivers. Some beg on Bulevar Juan Pablo II.

Domy Elizabeth Cortés, from Mexico City, described being despondent after her husband left her for another woman. The loss of his income meant she could feed her children only once a day. For weeks, she considered throwing herself and her two toddlers into a nearby sewage canal to drown together. Instead, she left her children with a brother and headed to Los Angeles. Day after day, mothers like Domy walk away from their children, some of them just a month old, and leave for the United States, not knowing if or when they will see them again.

With each step north, I became awed by the gritty determination these children possess in their struggle to get here. They are willing to endure misery and dangers for months on end. They come armed with their faith, a resolve not to return to Central America defeated, and a deep desire to be at their mothers' sides. One Honduran teenager I met in southern Mexico had been deported to Guatemala twenty-seven times. He said he wouldn't give up until he reached his mother in the United States. I began to believe that no number of border guards will deter children like Enrique, who are willing to endure so much to reach the United States. It is a powerful stream, one that can only be addressed at its source.

The migrants I spent time with also gave me an invaluable gift. They reminded me of the value of what I have. They taught me that people are willing to die in their quest to obtain it.

The single mothers who are coming to this country, and the children who follow them, are changing the face of immigration to the United States. Each year, the number of women and children who immigrate to the United States grows. They become our neighbors, children in our schools, workers in our homes. As they become a greater part of the fabric of the United States, their troubles and triumphs will be a part of this country's future. For Americans overall, this book should shed some light on this part of our society.

For Latina mothers coming to the United States, my hope is that they will understand the full consequences of leaving their children behind and make better-informed decisions. For in the end, these separations almost always end badly.

Every woman I interviewed in the United States who had left children behind had been sure the separation would be brief. Immigrants who come to the United States are by nature optimists. They have to be in order to leave everything they love and are familiar with for the unknown. The reality, however, is that it takes years and years until the children and mothers are together again. By the time that happens, if it happens, the children are usually very angry with their mothers. They feel abandoned. Their mothers are stunned by this judgment. They believe their children should show gratitude, not anger. After all, the mothers sacrificed being with their children, worked like dogs, all to help provide their children with a better life and future.

Latina migrants ultimately pay a steep price for coming to

the United States. They lose their children's love. Reunited, they end up in conflicted homes. Too often, the boys seek out gangs to try to find the love they thought they would find with their mothers. Too often, the girls get pregnant and form their own families. In many ways, these separations are devastating Latino families. People are losing what they value most.

Children who set out on this journey usually don't make it. They end up back in Central America, defeated. Enrique was determined to be with his mother again. Would he make it?

ENRIQUE'S
JOURNEY

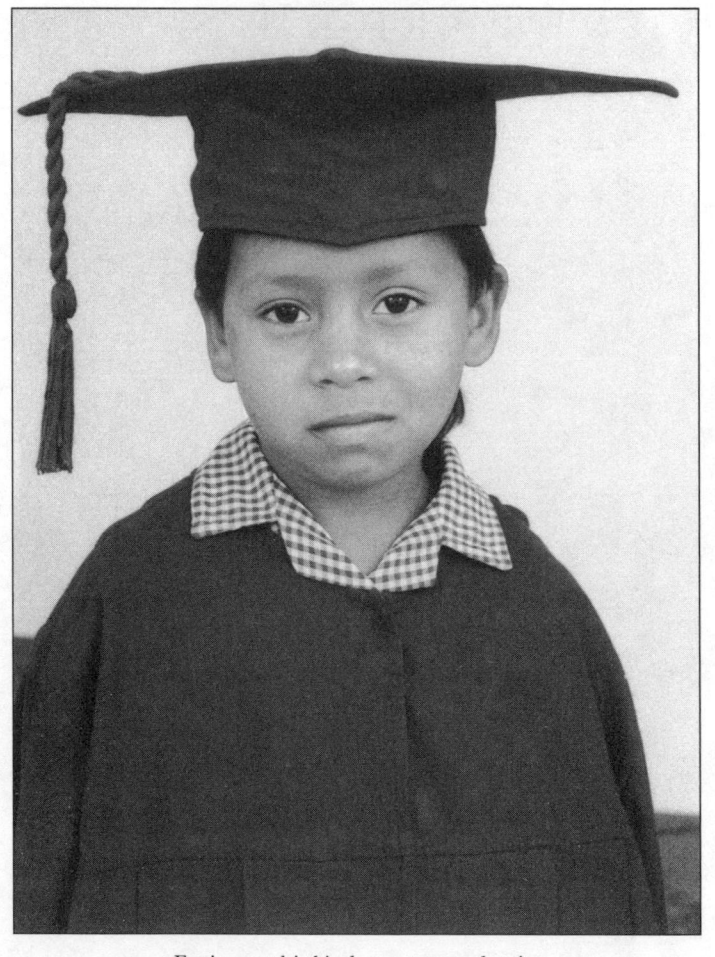

Enrique at his kindergarten graduation

O N E

The Boy Left Behind

The boy does not understand.

His mother is not talking to him. She will not even look at him. Enrique has no hint of what she is going to do.

Lourdes knows. She understands, as only a mother can, the terror she is about to inflict, the ache Enrique will feel, and finally the emptiness.

What will become of him? Already he will not let anyone else feed or bathe him. He loves her deeply, as only a son can. With Lourdes, he is openly affectionate. "*Dame pico, mami.* Give me a kiss, Mom," he pleads, over and over, pursing his lips. With Lourdes, he is a chatterbox. "*Mira, mami.* Look, Mom," he says softly, asking her questions about everything he sees. Without her, he is so shy it is crushing.

Slowly, she walks out onto the porch. Enrique clings to her pant leg. Beside her, he is tiny. Lourdes loves him so much she cannot bring herself to say a word. She cannot carry his picture. It would melt her resolve. She cannot hug him. He is five years old.

They live on the outskirts of Tegucigalpa, in Honduras. She can barely afford food for him and his sister, Belky, who is seven. She's never been able to buy them a toy or a birthday cake. Lourdes, twenty-four, scrubs other people's laundry in a muddy river. She goes door to door, selling tortillas, used clothes, and plantains.

She fills a wooden box with gum and crackers and cigarettes, and she finds a spot where she can squat on a dusty sidewalk next to the downtown Pizza Hut and sell the items to passersby. The sidewalk is Enrique's playground.

They have a bleak future. He and Belky are not likely to finish grade school. Lourdes cannot afford uniforms or pencils. Her husband is gone. A good job is out of the question.

Lourdes knows of only one place that offers hope. As a seven-year-old child, delivering tortillas her mother made to wealthy homes, she glimpsed this place on other people's television screens. The flickering images were a far cry from Lourdes's childhood home: a two-room shack made of wooden slats, its flimsy tin roof weighted down with rocks, the only bathroom a clump of bushes outside. On television, she saw New York City's spectacular skyline, Las Vegas's shimmering lights, Disneyland's magic castle.

Lourdes has decided: She will leave. She will go to the United States and make money and send it home. She will be gone for one year—less, with luck—or she will bring her children to be with her. It is for them she is leaving, she tells herself, but still she feels guilty.

She kneels and kisses Belky and hugs her tightly. Then she

turns to her own sister. If she watches over Belky, she will get a set of gold fingernails from *el Norte*.

But Lourdes cannot face Enrique. He will remember only one thing that she says to him: "Don't forget to go to church this afternoon."

It is January 29, 1989. His mother steps off the porch.

She walks away.

"*¿Dónde está mi mami?*" Enrique cries, over and over. "Where is my mom?"

His mother never returns, and that decides Enrique's fate. As a teenager—indeed, still a child—he will set out for the United States on his own to search for her. Virtually unnoticed, he will become one of an estimated 48,000 children who enter the United States from Central America and Mexico each year, illegally and without either of their parents. Roughly two thirds of them will make it past the U.S. Immigration and Naturalization Service.

Many go north seeking work. Others flee abusive families. Most of the Central Americans go to reunite with a parent, say counselors at a detention center in Texas where the INS houses the largest number of the unaccompanied children it catches. Of those, the counselors say, 75 percent are looking for their mothers. Some children say they need to find out whether their mothers still love them. A priest at a Texas shelter says they often bring pictures of themselves in their mothers' arms.

The journey is hard for the Mexicans but harder still for Enrique and the others from Central America. They must make an illegal and dangerous trek up the length of Mexico. Counselors and immigration lawyers say only half of them get help from smugglers. The rest travel alone. They are cold, hungry, and helpless. They are hunted like animals by corrupt police, bandits, and gang members deported from the United States. A University of Houston study found that most are robbed, beaten, or raped, usually several times. Some are killed.

They set out with little or no money. Thousands, shelter workers say, make their way through Mexico clinging to the sides and tops of freight trains. Since the 1990s, Mexico and the United States have tried to thwart them. To evade Mexican police and immigration authorities, the children jump onto and off of the moving train cars. Sometimes they fall, and the wheels tear them apart.

They navigate by word of mouth or by the arc of the sun. Often, they don't know where or when they'll get their next meal. Some go days without eating. If a train stops even briefly, they crouch by the tracks, cup their hands, and steal sips of water from shiny puddles tainted with diesel fuel. At night, they huddle together on the train cars or next to the tracks. They sleep in trees, in tall grass, or in beds made of leaves.

Some are very young. Mexican rail workers have encountered seven-year-olds on their way to find their mothers. A policeman discovered a nine-year-old boy near the downtown Los Angeles tracks. "I'm looking for my mother," he said. The youngster had left Puerto Cortes in Honduras three months before. He had been guided only by his cunning and the single thing he knew about her: where she lived. He had asked everyone, "How do I get to San Francisco?"

Typically, the children are teenagers. Some were babies when their mothers left; they know them only by pictures sent home. Others, a bit older, struggle to hold on to memories: One has slept in her mother's bed; another has smelled her perfume, put on her deodorant, her clothes. One is old enough to remember his mother's face, another her laugh, her favorite shade of lipstick, how her dress felt as she stood at the stove patting tortillas.

Many, including Enrique, begin to idealize their mothers. They remember how their mothers fed and bathed them, how they walked them to kindergarten. In their absence, these mothers become larger than life. Although in the United States the women struggle to pay rent and eat, in the imaginations of their children back home they become deliverance itself, the answer to every problem. Finding them becomes the quest for the Holy Grail.

CONFUSION

Enrique is bewildered. Who will take care of him now that his mother is gone? Lourdes, unable to burden her family with both of her children, has split them up. Belky stayed with Lourdes's mother and sisters. For two years, Enrique is entrusted to his father, Luis, from whom his mother has been separated for three years.

Enrique clings to his daddy, who dotes on him. A bricklayer, his father takes Enrique to work and lets him help mix mortar. They live with Enrique's grandmother. His father shares a bed with him and brings him apples and clothes. Every month, Enrique misses his mother less, but he does not forget her. "When is she coming for me?" he asks.

Lourdes and her smuggler cross Mexico on buses. Each afternoon, she closes her eyes. She imagines herself home at dusk, playing with Enrique under a eucalyptus tree in her mother's front yard. Enrique straddles a broom, pretending it's a donkey, trotting around the muddy yard. Each afternoon, she presses her eyes shut and tears fall. Each afternoon, she reminds herself that if she is weak, if she does not keep moving forward, her children will pay.

Lourdes crosses into the United States in one of the largest immigrant waves in the country's history. She enters at night through a rat-infested Tijuana sewage tunnel and makes her way to Los Angeles. There, in the downtown Greyhound bus terminal, the smuggler tells Lourdes to wait while he runs a quick errand. He'll be right back. The smuggler has been paid to take her all the way to Miami.

Three days pass. Lourdes musses her filthy hair, trying to blend in with the homeless and not get singled out by police. She prays to God to put someone before her, to show her the way. Whom can she reach out to for help? Starved, she starts walking. East of downtown, Lourdes spots a small factory. On the loading dock, under a gray tin roof, women sort red and green tomatoes. She begs for work. As she puts tomatoes into boxes, she hallucinates that she is slicing open a juicy one and sprinkling it with salt. The boss pays her $14 for two hours' work. Lourdes's brother has a friend in Los Angeles who helps Lourdes get a fake Social Security card and a job.

She moves in with a Beverly Hills couple to take care of their three-year-old daughter. Their spacious home has carpet on the floors and mahogany panels on the walls. Her employers are kind. They pay her $125 a week. She gets nights and weekends off. Maybe, Lourdes tells herself—if she stays long enough—they will help her become legal.

Every morning as the couple leave for work, the little girl cries for her mother. Lourdes feeds her breakfast and thinks of Enrique and Belky. She asks herself: "Do my children cry like this? I'm giving this girl food instead of feeding my own children." To get the girl to eat, Lourdes pretends the spoon is an airplane. But each time the spoon lands in the girl's mouth, Lourdes is filled with sadness.

In the afternoon, after the girl comes home from prekindergarten class, they thumb through picture books and play. The girl, so close to Enrique's age, is a constant reminder of her son. Many afternoons, Lourdes cannot contain her grief. She gives the girl a toy and dashes into the kitchen. There, out of sight, tears flow. After seven months, she cannot take it. She quits and moves to a friend's place in Long Beach.

Boxes arrive in Tegucigalpa bearing clothes, shoes, toy cars, a Robocop doll, a television. Lourdes writes: Do they like the things she is sending? She tells Enrique to behave, to study hard. She has hopes for him: graduation from high school, a white-collar job, maybe as an engineer. She pictures her son working in a crisp shirt and shiny shoes. She says she loves him.

Enrique asks about his mother. "She'll be home soon," his grandmother assures him. "Don't worry. She'll be back."

But his mother does not come. Her disappearance is incomprehensible. Enrique's bewilderment turns to confusion and then to adolescent anger.

When Enrique is seven, his father brings a woman home. To her, Enrique is an economic burden. One morning, she spills hot cocoa and burns him. His father throws her out. But their separation is brief.

"Mom," Enrique's father tells the grandmother, "I can't think of anyone but that woman."

Enrique's father bathes, dresses, splashes on cologne, and follows her. Enrique tags along and begs to stay with him. But his father tells him to go back to his grandmother.

His father begins a new family. Enrique sees him rarely, usually by chance. In time, Enrique's love turns to contempt. "He doesn't love me. He loves the children he has with his wife," he tells Belky. "I don't have a dad."

His father notices. "He looks at me as if he wasn't my son, as if he wants to strangle me," he tells Enrique's grandmother. Most of the blame, his father decides, belongs to Enrique's mother. "She is the one who promised to come back."

For Belky, their mother's disappearance is just as distressing. She lives with Aunt Rosa Amalia, one of her mother's sisters. On Mother's Day, Belky struggles through a celebration at school. That night she cries quietly, alone in her room. Then she scolds herself. She should thank her mother for leaving; without the money she sends for books and uniforms, Belky could not even attend school. She reminds herself of all the other things her mother ships south: Reebok tennis shoes, black sandals, the yellow bear and pink puppy stuffed toys on her bed. She commiserates with a friend whose mother has also left. They console each other. They know a girl whose mother died of a heart attack. At least, they say, ours are alive.

But Rosa Amalia thinks the separation has caused deep emotional problems. To her, it seems that Belky is struggling with an unavoidable question: How can I be worth anything if my mother left me?

"There are days," Belky tells Aunt Rosa Amalia, "when I wake up and feel so alone." Belky is temperamental. Sometimes she stops talking to everyone. When her mood turns dark, her grandmother warns the other children in the house, "*¡Pórtense bien porque la marea anda brava!* You better behave, because the seas are choppy!"

Confused by his mother's absence, Enrique turns to his

grandmother. Alone now, he and his father's elderly mother share a shack thirty feet square. María Marcos built it herself of wooden slats. Enrique can see daylight in the cracks. It has four rooms, three without electricity. There is no running water. Gutters carry rain off the patched tin roof into two barrels. A trickle of cloudy white sewage runs past the front gate. On a well-worn rock nearby, Enrique's grandmother washes musty used clothing she sells door to door. Next to the rock is the latrine—a concrete hole. Beside it are buckets for bathing.

The shack is in Carrizal, one of Tegucigalpa's poorest neighborhoods. Sometimes Enrique looks across the rolling hills to the neighborhood where he and his mother lived and where Belky still lives with their mother's family. They are six miles apart. They hardly ever visit.

Lourdes sends Enrique $50 a month, occasionally $100, sometimes nothing. It is enough for food but not for school clothes, fees, notebooks, or pencils, which are expensive in Honduras. There is never enough for a birthday present. But Grandmother María hugs him and wishes him a cheery ¡Feliz cumpleaños! "Your mom can't send enough," she says, "so we both have to work."

Enrique loves to climb his grandmother's guayaba tree, but there is no more time for play now. After school, Enrique sells tamales and plastic bags of fruit juice from a bucket hung in the crook of his arm. "¡Tamarindo! ¡Piña!" he shouts.

Sometimes Enrique takes his wares to a service station where diesel-belching buses rumble into Carrizal. Jostling among mango and avocado vendors, he sells cups of diced fruit.

After he turns ten, he rides buses alone to an outdoor food market. He stuffs tiny bags with nutmeg, curry powder, and paprika, then seals them with hot wax. He pauses at big black gates in front of the market and calls out, "*¿Va a querer especias?* Who wants spices?" He has no vendor's license, so he keeps moving, darting between wooden carts piled with papayas. Younger children, five and six years old, dot the curbs, thrusting fistfuls of tomatoes and chiles at shoppers. Others offer to carry purchases of fruits and vegetables from stall to stall in rustic wooden wheelbarrows in exchange for tips. "*Te ayudo?* May I help you?" they ask. Arms taut, backs stooped, the boys heave forward, their carts bulging.

In between sales, some of the young market workers sniff glue.

Grandmother María cooks plantains, spaghetti, and fresh eggs. Now and then, she kills a chicken and prepares it for him. In return, when she is sick, Enrique rubs medicine on her back. He brings water to her in bed. Two or three times a week, Enrique lugs buckets filled with drinking water, one on each shoulder, from the water truck at the bottom of the hill up to his grandmother's house.

Every year on Mother's Day, he makes a heart-shaped card at school and presses it into her hand. "I love you very much, Grandma," he writes.

But she is not his mother. Enrique longs to hear Lourdes's voice. Once he tries to call her collect from a public telephone in his neighborhood. He can't get the call to go through. His only way of talking to her is at the home of his mother's cousin María Edelmira Sánchez Mejía, one of the few family members who has a telephone. His mother seldom calls. One year she does not call at all.

"I thought you had died, girl!" María Edelmira says, when she finally does call.

Better to send money, Lourdes replies, than burn it up on

the phone. But there is another reason she hasn't called: her life in the United States is nothing like the television images she saw in Honduras.

Lourdes shares an apartment bedroom with three other women. She sleeps on the floor. A boyfriend from Honduras, Santos, joins her in Long Beach. Lourdes is hopeful. She's noticed that her good friend Alma saves much faster now that she has moved in with a Mexican boyfriend. The boyfriend pays Alma's rent and bills. Alma can shop for her two girls in Honduras at nice stores such as JCPenney and Sears. She's saving to build a house in Honduras.

Santos, who once worked with Lourdes's stepfather as a bricklayer, is such a speedy worker that in Honduras his nickname was *El Veloz*. With Santos here, Lourdes tells herself, she will save enough to bring her children within two years. If not, she will take her savings and return to Honduras to build a little house and corner grocery store.

Lourdes unintentionally gets pregnant. She struggles through the difficult pregnancy, working in a refrigerated fish factory, packing and weighing salmon and catfish all day. Her water breaks at five one summer morning. Lourdes's boyfriend, who likes to get drunk, goes to a bar to celebrate. He asks a female bar buddy to take Lourdes to the public hospital. Lourdes's temperature shoots up to 105 degrees. She becomes delirious. The bar buddy wipes sweat dripping from Lourdes's brow. "Bring my mother. Bring my mother," Lourdes moans. Lourdes has trouble breathing. A nurse slips an oxygen mask over her face. She gives birth to a girl, Diana.

After two days, Lourdes must leave the hospital. She is still sick and weak. The hospital will hold her baby one more day. Santos has never shown up at the hospital. He isn't answering their home telephone. His drinking buddy has taken Lourdes's clothes back to her apartment. Lourdes leaves the hospital wearing a blue paper disposable robe. She doesn't even have a pair of underwear. She sits in her apartment kitchen and sobs, longing for her mother, her sister, anyone familiar.

Santos returns the next morning, after a three-day drinking binge. "*Ya vino?* Has it arrived?" He passes out before Lourdes can answer. Lourdes goes, alone, to get Diana from the hospital.

Santos loses his job making airplane parts. Lourdes falls on a pallet and hurts her shoulder. She complains to her employer about the pain. Two months after Diana's birth, she is fired. She gets a job at a pizzeria and bar. Santos doesn't want her to work there. One night, Santos is drunk and jealous that Lourdes has given a male co-worker a ride home. He punches Lourdes in the chest, knocking her to the ground. The next morning, there is coagulated blood under the skin on her breast. "I won't put up with this," Lourdes tells herself.

When Diana is one year old, Santos decides to visit Honduras. He promises to choose wise investments there and multiply the several thousand dollars the couple has scrimped to save. Instead, Santos spends the money on a long drinking binge with a fifteen-year-old girl on his arm. He doesn't call Lourdes again.

By the time Santos is gone for two months, Lourdes can no longer make car and apartment payments. She rents a garage—really a converted single carport. The owners have thrown up some walls, put in a door, and installed a toilet. There is no kitchen. It costs $300 a month.

Lourdes and Diana, now two years old, share a mattress on the concrete floor. The roof leaks, the garage floods, and slugs inch up the mattress and into bed. She can't buy milk or diapers or take her daughter to the doctor when she gets sick. Sometimes they live on emergency welfare.

Unemployed, unable to send money to her children in Honduras, Lourdes takes the one job available: work as a *fichera* at a Long Beach bar called El Mar Azul Bar #1. It has two pool tables, a long bar with vinyl stools, and a red-and-blue neon façade. Lourdes's job is to sit at the bar, chat with patrons, and encourage them to keep buying grossly overpriced drinks for her. Her first day is filled with shame. She imagines that her brothers are sitting at the bar, judging her. What if someone she knows walks into the bar, recognizes her, and word somehow gets back to Lourdes's mother in Honduras? Lourdes sits in the darkest corner of the bar and begins to cry. "What am I doing here?" she asks herself. "Is this going to be my life?" For nine months, she spends night after night patiently listening to drunken men talk about their problems, how they miss their wives and children left behind in Mexico.

A friend helps Lourdes get work cleaning oil refinery offices and houses by day and ringing up gasoline and cigarette sales at a gas station at night. Lourdes drops her daughter off at school at 7 A.M., cleans all day, picks Diana up at 5 P.M., drops her at a babysitter, then goes back to work until 2 A.M. She fetches Diana and collapses into bed. She has four hours to sleep.

Some of the people whose houses she cleans are kind. One woman in Redondo Beach always cooks Lourdes lunch and leaves it on the stove for her. Another woman offers, "Anything you want to eat, there is the fridge." Lourdes tells both, "God bless you."

Others seem to revel in her humiliation. One woman in posh Palos Verdes demands that she scrub her living room and kitchen floors on her knees instead of with a mop. It exacerbates her arthritis. She walks like an old lady some days. The cleaning liquids cause her skin to slough off her knees, which sometimes bleed. The woman never offers Lourdes a glass of water.

There are good months, though, when she can earn $1,000 to $1,200 cleaning offices and homes. She takes extra jobs, one at a candy factory for $2.25 an hour. Besides the cash for Enrique, every month she sends $50 each to her mother and Belky.

Those are her happiest moments, when she can wire money. Her greatest dread is when there is no work and she can't. That and random gang shootings. *"La muerte nunca te avisa cuando viene,"* Lourdes says. "Death never announces when it is going to come." A small park near her apartment is a gang hangout. When Lourdes returns home in the middle of the night, gangsters come up and ask for money. She always hands over three dollars, sometimes five. What would happen to her children if she died?

The money Lourdes sends is no substitute for her presence. Belky, now nine, is furious about the new baby. Their mother might lose interest in her and Enrique, and the baby will make it harder to wire money and save so she can bring them north. "How can she have more children now?" Belky asks.

For Enrique, each telephone call grows more strained. Because he lives across town, he is not often lucky enough to be at María Edelmira's house when his mother phones. When he is, their talk is clipped and anxious. Quietly, however, one of these conversations plants the seed of an idea. Unwittingly, Lourdes sows it herself.

"When are you coming home?" Enrique asks. She avoids an answer. Instead, she promises to send for him very soon.

It had never occurred to him: If she will not come home,

then maybe he can go to her. Neither he nor his mother realizes it, but this kernel of an idea will take root. From now on, whenever Enrique speaks to her, he ends by saying, "I want to be with you."

"Come home," Lourdes's own mother begs her on the telephone. "It may only be beans, but you always have food here." Pride forbids it. How can she justify leaving her children if she returns empty-handed? Four blocks from her mother's place is a white house with purple trim. It takes up half a block behind black iron gates. The house belongs to a woman whose children went to Washington, D.C., and sent her the money to build it. Lourdes cannot afford such a house for her mother, much less herself.

But she develops a plan. She will become a resident and bring her children to the United States legally. Three times, she hires storefront immigration counselors who promise help. She pays them a total of $3,850. But the counselors never deliver.

One is a supposed attorney near downtown Los Angeles. Another is a blind man who says he once worked at the INS. Lourdes's friends say he's helped them get work papers. A woman in Long Beach, whose house she cleans, agrees to sponsor her residency. The blind man dies of diabetes. Soon after, Lourdes gets a letter from the INS. Petition denied.

She must try again. A chance to get her papers comes from someone Lourdes trusts. Dominga is an older woman with whom Lourdes shares an apartment. Dominga has become Lourdes's surrogate mother. She loans Lourdes money when she runs short. She gives her advice on how to save so she can bring her children north. When Lourdes comes home late, she leaves her tamales or soup on the table, under the black velvet picture of the Last Supper.

Dominga is at the Los Angeles INS office. She's there to try to help a son arrested in an immigration raid. A woman walks up to her in the hallway. My name, she tells Dominga, is Gloria Patel. I am a lawyer. I have friends inside the INS who can help your son become legal. In fact, I work for someone inside the INS. She hands Dominga her business card. IMMIGRATION CONSULTANT. LEGAL PROFESSIONAL SERVICES. It has a drawing of the Statue of Liberty. Residency costs $3,000 per person up front, $5,000 total. Find five or six interested immigrants, the woman tells Dominga, and I'll throw in your son's residency papers for free.

"I found a woman, a great attorney!" Dominga tells Lourdes. "She can make us legal in one month." At most, three months. Dominga convinces other immigrants in her apartment complex to sign up. Initially, the recruits are skeptical. Some accompany Dominga to Patel's office. It is a suite in a nice building that also houses the Guatemalan Consulate. The waiting room is full. Two men loudly discuss how Patel has been successful in legalizing their family members. Patel shows Dominga papers—proof, she says, that her son's legalization process is already under way.

They leave the office grateful that Patel has agreed to slash her fee to $3,500 and require only $1,000 per person as a first installment. Lourdes gives Patel what she has: $800.

Soon Patel demands final payments from everyone to keep going. Lourdes balks. Should she be sending this money to her children in Honduras instead? She talks to Patel on the phone. She claims to be Salvadoran but sounds Colombian.

Patel is a smooth talker. "How are you going to lose out on this amazing opportunity? Almost no one has this opportunity! And for this incredible price."

"It's that there are a lot of thieves here. And I don't earn much."

"Who said I'm going to rob you?"

Lourdes prays. *God, all these years, I have asked you for only one thing: to be with my children again.* She hands over another $700. Others pay the entire $3,500.

Patel promises to send everyone's legalization papers in the mail. A week after mailing in the last payments, several migrants go back to her office to see how things are going. The office is shuttered. Gloria Patel is gone. Others in the building say she had rented space for one month. The papers the migrants were shown were filled-out applications, nothing more.

Lourdes berates herself for not dating an American who asked her out long ago. She could have married him, maybe even had her children here by now . . .

Lourdes wants to give her son and daughter some hope. "I'll be back next Christmas," she tells Enrique.

Enrique fantasizes about Lourdes's expected homecoming in December. In his mind, she arrives at the door with a box of Nike shoes for him. "Stay," he pleads. "Live with me. Work here. When I'm older, I can help you work and make money."

Christmas arrives, and he waits by the door. She does not come. Every year, she promises. Each year, he is disappointed. Confusion finally grows into anger. "I need her. I miss her," he tells his sister. "I want to be with my mother. I see so many children with mothers. I want that."

One day, he asks his grandmother, "How did my mom get to the United States?" Years later, Enrique will remember his grandmother's reply—and how another seed was planted: "Maybe," María says, "she went on the trains."

"What are the trains like?"

"They are very, very dangerous," his grandmother says. "Many people die on the trains."

When Enrique is twelve, Lourdes tells him yet again that she will come home.

"*Sí,*" he replies. "*Va, pues.* Sure. Sure."

Enrique senses a truth: Very few mothers ever return. He tells her that he doesn't think she is coming back. To himself, he says, "It's all one big lie."

The calls grow tense. "Come home," he demands. "Why do you want to be there?"

"It's all gone to help raise you."

Lourdes has nightmares about going back, even to visit, without residency documents. In the dreams, she hugs her children, then realizes she has to return to the United States so they can eat well and study. The plates on the table are empty. But she has no money for a smuggler. She tries to go back on her own. The path becomes a labyrinth. She runs through zigzagging corridors. She always ends up back at the starting point. Each time, she awakens in a sweat.

Another nightmare replays an incident when Belky was two years old. Lourdes has potty-trained her daughter. But Belky keeps pooping in her pants. "*Puerca!* You pig!" Lourdes scolds her daughter. Once, Lourdes snaps. She kicks Belky in the bottom. The toddler falls and hits her face on the corner of a door. Her lip splits open. Lourdes can't reach out and console her daughter. Each time, she awakens with Belky's screams ringing in her ears.

All along, Enrique's mother has written very little; she is barely literate and embarrassed by it. Now her letters stop.

Every time Enrique sees Belky, he asks, "When is our mom coming? When will she send for us?"

Lourdes does consider hiring a smuggler to bring the children but fears the danger. The coyotes, as they are called, are often alcoholics or drug addicts. Usually, a chain of smugglers is used to make the trip. Children are passed from one stranger to another. Sometimes the smugglers abandon their charges.

Lourdes is continually reminded of the risks. One of her best friends in Long Beach pays for a smuggler to bring her sister from El Salvador. During her journey, the sister calls Long Beach to give regular updates on her progress through Mexico. The calls abruptly stop.

Two months later, the family hears from a man who was among the group headed north. The smugglers put twenty-four migrants into an overloaded boat in Mexico, he says. It tipped over. All but four drowned. Some bodies were swept out to sea. Others were buried along the beach, including the missing sister. He leads the family to a Mexican beach. There they unearth the sister's decomposed body. She is still wearing her high school graduation ring.

Another friend is panic-stricken when her three-year-old son is caught by Border Patrol agents as a smuggler tries to cross him into the United States. For a week, Lourdes's friend doesn't know what's become of her toddler.

Lourdes learns that many smugglers ditch children at the first sign of trouble. Government-run foster homes in Mexico get migrant children whom authorities find abandoned in airports and bus stations and on the streets. Children as young as three, bewildered, desperate, populate these foster homes.

Víctor Flores, four years old, maybe five, was abandoned on a bus by a female smuggler. He carries no identification, no telephone number. He ends up at Casa Pamar, a foster home in Tapachula, Mexico, just north of the Guatemalan border. It broadcasts their pictures on Central American television so family members might rescue them.

The boy gives his name to Sara Isela Hernández Herrera, a coordinator at the home, but says he does not know how old he is or where he is from. He says his mother has gone to the United States. He holds Hernández's hand with all his might and will not leave her side. He asks for hugs. Within hours, he begins calling her Mama.

When she leaves work every afternoon, he pleads in a tiny voice for her to stay—or at least to take him with her. She gives him a jar of strawberry marmalade and strokes his hair. "I have a family," he says, sadly. "They are far away."

Francisco Gaspar, twelve, from Concepción Huixtla in Guatemala, is terrified. He sits in a hallway at a Mexican immigration holding tank in Tapachula. With a corner of his Charlie Brown T-shirt, he dabs at tears running down his chin. He is waiting to be deported. His smuggler left him behind at Tepic, in the western coastal state of Nayarit. "He didn't see that I hadn't gotten on the train," Francisco says between sobs. His short legs had kept him from scrambling aboard. Immigration agents caught him and bused him to Tapachula.

Francisco left Guatemala after his parents died. He pulls a tiny scrap of paper from a pants pocket with the telephone number of his uncle Marcos in Florida. "I was going to the United States to harvest chiles," he says. "Please help me! Please help me!"

Clutching a handmade cross of plastic beads on a string around his neck, he leaves his chair and moves frantically from one stranger to another in the hallway. His tiny chest heaves. His face contorts in agony. He is crying so hard that he struggles for breath. He asks each of the other migrants to help him get back to his smuggler in Tepic. He touches their hands. "Please take me back to Tepic! Please! Please!"

For Lourdes, the disappearance of her ex-boyfriend, Santos, hits closest to home. When Diana is four years old, her father returns to Long Beach. Soon after, Santos is snared in an INS raid of day laborers waiting for work on a street corner and deported. Lourdes hears he has again left Honduras headed for the United States. He never arrives. Not even his mother in Honduras knows what has happened to him. Eventually, Lourdes concludes that he has died in Mexico or drowned in the Rio Grande.

"Do I want to have them with me so badly," she asks herself of her children, "that I'm willing to risk their losing their lives?" Besides, she does not want Enrique to come to California. There are too many gangs, drugs, and crimes.

In any event, she has not saved enough. The cheapest coyote, immigrant advocates say, charges $3,000 per child. Female coyotes want up to $6,000. A top smuggler will bring a child by commercial flight for $10,000. She must save enough to bring both children at once. If not, the one left in Honduras will think she loves him or her less.

Enrique despairs. He will simply have to do it himself. He will go find her. He will ride the trains. "I want to come," he tells her.

Don't even joke about it, she says. It is too dangerous. Be patient.

REBELLION

Now Enrique's anger boils over. He refuses to make his Mother's Day card at school. He begins hitting other kids. At recess, he lifts schoolgirls' skirts. When a teacher tries to make him behave by smacking him with a large ruler, Enrique grabs the end of the ruler and refuses to let go, making the teacher cry.

He stands on top of the teacher's desk and bellows, "Who is Enrique?"

"You!" the class replies.

Three times, he is suspended. Twice he repeats a grade. But Enrique never abandons his promise to study. Unlike half the children from his neighborhood, he completes elementary school. There is a small ceremony. A teacher hugs him and mutters, "Thank God, Enrique's out of here."

He stands proud in a blue gown and mortarboard. But nobody from his mother's family comes to the graduation.

Now he is fourteen, a teenager. He spends more time on the streets of Carrizal, which is controlled by the Poison gang and is quickly becoming one of Tegucigalpa's toughest neighborhoods. His grandmother tells him to come home early. But he plays soccer until midnight. He refuses to sell spices. It is embarrassing when girls see him peddle fruit cups or when they hear someone call him "the tamale man." Sometimes his grandmother pulls out a belt at night when Enrique is naked in bed and therefore unable to quickly escape her punishment by running outside. "*Ahora vamos a areglar las cuentas.* Now we are going to settle the score," she says. She keeps count, inflicting one lash for each time Enrique has misbehaved.

Enrique has no parent to protect him on the streets of Carrizal. He makes up for it by cultivating a tougher image. When he walks alongside his grandmother, he hides his Bible under his shirt so no one will know they are headed to church.

Soon, he stops going to church at all.

"Don't hang out with bad boys," Grandmother María says.

"You can't pick my friends!" Enrique retorts. She is not his mother, he tells her, and she has no right to tell him what to do. He stays out all night.

His grandmother waits up for him, crying. "Why are you doing this to me?" she asks. "Don't you love me? I am going to send you away."

"Send me! No one loves me."

But she says she does love him. She only wants him to work and to be honorable, so that he can hold his head up high.

He replies that he will do what he wants.

Enrique has become her youngest child. "Please bury me," she says. "Stay with me. If you do, all this is yours." She prays that she can hold on to him until his mother sends for him. But her own children say Enrique has to go: she is seventy, and he will bury her, all right, by sending her to the grave.

Sadly, she writes to Lourdes: You must find him another home.

To Enrique, it is another rejection. First his mother, then his father, and now his grandmother.

Lourdes arranges for her eldest brother, Marco Antonio Zablah, to take him in. Marco will help Enrique, just as he helped Lourdes when she was Enrique's age. Marco once took in Lourdes to help ease the burden on their mother, who was struggling to feed so many children.

Her gifts arrive steadily. She sends Enrique an orange polo shirt, a pair of blue pants, a radio cassette player. She is proud that her money pays Belky's tuition at a private high school and eventually a college, to study accounting. In a country where nearly half live on $1 or less a day, kids from poor neighborhoods almost never go to college.

Money from Lourdes helps Enrique, too, and he realizes it. If she were here, he knows where he might well be: scavenging in the trash dump across town. Lourdes knows it, too; as a girl, she herself worked the dump. Enrique knows children as young as six or seven whose single mothers have stayed at home and who have had to root through the waste in order to eat.

Truck after truck rumbles onto the hilltop. Dozens of adults and children fight for position. Each truck dumps its load. Feverishly, the scavengers reach up into the sliding ooze to pluck out bits of plastic, wood, and tin. The trash squishes beneath their feet, moistened by loads from hospitals, full of blood and placentas. Occasionally a child, with hands blackened by garbage, picks up a piece of stale bread and eats it. As the youngsters sort through the stinking stew, thousands of sleek, black buzzards soar in a dark, swirling cloud and defecate on the people below.

Enrique sees other children who must work hard jobs. A block from where Lourdes grew up, children gather on a large pile of sawdust left by a lumber mill. Barefoot atop the peach-colored mound, their faces smeared with dirt, they quickly scoop the sawdust into rusty tin cans and dump it into big white plastic bags. They lug the bags half a mile up a hill. There, they sell the sawdust to families, who use it as kindling or to dry mud around their houses. An eleven-year-old boy has been hauling sawdust for three years, three trips up the hill each day. The earnings buy clothes, shoes, and paper for school.

Others in the neighborhood go door-to-door, offering to burn household trash for change. One afternoon, three children, ages eight to ten, line up in front of their mother, who loads them down with logs of wood to deliver. "Give me three!" one boy says. She lays a rag and then several pieces of wood atop his right shoulder.

In one neighborhood near where Enrique's mother grew up, fifty-two children arrive at kindergarten each morning. Forty-four arrive barefoot. An aide reaches into a basket and places a pair of shoes into each one's hands. At 4 P.M., before they leave, the children must return the shoes to the basket. If they take the shoes home, their mothers will sell them for food.

Black rats and a pig root around in a ravine where the children play.

At dinnertime, the mothers count out three tortillas for each child. If there are no tortillas, they try to fill their children's bellies with a glass of water with a teaspoon of sugar mixed in.

A year after Enrique goes to live with his uncle, Lourdes calls—this time from North Carolina. "California is too hard," she says. "There are too many immigrants." Employers pay poorly and treat them badly. Even with two jobs, she couldn't save. She has followed a female friend to North Carolina and started over again. It is her only hope of bettering her lot and seeing her children again. She sold everything in California— her old Ford, a chest of drawers, a television, the bed she shares with her daughter. It netted $800 for the move.

Here people are less hostile. She can leave her car, even her house, unlocked. Work is plentiful. She quickly lands a job as a waitress at a Mexican restaurant. She finds a room to rent in a trailer home for just $150 a month—half of what the small garage cost her in Los Angeles. She starts to save. Maybe if she amasses $4,000, her brother Marco will help her invest it in

Honduras. Maybe she'll be able to go home. Lourdes gets a better job on an assembly line for $9.05 an hour—$13.50 when she works overtime.

Going home would resolve a problem that has weighed heavily on Lourdes: Diana's delayed baptism. Lourdes has held off, hoping to baptize her daughter in Honduras with Honduran godparents. A baptism would lift Lourdes's constant concern that Diana's unexpected death will send her daughter to purgatory.

Lourdes has met someone, a house painter from Honduras, and they are moving in together. He, too, has two children in Honduras. He is kind and gentle, a quiet man with good manners. He gives Lourdes advice. He helps ease her loneliness. He takes Lourdes and her daughter to the park on Sundays. For a while, when Lourdes works two restaurant jobs, he picks her up when her second shift ends at 11 P.M., so they can share a few moments together. They call each other "honey." They fall in love.

Enrique misses Lourdes enormously. But Uncle Marco and his girlfriend treat him well. Marco is a money changer on the Honduran border. It has been lucrative work, augmented by a group that for years has been in constant need of his services: U.S.-funded Nicaraguan *contras* across the border. Marco's family, including a son, lives in a five-bedroom house in a middle-class neighborhood of Tegucigalpa. Uncle Marco gives Enrique a daily allowance, buys him clothes, and sends him to a private military school in the evenings.

By day, Enrique runs errands for his uncle, washes his five cars, follows him everywhere. His uncle pays as much attention to him as he does his own son, if not more. Often, Marco plays billiards with Enrique. They watch movies together. Enrique sees New York City's spectacular skyline, Las Vegas's shimmering lights, Disneyland's magic castle. *Negrito,* Marco calls Enrique fondly, because of his dark skin. Marco and Enrique stand the same way, a little bowlegged, with the hips tucked forward. Although he is in his teens, Enrique is small, just shy of five feet, even when he straightens up from a slight stoop. He has a big smile and perfect teeth.

His uncle trusts him, even to make bank deposits. He tells Enrique, "I want you to work with me forever." Enrique senses that Uncle Marco loves him, and he values his advice.

One week, as his uncle's security guard returns from trading Honduran lempiras, robbers drag the guard off a bus and kill him. The guard has a son twenty-three years old, and the slaying impels the young man to go to the United States. He comes back before crossing the Rio Grande and tells Enrique about riding on trains, leaping off rolling freight cars, and dodging *la migra,* Mexican immigration agents.

Because of the security guard's murder, Marco swears that he will never change money again. A few months later, though, he gets a call. For a large commission, would he exchange $50,000 in lempiras on the border with El Salvador? Uncle Marco promises that this will be the last time.

Enrique wants to go with him, but his uncle says he is too young. He takes Victor, one of his own brothers, instead. Robbers riddle their car with bullets. Enrique's uncles careen off the road. The thieves shoot Uncle Marco three times in the chest and once in the leg. They shoot Victor in the face. Both die. Now Uncle Marco is gone.

In nine years, Lourdes has saved $700 toward bringing her children to the United States. Instead, she uses it to help pay for her brothers' funerals.

Lourdes goes into a tailspin. Marco had visited her once, shortly after she arrived in Long Beach. She had not seen Victor since leaving Honduras. If the dead can appear to the living, Lourdes beseeches God through tears, allow Victor to show himself so she can say good-bye. "*Mira, hermanito,* I know you are dead. But I want to see you one more time. Come to me. I promise I won't be afraid of you," Lourdes says.

Lourdes angrily swears off Honduras. How could she ever live in such a lawless place? People there are killed like dogs. There are no repercussions. The only way she'll go back now, she tells herself, is by force, if she is deported. Soon after her brothers' deaths, the restaurant where Lourdes works is raided by immigration agents. Every worker is caught up in the sweep. Lourdes is the only one spared. It is her day off.

Lourdes decides to wait no longer. With financial help from her boyfriend, she baptizes seven-year-old Diana. The girl's godparents are a trustworthy Mexican house painter and his wife. Lourdes dresses Diana in a white floor-length dress and tiara. A priest sprinkles her daughter with holy water. Lourdes feels that one worry, at least, has been lifted.

Still, her resolve to stay in the United States brings a new nightmare. One morning at four, she hears her mother's voice. It is loud and clear. Her mother utters her name three times: *Lourdes. Lourdes. Lourdes.* "Huh?" Lourdes, half awake, bolts up in bed, screaming. This must be an omen that her mother has just died. She is inconsolable. Will she ever see her mother again?

Back in Honduras, within days of the two brothers' deaths, Uncle Marco's girlfriend sells Enrique's television, stereo, and Nintendo game—all gifts from Marco. Without telling him why, she says, "I don't want you here anymore." She puts his bed out on the street.

ADDICTION

Enrique, now fifteen, gathers his clothing and goes to his maternal grandmother. "Can I stay here?" he asks.

This had been his first home, the small stucco house where he and Lourdes lived until Lourdes stepped off the front porch and left. His second home was the wooden shack where he and his father lived with his father's mother, until his father found a new wife and left. His third home was the comfortable house where he lived with his uncle Marco.

Now he is back where he began. Seven people live here already: his grandmother, Águeda Amalia Valladares; two divorced aunts; and four young cousins. They are poor. Gone are Marco's contributions, which helped keep the household financially afloat. Águeda has a new expense: she must raise the young child left by her dead son Victor. The boy's mother left him as a baby to go to the United States and hasn't shown any interest since. "We need money just for food," says his grandmother, who suffers from cataracts. Nonetheless, she takes Enrique in.

She and the others are consumed by the slayings of the two uncles; they pay little attention to Enrique. He grows quiet, introverted. He does not return to school. At first, he shares the front bedroom with an aunt, Mirian, twenty-six. One day she awakens at 2 A.M. Enrique is sobbing quietly in his bed, cradling a picture of Uncle Marco in his arms. Enrique cries off and on for six months. His uncle loved him; without his uncle, he is lost.

Grandmother Águeda quickly sours on Enrique. She grows angry when he comes home late, knocking on her door, rousing the household. About a month later, Aunt Mirian wakes up again in the middle of the night. This time she smells acetone and hears the rustle of plastic. Through the dimness, she sees Enrique in his bed, puffing on a bag. He is sniffing glue.

Enrique is banished to a tiny stone building seven feet behind the house but a world away. It was once a cook shack, where his grandmother prepared food on an open fire. Its walls and ceiling are charred black. It has no electricity. The wooden door pries only partway open. It is dank inside. The single window has no glass, just bars. A few feet beyond is his privy—a hole with a wooden shanty over it.

The stone hut becomes his home. Now Enrique can do whatever he wants. If he is out all night, no one cares. But to him, it feels like another rejection.

At his uncle's funeral, he notices a shy girl with cascading curls of brown hair. She lives next door with her aunt. She has an inviting smile, a warm manner. At first, María Isabel, seventeen, can't stand Enrique. She notices how the teenager, who comes from his uncle Marco's wealthier neighborhood, is neatly dressed and immaculately clean, and wears his hair long. He seems arrogant. "*Me cae mal.* I don't like him," she tells a friend. Enrique is sure she has assumed that his nice clothes and his seriousness mean he's stuck-up. He persists. He whistles softly as she walks by, hoping to start a conversation. Month after month, Enrique asks the same question: "Would you be my girlfriend?"

"I'll think about it."

The more she rejects him, the more he wants her. He loves her girlish giggle, how she cries easily. He hates it when she flirts with others.

He buys her roses. He gives her a shiny black plaque with a drawing of a boy and girl looking tenderly at each other. It reads, "The person I love is the center of my life and of my heart. The person I love IS YOU." He gives her lotions, a stuffed teddy bear, chocolates. He walks her home after school from night classes two blocks away. He takes her to visit his paternal grandmother across town. Slowly, María Isabel warms to him.

The third time Enrique asks if she will be his girlfriend, she says yes.

For Enrique, María Isabel isn't just a way to stem the loneliness he's felt since his mother left him. They understand each other, they connect. María Isabel has been separated from her parents. She, too, has had to shuffle from home to home.

When she was seven, María Isabel followed her mother, Eva, across Honduras to a borrowed hut on a Tegucigalpa mountainside. Like Enrique's mother, Eva was leaving an unfaithful husband.

The hut was twelve by fifteen feet. It had one small wooden window and dirt floors. There was no bathroom. They relieved themselves and showered outdoors or at the neighbor's. There was no electricity. They cooked outside using firewood. They hauled buckets of water up from a relative's home two blocks down the hill. They ate beans and tortillas. Eva, asthmatic, struggled to keep the family fed.

Nine people slept in the hut. They crowded onto two beds and a slim mattress jammed each night into the aisle between the beds. To fit, everyone slept head to foot. María Isabel shared one of the beds with three other women.

When she was ten, María Isabel ran to catch a delivery truck. "Firewood!" she yelled out to a neighbor, Ángela Emérita Nuñez, offering to get some for her.

After that, each morning María Isabel asked if Ángela had a chore for her. Ángela liked the sweet, loving girl with coils of hair who always smiled. She admired the fact that she was a hard worker and a fighter, a girl who thrived when her own twin died a month after birth. *"Mira,"* María Isabel says, *"yo por pereza no me muero del hambre.* I will never die out of laziness." María Isabel fed and bathed Ángela's daughter, helped make tortillas and mop the red-and-gray tile floors. María Isabel often ate at Ángela's. Eventually, María Isabel spent many nights a week at Ángela's roomier house, where she had to share a bed with only one other person, Ángela's daughter.

María Isabel graduated from the sixth grade. Her mother proudly hung María Isabel's graduation certificate on the wall of the hut. A good student, she hadn't even asked her mother about going on to junior high. "How would she speak of that? We had no chance to send a child to school that long," says Eva, who never went to school a day and began selling bread from a basket perched on her head when she was twelve.

At sixteen, a fight forced María Isabel to move again. The spat was with an older cousin, who thought María Isabel was showing interest in her boyfriend. Eva scolded her daughter. María Isabel decided to move across town with her aunt Gloria, who lived next door to Enrique's maternal grandmother. María Isabel would help Gloria with a small food store she ran out of the front room of her house. To Eva, her daughter's departure was a relief. The family was eating, but not well. Eva was thankful that Gloria had lightened her load.

Gloria's house is modest. The windows have no panes, just wooden shutters. But to María Isabel, Gloria's two-bedroom home is wonderful. She and Gloria's daughter have a bedroom to themselves. Besides, Gloria is more easygoing about letting María Isabel go out at night to an occasional dance or party, or to the annual county fair. Eva wouldn't hear of such a thing, fearful the neighbors would gossip about her daughter's morals.

A cousin promises to take María Isabel to a talk about birth control. María Isabel wants to prevent a pregnancy. Enrique desperately wants to get María Isabel pregnant. If they have a child together, surely María Isabel won't abandon him. So many people have abandoned him.

Near where Enrique lives is a neighborhood called El Infiernito, Little Hell. Some homes there are teepees, stitched together from rags. It is controlled by a street gang, the Mara Salvatrucha. Some members were U.S. residents, living in Los Angeles until 1996, when a federal law began requiring judges to deport them if they committed serious crimes. Now they are active throughout much of Central America and Mexico. Here in El Infiernito, they carry *chimbas,* guns fashioned from plumbing pipes, and they drink *charamila,* diluted rubbing alcohol. They ride the buses, robbing passengers. Sometimes they assault people as they are leaving church after Mass.

Enrique and a friend, José del Carmen Bustamante, sixteen, venture into El Infiernito to buy marijuana. It is dangerous. On one occasion, José, a timid, quiet teenager, is threatened by a man who wraps a chain around his neck. The boys never linger. They take their joints partway up a hill to a billiard hall, where they sit outside smoking and listening to the music that drifts through the open doors.

With them are two other friends. Both have tried to ride freight trains to *el Norte.* One is known as El Gato, the Cat. He talks about *migra* agents shooting over his head and how easy it is to be robbed by bandits. In Enrique's marijuana haze, train riding sounds like an adventure. He and José resolve to try it soon.

Some nights, at ten or so, they climb a steep, winding path to the top of another hill. Hidden beside a wall scrawled with graffiti, they inhale glue late into the night. One day María Isabel turns a street corner and bumps into him. She is overwhelmed. He smells like an open can of paint.

"What's that?" she asks, reeling away from the fumes. "Are you on drugs?"

"No!" Enrique says.

Many sniffers openly carry their glue in baby food jars. They pop the lids and press their mouths to the small openings. Enrique tries to hide his habit. He dabs a bit of glue into a plastic bag and stuffs it into a pocket. Alone, he opens the end over his mouth and inhales, pressing the bottom of the bag toward his face, pushing the fumes into his lungs.

Belky, Enrique's sister, notices cloudy yellow fingerprints on María Isabel's jeans: glue, a remnant of Enrique's embrace.

María Isabel sees him change. His mouth is sweaty and sticky. He is jumpy and nervous. His eyes grow red. Sometimes they are glassy, half closed. Other times he looks drunk. If she asks a question, the response is delayed. His temper is quick. On a high, he grows quiet, sleepy, and distant. When he comes down, he becomes hysterical and insulting.

Drogo, one of his aunts calls him. Drug addict.

Enrique stares silently. "No one understands me," he tells Belky when she tries to keep him from going out.

His grandmother points to a neighbor with pale, scaly skin who has sniffed glue for a decade. The man can no longer stand up. He drags himself backward on the ground, using his forearms. "Look! That's how you're going to end up," his grandmother tells Enrique.

Enrique fears that he will become like the hundreds of glue-sniffing children he sees downtown.

Some sleep by trash bins. A gray-bearded priest brings them sweet warm milk. He ladles it out of a purple bucket into big bowls. On some days, two dozen of them line up behind his van. Many look half asleep. Some can barely stand. The acrid smell of the glue fills the air. They shuffle forward on blackened feet, sliding the lids off their glue jars to inhale. Then they pull the steaming bowls up to their filthy lips. If the priest tries to take away their glue jars, they cry. Older children beat or sexually abuse the younger ones. In six years, the priest has seen twenty-six die from drugs.

Sometimes Enrique hallucinates that someone is chasing him. He imagines gnomes and fixates on ants. He sees a cartoonlike Winnie-the-Pooh soaring in front of him. He walks, but he cannot feel the ground. Sometimes his legs will not respond. Houses move. Occasionally, the floor falls.

Once he almost throws himself off the hill where he and his friend sniff glue. For two particularly bad weeks, he doesn't recognize family members. His hands tremble. He coughs black phlegm.

No one tells Enrique's mother. Why worry her? Lourdes has enough troubles. She is three months behind in school payments for Belky, and the school is threatening not to let her take final exams.

AN EDUCATION

Enrique marks his sixteenth birthday. All he wants is his mother. One Sunday, he and his friend José put train riding to the test. They leave for *el Norte*.

At first, no one notices. They take buses across Guatemala to the Mexican border. "I have a mom in the United States," Enrique tells a guard.

"Go home," the man replies.

They slip past the guard and make their way twelve miles into Mexico to Tapachula. There they approach a freight train near the depot. But before they can reach the tracks, police stop them. The officers rob them, the boys say later, but then let them go—José first, Enrique afterward.

They find each other and another train. Now, for the first time, Enrique clambers aboard. The train crawls out of the Tapachula station. From here on, he thinks, nothing bad can happen.

They know nothing about riding the rails. José is terrified. Enrique, who is braver, jumps from car to car on the slow-moving train. He slips and falls—away from the tracks, luckily—and lands on a backpack padded with a shirt and an extra pair of pants.

He scrambles aboard again. But their odyssey comes to a humiliating halt. Near Tierra Blanca, a small town in Veracruz, authorities snatch them from the top of a freight car. The officers take them to a cell filled with MS gangsters, then deport them. Enrique is bruised and limping, and he misses María Isabel. They find coconuts to sell for bus fare and go home.

A DECISION

Enrique sinks deeper into drugs. By mid-December, he owes his marijuana supplier 6,000 lempiras, about $400. He has only 1,000 lempiras. He promises the rest by midweek but cannot keep his word. The following weekend, he encounters the dealer on the street.

"I'm going to kill you," the dealer tells Enrique. "You lied to me."

"Calm down," Enrique says, trying not to show any fear. "I'll give you your money."

"If you don't pay up," the supplier vows, "I'll kill your sister."

The dealer mistakenly thinks that Enrique's cousin Tania Ninoska Turcios, eighteen, is his sister. Both girls are finishing high school, and most of the family is away at a Nicaraguan hotel celebrating their graduation.

Enrique pries open the back door to the house where his uncle Carlos Orlando Turcios Ramos and aunt Rosa Amalia live. He hesitates. How can he do this to his own family? Three times, he walks up to the door, opens it, closes it, and leaves. Each time, he takes another deep hit of glue. He knows the dealer who threatened him has spent time in jail and owns a .57-caliber gun.

"It's the only way out," he tells himself finally, his mind spinning.

Finally, he enters the house, picks open the lock to a bedroom door, then jimmies the back of his aunt's armoire with a knife. He stuffs twenty-five pieces of her jewelry into a plastic bag and hides it under a rock near the local lumberyard.

At 10 P.M., the family returns to find the bedroom ransacked.

Neighbors say the dog did not bark.

"It must have been Enrique," Aunt Rosa Amalia says. She calls the police. Uncle Carlos and several officers go to find him.

"What's up?" he asks. He has come down off his high.

"Why did you do this? Why?" Aunt Rosa Amalia yells.

"It wasn't me." As soon as he says it, he flushes with shame and guilt. The police handcuff him. In their patrol car, he trembles and begins to cry. "I was drugged. I didn't want to do it." He tells the officers that a dealer wanting money had threatened to kill Tania.

He leads police to the bag of jewelry.

"Do you want us to lock him up?" the police ask.

Uncle Carlos thinks of Lourdes. They cannot do this to her. Instead, he orders Tania to stay indoors indefinitely, for her own safety.

But the robbery finally convinces Uncle Carlos that Enrique needs help. He finds him a $15-a-week job at a tire store. He eats lunch with him every day—chicken and homemade soup. He tells the family they must show him their love.

During the next month, January 2000, Enrique tries to quit drugs. He cuts back, but then he gives in. Every night, he comes home later. María Isabel begs him not to go up the hill where he sniffs glue. He promises not to but does anyway. He looks at himself in disgust. He is dressing like a slob—his life is unraveling.

He is lucid enough to tell Belky that he knows what he has to do: he has to go find his mother.

Aunt Ana Lucía agrees. Ana Lucía is wound tight. She and Enrique have clashed for months. Ana Lucía is the only breadwinner in the household. Even with his job at the tire store, Enrique is an economic drain. Worse, he is sullying the only thing her family owns: its good name.

They speak bitter words that both, along with Enrique's grandmother Águeda, will recall months later.

"Where are you coming from, you old bum?" Ana Lucía asks as Enrique walks in the door. "Coming home for food, huh?"

"Be quiet!" he says. "I'm not asking anything of you."

"You're a lazy bum! A drug addict! No one wants you here." All the neighbors can hear. "This isn't your house. Go to your mother!"

"I don't live with you. I live alone."

"You eat here."

Over and over, in a low voice, Enrique says, half pleading, "You better be quiet." Finally, he snaps. He kicks Ana Lucía twice, squarely in the buttocks. She shrieks.

His grandmother runs out of the house. She grabs a stick and threatens to club him if he touches Ana Lucía again. Enrique turns on his heel. "No one cares about me!" he says. He stomps away. Ana Lucía threatens to throw his clothes out onto the street. Now even his grandmother wishes he would go to the United States. He is hurting the family—and himself. She says, "He'll be better off there."

GOOD-BYE

María Isabel finds him sitting on a rock at a street corner, weeping, rejected again. She tries to comfort him. He is high on glue. He tells her he sees a wall of fire. His mother has just passed through it. She is lying on the other side, and she is dying. He approaches the fire to save her, but someone walks toward him through the flames and shoots him. He falls, then rises again, unhurt. His mother dies. "*¿Por qué me dejó?*" he cries out. "Why did she leave me?"

Even Enrique's sister and grandmother have urged María Isabel to leave Enrique, to find someone better. "What do you see in him? Don't you see he uses drugs?" people ask her. Her uncle is also wary of the drug-addicted teenager. He and Enrique both work at the same mechanic's shop, but the uncle never offers him a lift in his car to their job.

María Isabel can't leave him, despite his deep flaws. He is macho and stubborn. When they fight, he gives her the silent treatment. She has to break the ice. He is her third boyfriend but her first love. Enrique also provides a refuge from her own problems. Her aunt Gloria's son is an alcoholic. He throws things. He steals things. There are a lot of fights.

María Isabel loses herself in Enrique. At night, they sit on some big rocks outside his grandmother's home, where they have a bit of privacy, and talk. Enrique talks about his mother, his life with his grandmother María and his uncle Marco. "Why don't you leave your vices?" María Isabel asks. "It's hard," he answers quietly. When they walk by his drug haunts, she holds his hand tighter, hoping it will help.

Enrique feels shame for what he has done to his family and what he is doing to María Isabel, who might be pregnant. María Isabel pleads with him to stay. She won't abandon him. She tells Enrique she will move into the stone hut with him. But Enrique fears he will end up on the streets or dead. Only his mother can help him. She is his salvation. "If you had known my mom, you would know she's a good person," he says to his friend José. "I love her."

Enrique has to find her.

Each Central American neighborhood has a smuggler. In Enrique's neighborhood, it's a man who lives at the top of a hill. For $5,000, he will take anyone to *los Estados*. But Enrique can't imagine that kind of money.

He sells the few things he owns: his bed, a gift from his mother; his leather jacket, a gift from his dead uncle; his rustic armoire, where he hangs his clothes. He crosses town to say good-bye to Grandmother María. Trudging up the hill to her house, he encounters his father. "I'm leaving," he says. "I'm going to make it to the U.S." He asks him for money.

His father gives him enough for a soda and wishes him luck.

"Grandma, I'm leaving," Enrique says. "I'm going to find my mom."

Don't go, she pleads. She promises to build him a one-room house in the corner of her cramped lot. But he has made up his mind.

She gives him 100 lempiras, about $7—all the money she has.

"I'm leaving already, sis," he tells Belky the next morning.

She feels her stomach tighten. They have lived apart most of their lives, but he is the only one who understands her loneliness. Quietly, she fixes a special meal: tortillas, a pork cutlet, rice, fried beans with a sprinkling of cheese. "Don't leave," she says, tears welling up in her eyes.

"I have to."

It is hard for him, too. Every time he has talked to his mother, she has warned him not to come—it's too dangerous. But if somehow he gets to the U.S. border, he will call her. Being so close, she'll have to welcome him. "If I call her from there," he says to José, "how can she not accept me?"

He makes himself one promise: "I'm going to reach the United States, even if it takes one year." Only after a year of trying would he give up and go back.

Quietly, Enrique, the slight kid with a boyish grin, fond of kites, spaghetti, soccer, and break dancing, who likes to play in the mud and watch Mickey Mouse cartoons with his four-year-old cousin, packs up his belongings: corduroy pants, a T-shirt, a cap, gloves, a toothbrush, and toothpaste.

For a long moment, he looks at a picture of his mother, but he does not take it. He might lose it. He writes her telephone number on a scrap of paper. Just in case, he also scrawls it in ink on the inside waistband of his pants. He has $57 in his pocket.

On March 2, 2000, he goes to his grandmother Águeda's house. He stands on the same porch that his mother disappeared from eleven years before. He hugs María Isabel and Aunt Rosa Amalia. Then he steps off.

Seeking Mercy

The day's work is done at Las Anonas, a railside hamlet of thirty-six families in the state of Oaxaca, Mexico, when a field hand, Sirenio Gómez Fuentes, sees a startling sight: a battered and bleeding boy, naked except for his undershorts.

It is Enrique. He limps forward on bare feet, stumbling first one way, then another. His right shin is gashed. His upper lip is split. The left side of his face is swollen. He is crying.

His eyes are red, filled with blood. He dabs open wounds on his face with a filthy sweater he has found on the tracks. Gómez hears him whisper, "Give me water, please."

The knot of apprehension in Sirenio Gómez melts into pity. He runs into his thatched hut, fills a cup, and gives it to Enrique.

"Do you have a pair of pants?" Enrique asks.

Gómez dashes back inside and fetches some. There are

holes in the crotch and the knees, but they will do. Then, with kindness, Gómez directs Enrique to Carlos Carrasco, the mayor of Las Anonas. Whatever has happened, maybe he can help.

Enrique hobbles down a dirt road into the heart of the little town. He encounters a man wearing a white straw hat on a horse. Could he help him find the mayor? "That's me," the man says. He stops and stares. "Did you fall from the train?"

Again, Enrique begins to cry. Mayor Carrasco dismounts. He takes Enrique's arm and guides him to his home, next to the town church. "Mom!" he shouts. "There's a poor kid out here! He's all beaten up." Lesbia Sibaja, the mayor's mother, hears his urgent tone and rushes outside.

Enrique's cheeks and lips are swelling badly. *He's going to die,* Carrasco thinks. Carrasco drags a wooden pew out of the church, pulls it into the shade of a tamarind tree, and helps Enrique onto it.

The mayor's mother puts a pot of water on to boil and sprinkles in salt and herbs to clean his wounds. She brings Enrique a bowl of hot broth, filled with bits of meat and potatoes. He spoons the brown liquid into his mouth, careful not to touch his broken teeth. He cannot chew.

Townspeople come to see. They stand in a circle. "Is he alive?" asks Gloria Luis, a stout woman with long black hair. "Why don't you go home? Wouldn't that be better?" Other women press him to return to Honduras.

"I'm going to find my mom," Enrique says, quietly.

He is seventeen. It is March 24, 2000. Eleven years before, he tells the townspeople, his mother left home in Tegucigalpa, Honduras, to work in the United States. She did not come back, and now he is riding freight trains up through Mexico to find her.

Gloria Luis looks at Enrique and thinks about her own children.

She earns little; most people in Las Anonas make 30 pesos a day, roughly $3, working the fields. She digs into a pocket and presses 10 pesos into Enrique's hand.

Several other women open his hand, adding 5 or 10 pesos each.

Mayor Carrasco gives Enrique a shirt and shoes. He has cared for injured migrants before. Some have died. Giving Enrique clothing will be futile, Carrasco thinks, if he can't find someone with a car who can get the boy to medical help.

Adan Díaz Ruiz, mayor of San Pedro Tapanatepec, the county seat, happens by in his pickup.

Carrasco begs a favor: Take this kid to a doctor.

Díaz balks. He is miffed. "This is what they get for doing this journey," he says. Enrique cannot pay for any treatment. The migrants most badly mangled by the train run up bills of $1,000 to $1,500 each when they end up at a public hospital one and a half hours away. Why, Díaz wonders, do these Central American governments send us all their problems?

Looking at the small, soft-spoken boy lying on the bench, he reminds himself that a live migrant is better than a dead one. In eighteen months, Díaz has had to bury eight of them, nearly all mutilated by the trains. Already today, he has been told to expect the body of yet another, in his late thirties.

Sending this boy to a local doctor would cost the county $60. Burying him in a common grave would cost three times as much. First Díaz would have to pay someone to dig the grave, then someone to handle the paperwork, then someone to stand guard while Enrique's unclaimed body is displayed on the steamy patio of the San Pedro Tapanatepec cemetery for seventy-two hours, as required by law.

All the while, people visiting the graves of their loved ones would complain about the smell of another rotting migrant.

"We will help you," he tells Enrique finally.

He turns him over to his driver, Ricardo Díaz Aguilar. Inside the mayor's pickup, Enrique sobs, but this time with relief. He says to the driver, "I thought I was going to die."

An officer of the judicial police approaches in a white pickup. Enrique cranks down his window. Instantly, he recoils. He recognizes both the officer with buzz-cut hair and the truck.

The officer, too, seems startled. Both stare silently at each other.

For a moment, the officer and the mayor's driver discuss the new dead migrant. Quickly, the policeman pulls away.

"That guy robbed me yesterday," Enrique says.

The policeman and a partner had seen Enrique and four other migrants drying off after bathing in a river five miles to the south. "Get over here," the buzz-cut officer barked, waving a pistol. One of the migrants bolted. Enrique obeyed, afraid of what might happen if he tried to run. The officers put the migrants in the back of their truck. They demanded 100 pesos to let them go. Enrique was relieved that one of the fellow migrants had the money and handed it over. "You won't tell anyone," the officer warned.

The mayor's driver is not surprised. The judicial police, he says, routinely stop trains to rob and beat migrants. The *judiciales*—the Agencia Federal de Investigación—deny it.

Enrique has already had other run-ins with corrupt Mexican cops. Once, he was just fifteen miles inside Mexico, in Tapachula, when two municipal police officers grabbed him and put him in the back of their pickup.

"Where are you from?" they demanded. "How much do

you have on you? Give it to us and we will let you go." They stole everything he had, $4.

Four of five migrants who arrive at the Albergue Belén shelter in Tapachula have already been robbed, beaten, or extorted by police, says the shelter priest, Flor María Rigoni. At the Tapachula train station, fights break out between municipal and state police officers over who gets to rob a group of migrants. Migrants describe being locked up by police officers until a relative in the United States can wire the kidnapper's fee and buy their freedom.

For immigration agents, squeezing cash from migrants is central to day-to-day operations, helping underpaid agents buy big houses and nice cars. At highway checkpoints, agents charge smugglers $50 to $200 per migrant to pass through. The checkpoint boss typically gets half the take; his workers split the rest. Officials who try to stop abuses receive repeated death threats. One government worker in the Mexican state of Tabasco, who in 1999 denounced corruption by certain judicial police agents, was dead a few days later in a mysterious car accident. "If you speak out too much against police corruption, you wake up with a machete in your back," says Father Rigoni.

In San Pedro Tapanatepec, the driver seeking a doctor for Enrique finds the last clinic still open that night.

PERSEVERANCE

When Enrique's mother left, he was a child. Six months ago, the first time he set out to find her, he was still a callow kid. Now he is a veteran of a perilous pilgrimage by children, many of whom come looking for their mothers and travel any way they can. The thousands who ride freight trains must hop between seven and thirty trains to get through Mexico. The luckiest make it in a month. Others, who stop to work along the way, take a year or longer.

Some go up to five days without eating. Their prize possessions are scraps of paper, wrapped in plastic, often tucked into a shoe. On the scraps are telephone numbers: their only way to contact their mothers. Some do not have even that.

None of the youngsters has proper papers. Many are caught by the Mexican police or by *la migra*, the Mexican immigration authorities, who take them south to Guatemala. Most try again.

Like many others, Enrique has made several attempts.

The first: He set out from Honduras with a friend, José del Carmen Bustamante. They remember traveling thirty-one days and about a thousand miles through Guatemala into the state of Veracruz in central Mexico, where *la migra* captured them on top of a train and sent them back to Guatemala on what migrants call *El Bus de Lágrimas*, the Bus of Tears. These buses make as many as eight runs a day, deporting more than 100,000 unhappy passengers every year.

The second: Enrique journeyed by himself. Five days and 150 miles into Mexico, he committed the mistake of falling asleep on top of a train with his shoes off. Police stopped the train near the town of Tonalá to hunt for migrants, and Enrique had to jump off. Barefoot, he could not run far. He hid overnight in some grass, then was captured and put on the bus back to Guatemala.

The third: After two days, police surprised him while he was asleep in an empty house near Chahuites, 190 miles into Mexico. They robbed him, he says, and then turned him over to *la migra*, who put him, once more, on the bus to Guatemala.

The fourth: After a day and twelve miles, police caught him sleeping on top of a mausoleum in a graveyard near the depot in Tapachula, Mexico, known as the place where a migrant woman had been raped and, two years before that, another had been raped and stoned to death. *La migra* took Enrique back to Guatemala.

The fifth: *La migra* captured him as he walked along the tracks in Querétaro, north of Mexico City. Enrique was 838 miles and almost a week into his journey. He had been stung in the face by a swarm of bees. For the fifth time, immigration agents shipped him back to Guatemala.

The sixth: He nearly succeeded. It took him more than five days. He crossed 1,564 miles. He reached the Rio Grande and actually saw the United States. He was eating alone near some railroad tracks when *migra* agents grabbed him. They sent him to a detention center called El Corralón, the Corral, in Mexico City. The next day they bused him for fourteen hours, all the way back to Guatemala.

The bus unloaded him back across the Río Suchiate in the rugged frontier town of El Carmen. The river marks the Guatemalan border, just as the Rio Grande defines the Mexican border to the north. A sign in block letters on top of a hill says BIENVENIDOS A GUATEMALA.

It was as if he had never left.

He has slept on the ground; in a sewage culvert, curled up with other migrants; on top of gravestones. Once, on top of a moving train, he grew so hungry that he jumped forward to the first car, leaped off, and raced to pick a pineapple. He was able to reboard one of the train's last cars. Another time, he had gone two days without water. His throat felt as if it was swelling shut. There were no houses in sight. He found a small cattle trough. It was frothy with cow spit. Under the froth was green algae. Beneath the algae was stagnant, yellow water. He brought handfuls to his parched lips. He was so thirsty it tasted wonderful.

Each time he is deported, Enrique knows he must quickly get back over the river, into Mexico, away from Guatemala's lawless border towns. Once he was deported at 2 A.M. and spent the night cowering, sleepless, near the border guard station, afraid for his life.

Migrants usually head to the border town of Tecún Umán to cross the river. Its lifeblood is trafficking in arms, drugs, and people. It teems with violence, prostitutes, and destitute migrants. They die at a rate of two or three a week. Tecún Umán is controlled by two rival gangs, both born in Los Angeles: the Mara Salvatrucha and 18th Street.

In Tecún Umán, the river is wider, slower, easier to ford. A platoon of large passenger tricycles wheels migrants from the bus stop to the riverbank, swerving along the main, rutted, dirt road to avoid pigs and trash burning in the middle of the street.

The bank's muddy shores reek of sewage. Salsa music blares from restaurants that double as houses of prostitution. Some Central American children, penniless, get stuck here, turning tricks, doing drugs, and stealing, says Marvin Godínez, legal assistant at Tecún Umán's Casa del Migrante shelter. Workers unload scores of tricycles piled high with toilet paper and Pepsi-Cola and load them onto rafts bound for Mexico. The rafts are a few planks of wood lashed on top of two tractor tire inner tubes. Dozens of the rafts crisscross the river. A man uses a long cane to push against the river bottom or ties himself to the front of the raft with a long rope and swims. Migrants prefer to pay to cross in a raft than risk the river alone.

Enrique prefers to cross the river in El Carmen, where the

bus leaves him, even though there are no rafts and the Río Suchiate is more narrow, fast, and rocky. The water is the color of coffee with too much cream. The nasty river reaches his chest. Each time he crosses, as the rainy season approaches, the river is higher and higher. He always crosses with one or two other migrants, in case he slips and starts to drown. Chin high, he staggers across, stumbling on the uneven riverbed, lurching into the hollows, straining against the current. Exhausted, he reaches the far bank.

This is his seventh try, and it is on this attempt that he suffers the injuries that leave him in the hands of the kind people of Las Anonas.

Here is what Enrique recalls:

It is night. He is riding on a freight train. A stranger climbs up the side of his tanker car and asks for a cigarette. The man moves quickly, but Enrique is not alarmed. Sometimes migrants riding on the trains climb from car to car, trying to move forward or backward.

Trees hide the moon, and Enrique does not see two men who are behind the stranger, or three more creeping up the other side of the car. Scores of migrants cling to the train, but no one is within shouting distance.

One of the men reaches a grate where Enrique is sitting. He grabs Enrique with both hands. Someone seizes him from behind. They slam him facedown. All six surround him. Take off everything, one says. Another swings a wooden club. It cracks into the back of Enrique's head. Hurry, somebody demands. The club smacks his face.

Enrique feels someone yank off his shoes. Hands paw through his pants pockets. One of the men pulls out a small scrap of paper. It has his mother's telephone number. Without it, he has no way to locate her. The man tosses the paper into the air. Enrique sees it flutter away.

The men pull off his pants. His mother's number is inked inside the waistband. But there is little money. Enrique has less than 50 pesos on him, only a few coins that he has gathered begging. The men curse and fling the pants overboard.

The blows land harder.

"Don't kill me," Enrique pleads.

"Shut up!" someone says.

His cap flies away. Someone rips off his shirt. Another blow finds the left side of his face. It shatters three teeth. They rattle like broken glass in his mouth. The men pummel him for what seems like ten minutes. The robbery has turned into blood sport.

One of the men stands over Enrique, straddling him. He wraps the sleeve of a jacket around Enrique's neck and starts to twist.

Enrique wheezes, coughs, and gasps for air. His hands move feverishly from his neck to his face as he tries to breathe and buffer the blows.

"Throw him off the train," one man yells.

Enrique thinks of his mother. He will be buried in an unmarked grave, and she will never know what happened. "Please," he asks God, "don't let me die without seeing her again."

The man with the jacket slips. The noose loosens.

Enrique struggles to his knees. He has been stripped of everything but his underwear. He manages to stand, and he runs along the top of the fuel car, desperately trying to balance on the smooth, curved surface. Loose tracks flail the train from side to side. There are no lights. He can barely see his feet. He stumbles, then regains his footing.

In half a dozen strides, he reaches the rear of the car.

The train is rolling at nearly 40 miles per hour. The next car is another fuel tanker. Leaping from one to the other at such speed would be suicidal. Enrique knows he could slip, fall between them, and be sucked under.

He hears the men coming. Carefully, he jumps down onto the coupler that holds the cars together, just inches from the hot, churning wheels. He hears the muffled pop of gunshots and knows what he must do. He leaps from the train, flinging himself outward into the black void.

He hits dirt by the tracks and crumples to the ground. He crawls thirty feet. His knees throb. Finally, he collapses under a small mango tree.

Enrique cannot see blood, but he senses it everywhere. It runs in a gooey dribble down his face and out of his ears and nose. It tastes bitter in his mouth. Still, he feels overwhelming relief: the blows have stopped.

He recalls sleeping for maybe twelve hours, then stirring and trying to sit. His mind wanders to his mother, then to his family and María Isabel, who might be pregnant. "How will they know where I have died?"

Enrique's girlfriend, María Isabel, is sure Enrique hasn't really left Honduras. This is all a joke. He has probably gone to visit a friend. He'll be back any day.

A couple of weeks after Enrique disappears, his paternal grandmother, María, traverses Tegucigalpa to talk to Enrique's relatives and María Isabel. Has anyone heard anything from Enrique, who came to bid her good-bye before leaving for the United States?

It is no joke.

María Isabel knows Enrique longed to be with his mother.

He spoke often of going north to be with Lourdes. Still, how could he leave her? What if he is harmed or killed crossing Mexico? What if she never sees him again?

She cries and blames herself for Enrique's departure. Then she prays. "God," she whispers, "grant me one wish. Get Mexican immigration authorities to catch Enrique and deport him back to Honduras. Send him back to me." It is a well-worn prayer in Honduras, especially by children whose mothers have just left them to head north.

María Isabel doesn't feel well, forcing her to quit night school. She loses weight. What if she *is* pregnant and Enrique dies trying to make it to his mother?

A friend offers a solution. The two of them will journey to the United States together. Maybe, the friend says, they will find Enrique as they make their way through Mexico. María Isabel has no money. Her friend, who works at a clothing store, says she has cash. She has saved 10,000 lempiras, roughly $570. It's not enough to hire a smuggler. But if María Isabel will accompany her north, the friend says, she will share it. "We'll be happier there. There, we'll have everything," the friend says.

María Isabel has decided. They set a date to leave. She will go and find Enrique.

A MISTAKE

Enrique falls back asleep, then wakes again. The sun is high and hot. Enrique's left eyelid won't open. He can't see very well. His battered knees don't want to bend.

He grabs a stick and pulls himself up. Slowly, barefoot, and with swollen knees, he hobbles north along the rails. He sees a rancher and asks for water. Get lost, the rancher says. Enrique grows dizzy and confused. He walks the other way, south along the tracks. After what seems to be several hours, he is back again where he began, at the mango tree.

Just beyond it, in the opposite direction, is a thatched hut surrounded by a white fence. It belongs to field hand Sirenio Gómez Fuentes, who watches as the bloodied boy walks toward him.

At the one-room medical clinic, Dr. Guillermo Toledo Montes leads Enrique from the outside porch, where patients wait to be seen, to an examination table inside.

Enrique's left eye socket has a severe concussion. The eyelid is injured and might droop forever. His back is covered with bruises. He has several lesions on his right leg and an open wound hidden under his hair. Two of his top teeth are broken. So is one on the bottom.

Dr. Toledo jabs a needle under the skin near Enrique's eye, then into his forehead. He injects a local anesthetic. He scrubs dirt out of the wounds and thinks of the migrants he has treated who have died. This one is lucky. "You should give thanks you are alive," he says.

Sometimes the doctor hands the most difficult cases to a hospital in Arriaga, a town one and a half hours away. Arriaga's Red Cross workers retrieve, on average, ten migrants per month who have fallen or been beaten up by bandits or gangsters. "They threw me off the train," they explain. Some have been shot. Others have had their hands cut open trying to protect themselves from machete blows. Injured migrants who land in isolated stretches of the tracks and cannot move wait one or two days until someone finally walks by.

In Las Anonas, the Red Cross retrieves a seventeen-year-old Honduran boy who lost his left leg. They come for a woman who is convulsing. She has not eaten for six days and has fallen off the train.

They pick up three migrants mutilated by the train in as many days. One loses a leg, another his hand; the third has been cut in half. Sometimes the ambulance workers must pry a flattened hand or leg off the rails to move the migrant. Other times, the migrant is dead by the time they arrive. They aren't supposed to transport dead people. Still, sometimes, they take the body away, so coyotes and vultures won't eat it.

The Arriaga hospital chronicles a parade of misery. Two weeks before Enrique's March beating, a Salvadoran was found crumpled and unconscious and by the tracks, his left arm broken. In April, a Honduran broke his foot falling from the train. Another, assaulted by someone wielding a machete atop the trains, arrived with the ligaments in his right hand severed. In May, a Honduran had a fractured right clavicle. In June, a Nicaraguan had a broken right rib. In July, a seventeen-year-old Honduran lost both legs. In August, a Salvadoran arrived with his leg hanging by a bit of skin and muscle. In October, two Salvadoran youths on top of a train were electrocuted by a high-tension wire. One had second-degree burns over 47 percent of his body. In December, a Honduran arrived with both legs and ankles broken. Most often, says social worker Isabel Barragán Torres, migrants lose their left legs to the train.

Some amputees stay in the area, too ashamed to go back and let their families see what has become of them. To the many injured who do return to Central America, the hospital social worker pleads, "Tell other people there not to travel this way."

"Why don't you go home?" the doctor treating Enrique asks.

"No." Enrique shakes his head. "I don't want to go back." Politely he asks if there is a way that he can pay for his care, as well as the antibiotics and the anti-inflammatory drugs.

The doctor shakes his head. "What do you plan to do now?"

Catch another freight train, Enrique says. "I want to get to my family. I am alone in my country. I have to go north."

The police in San Pedro Tapanatepec do not hand him over to *la migra*. Instead, he sleeps that night on the concrete floor of their one-room command post. At dawn, he leaves, hoping to catch a bus back to the railroad tracks. As he walks, people stare at his injured face. Without a word, one man hands him 50 pesos. Another gives him 20. He limps on, heading for the outskirts of town.

The pain is too great, so he flags down a car. "Will you give me a ride?"

"Get in," the driver says.

Enrique does. It is a costly mistake. The driver is an off-duty immigration officer. He pulls into a *migra* checkpoint and turns Enrique over. You can't keep going north, the agents say.

Next time, he prays, he will make it.

He is ushered onto another bus, with its smell of sweat and diesel fumes. He is relieved that there are no Central American gangsters on board. Sometimes they let themselves be caught by *la migra* so they can beat and rob the migrants on the buses. They move from seat to seat, threatening the passengers with ice picks and demanding everything they have.

Enrique's bus picks up other deportees at *migra* stations along the way. As Mexican officials call out their names, the migrants step out of large cells, some with open-trench toilets brimming with feces and urine. They are handed their belongings. Apart from the clothes they wear, all that many have left are their belts.

Some migrants realize, sitting on the bus, that they can take no more. They are out of money. They have passed through cold, heat, hunger. They slump in their seats, weak. Often something tragic has broken their willpower: a violent assault, a rape, or a fall from a train. They no longer believe it's possible to reach America.

Others have been on the bus dozens of times. They vow to keep trying, no matter what. They rest on the bus, recharging for the road ahead. They plot how they will try again, using knowledge gained from previous attempts.

There are twenty migrants on Enrique's bus, and they are depressed. They talk of giving up, heading back to El Salvador or Nicaragua. For long stretches, the bus is quiet, save for the rattle of the muffler.

In spite of everything, Enrique has failed again—he will not reach the United States this time, either. He tells himself over and over that he'll just have to try again.

THREE

Facing the Beast

Enrique wades chest-deep across a river. He is five feet tall and stoop-shouldered and cannot swim. The logo on his cap boasts hollowly, NO FEAR.

The river, the Río Suchiate, forms the border. Behind him is Guatemala. Ahead is Mexico, with its southernmost state of Chiapas. *"Ahora nos enfrentamos a la bestia,"* migrants say when they enter Chiapas. "Now we face the beast."

Painfully, Enrique, seventeen years old, has learned a lot about "the beast." In Chiapas, bandits will be out to rob him, police will try to shake him down, and street gangs might kill him. But he will take those risks, because he needs to find his mother.

This is Enrique's eighth attempt to reach *el Norte*. First, always, comes the beast. About Chiapas, Enrique has discovered several important things.

In Chiapas, do not take buses, which must pass through nine permanent immigration checkpoints. A freight train faces checkpoints as well, but Enrique can jump off as it brakes, and if he runs fast enough, he might sneak around and meet the train on the other side.

In Chiapas, never ride alone. His best odds are at night or in fog, when Enrique can see immigration agents' flashlights but they cannot see him. Storms are best, even when they bring lightning and he is riding on a tank car full of gas; rain keeps immigration agents indoors.

In Chiapas, do not trust anyone in authority and beware even the ordinary residents, who tend to dislike migrants.

Once the Río Suchiate is safely behind him, Enrique beds down for the night in a cemetery near the depot in the town of Tapachula, tucking the NO FEAR cap beneath him so it will not be stolen.

On previous trips, Enrique slept close to the train station, which is several blocks from the cemetery. Once, he rested in a clump of grass next to the dilapidated depot. Another time, he found an abandoned house nearby. He lay down a scrap of cardboard and used another piece as a blanket to keep mosquitoes away. From there, he could watch for trains leaving for the north. Missing one meant waiting two or three days for the next train.

But Enrique has been caught twice near the depot in police sweeps. The officers seal off surrounding streets and leave little room for escape.

The cemetery, Enrique decides, is a better bet. He is close enough to hear diesel engines growl and horns blare whenever a train pulls out but far enough to avoid police who hover around the station looking for migrants. Enrique hopes there will be a train tomorrow. He stuffs a few rags under his head for a pillow and slips into sleep.

"Wake up." The warning is only a whisper, but Enrique hears it. The words are from a gangster sleeping next to him, on top of a mausoleum.

Five pickups have coasted silently up to the cemetery with their lights out, filled with municipal police. Now, just before dawn, the officers start moving in. "Spread out!" They stride through a tangled maze of pathways, fanning out among the graves, carrying AR15 rifles, 12-gauge shotguns, and .38-caliber pistols.

The cemetery is beautiful. The moon is yellow. The sky is midnight blue. Enrique can see stars around the ceiba trees shrouding the headstones. Crosses, entire crypts, are painted periwinkle, neon green, purple. Wind touches the tree branches, and they murmur in the gathering light. A bigger gust moves the vast limbs, and the sound builds slowly until the wind commands the branches to dance and the leaves to titter. The burial ground greets the sun with a symphony.

Police radios crackle. Enrique peeks over the edge of the mausoleum.

The graveyard might be beautiful, but it is filled with peril. A seventeen-year-old girl waiting for a train was dragged out among the headstones three years ago, then raped and murdered. The year before that, a young man's forehead was beaten in with a metal tube. Before that, a rag was stuffed into a young woman's mouth and she was raped, then beaten to death with stones.

But Enrique has found four members of the Mara Salvatrucha gang, who use the graveyard as their hideout. On an earlier trip, he had met El Brujo, one of their comrades. They will provide protection, even in the darkest corners of this burial ground, where migrants pile excrement, old clothes, and sardine cans, where visitors leave candles burning on top of tombs, and where a witch comes to sacrifice chickens. Without these gangsters, Enrique would never venture here, behind the black iron gates.

In this migrant dormitory, he has washed his mouth with urine, a home remedy for his still aching, broken teeth. He has passed up graves covered by foot-high rectangular blocks, called *mesas*, with triangular headstones that would make good pillows. Instead, he has chosen the roof of the mausoleum, a one-room crypt holding the remains of four members of the Conchalitos family, the owners of a local restaurant. He and Big Daddy, fifteen, of the Mara Salvatrucha have settled on top. One stucco wall is tagged, in aerosol spray, MARA SALVA-TRUCHA and EL YAGA, a local leader.

But these words provide no protection against what he and Big Daddy see happening below. The police, in blue uniforms, are encircling them and thirty-odd additional migrants who have spent the night among the dead. Some of the migrants are trying to run, stampeding among the graves. Enrique knows that is futile; the last time he tried running from the police in the cemetery, he was caught and deported.

He and Big Daddy flatten themselves on the mausoleum roof.

Enrique tries not to breathe.

But some of the police look their way. Enrique and Big Daddy pretend that the officers do not notice them.

Then Big Daddy sees one of the policemen peer up over the edge of the crypt and straight at him. Big Daddy can't help himself. He giggles.

"Get down," the officer says.

There is no escape. Enrique and the others are marched off to the Tapachula jail. "Name? Age? Where are you from?" They are led through four metal doors into a courtyard, then into three small cells. Stink wafts from toilet pits. Men and boys press against the metal bars, trying to get fresh air.

Finally, everyone is taken to a jail next door, run by *la migra*. The jail has several holding cells, rooms with concrete benches and iron doors. Each cell is packed. The agents take Enrique and about twenty others to a patio. As they mill about, a rumor circulates: a train is leaving at 10 A.M.

"I can't miss it," Enrique says to himself.

He sees an old bicycle leaning against the patio wall. Now he watches *la migra* carefully. When they are distracted, he climbs on top of the bicycle. Other migrants hoist him higher. He grabs a water pipe and pulls himself over the wall and onto the roof of an adjoining house. He jumps to the ground. His head pounds; it is still swollen from being battered.

But he is free.

Enrique runs back to the cemetery, a way station for migrants. At sunup on any given day, it seems as uninhabited as a country graveyard. But then, at the first rumble of a departing train and the hiss of air from its brake lines, it erupts with life. Dozens of migrants, children among them, emerge from the bushes, from behind the ceiba trees, and from among the tombs.

They run on trails between the graves and dash headlong down the slope. A sewage canal, twenty feet wide, separates them from the rails. They jump across seven stones in the canal, from one to another, over a nauseating stream of black. They gather on the other side, shaking the water from their feet. Now they are only yards from the rail bed.

On this day, March 26, 2000, Enrique is among them. He

sprints alongside rolling freight cars and focuses on his footing. The roadbed slants down at 45 degrees on both sides. It is scattered with rocks as big as his fist. He cannot maintain his balance and keep up, so he aims his tattered tennis shoes at the railroad ties. Spaced every few feet, the ties have been soaked with creosote, and they are slippery.

Here the locomotives accelerate. Sometimes they reach 25 miles per hour. Enrique knows he must heave himself up onto a car before the train comes to an orange bridge that crosses the Coatán River, just beyond the end of the cemetery. He has learned to make his move early, before the train gathers speed.

Most freight cars have two ladders on a side, each next to a set of wheels. Enrique always chooses a ladder at the front. If he misses and his feet land on the rails, he still has an instant to jerk them away before the back wheels arrive. But if he runs too slowly, the ladder will yank him forward and send him sprawling. Then the front wheels, or the back ones, could take an arm, a leg, perhaps his life.

"Se lo comió el tren," other migrants will say. "The train ate him up."

Already, Enrique has four jagged scars on his shins from frenzied efforts to board trains.

The lowest rung of the ladder is waist-high. When the train leans away, it is higher. If it banks a curve, the wheels kick up hot white sparks, burning Enrique's skin. He has learned that if he considers all of this too long, he will fall behind—and the train will pass him by. This time, he trots alongside a gray hopper car. He grabs one of its ladders, summons all of his strength, and pulls himself up. One foot finds the bottom rung, then the other.

He is aboard.

Enrique looks ahead on the train. Men and boys are hanging on to the sides of tank cars, trying to find a spot to sit or stand. Some of the youngsters could not land their feet on the ladders and have pulled themselves up rung by rung on their knees, which are bruised and bloodied.

Suddenly, Enrique hears screams. Three cars away, a boy, twelve or thirteen years old, has managed to grab the bottom rung of a ladder on a fuel tanker, but he cannot haul himself up. Air rushing beneath the train is sucking his legs under the car. It is tugging at him harder, drawing his feet toward the wheels.

"Pull yourself up!" a man says.

"Don't let go!" another man shouts. He and others crawl along the top of the train to a nearby car. They shout again. They hope to reach the boy's car before he is so exhausted he must let go. By then, his tired arms would have little strength left to push away from the train's wheels.

The boy dangles from the ladder. He struggles to keep his grip. Carefully, the men crawl down and reach for him. Slowly, they lift him up. The rungs batter his legs, but he is alive. He still has his feet.

GETTING ABOARD

There are no women on board the train today; it is too dangerous. There are several children, some much younger than Enrique. One is only eleven. He is among the 20 to 30 percent of those boarding the trains in Tapachula who are fifteen or under, by estimate of Grupo Beta, a government migrant rights group in Chiapas. This eleven-year-old tells Enrique that he, too, was left behind with his grandmother in Honduras. He, too, is going alone to find his mother in the United States. He tells Enrique that he is frantic to see her.

Enrique has encountered children as young as nine. Some speak only with big brown eyes or a smile. Others talk openly about their mothers: "I felt alone. I only talked to her on the phone. I didn't like that. I want to see her. When I see her, I'm going to hug her a lot, with everything I have."

Enrique guesses there are more than two hundred migrants on board, a tiny army of them who charged out of the cemetery with nothing but their cunning. Arrayed against them is *la migra,* along with crooked police, street gangsters, and bandits. They wage what a priest at a migrant shelter calls *la guerra sin nombre,* the war with no name. Chiapas, he says, "is a cemetery with no crosses, where people die without even getting a prayer." A 1999 human rights report said that migrants trying to make it through Chiapas face "an authentic race against time and death."

All of this is nothing, however, against Enrique's longing for his mother, who left him behind eleven years ago. Although his efforts to survive often force her out of his mind, at times he thinks of her with a loneliness that is overwhelming. He remembers when she would call Honduras from the United States, the concern in her voice, how she would not hang up before saying, "I love you. I miss you."

Enrique considers carefully. Which freight car will he ride on? This time he will be more cautious than before.

Boxcars are the tallest. Their ladders do not go all the way up. *Migra* agents would be less likely to climb to the top. And he could lie flat on the roof and hide. From there he could see the agents approaching, and if they started to climb up, he could jump to another car and run.

But boxcars are dangerous. They have little on top to hold on to. Inside a boxcar might be better. But police, railroad security agents, or *la migra* could bar the doors, trapping him inside.

Another migrant, Darwin Zepeda López, recounts what can happen in a locked boxcar.

Coyotes, or smugglers, mistook him for a paying customer and herded him along with their clients toward four boxcars, their doors open. Then they loaded him and about forty of the others into one of the cars. Zepeda, twenty-two, says he heard the metal doors slide, then clang shut. The smugglers locked them in from the outside, so the boxcar would not look suspicious. It was April 2000 in southern Mexico, and the outdoor temperature was climbing past 100 degrees. Inside, the car was turning into an oven.

As the train rolled north, the migrants drank their water bottles dry. The air in the car turned rank with sweat. Zepeda could hardly breathe. People began screaming and shouting for help. Some knelt and pleaded with God to stop the train.

Fistfights broke out in his boxcar as the riders jockeyed to suck fresh air through tiny rust holes over the doors. After four hours, he says, a woman with asthma begged for water, then slumped to the floor, unconscious. Others pried open her mouth and tried to give her the few drops they could find. Finally, they left her for dead. Some stood on her to reach the highest airholes.

In the next five hours, before immigration agents and Mexican soldiers stopped the train and opened the doors, Zepeda saw seven migrants fall to the floor. The boxcar, he says, looked like a rolling morgue.

Enrique looks elsewhere. A good place to hide could be under the cars, up between the axles, balancing on a foot-wide iron shock absorber. But Enrique might be too big to fit. Besides, trains kick up rocks. Worse, if his arms grew tired or if he fell asleep, he would drop directly under the wheels. He tells himself, "That's crazy."

He could sit on a round compressor at the end of some hoppers, his feet dangling just above the train wheels. Or stand on a tiny ledge, barely big enough for his feet, on the end of other hopper cars. His hands would turn numb and callous after hours of hanging on.

Enrique settles for the top of a hopper. He finds one that is full, making it more stable. He holds on to a grate running along the rim. From his perch fourteen feet up, he can see anyone approaching on either side of the tracks up ahead or from another car. Below, at each end, the hopper's wheels are exposed: shiny metal, three feet in diameter, five inches thick, churning. He stays as far away as he can.

He doesn't carry anything that might keep him from running fast. At most, if it is exceptionally hot, he ties a nylon string on an empty plastic bottle, wraps it around his arm, and fills the bottle with water when he can.

Some migrants climb on board with a toothbrush tucked into a pocket. A few allow themselves a small reminder of family. One father wraps his eight-year-old daughter's favorite hair band around his wrist. Others bring a small Bible with telephone numbers, penciled in the margins, of their mothers or fathers or other relatives in the United States. Maybe nail clippers, a rosary, or a scapular with a tiny drawing of San Cristóbal, the patron saint of travelers, or of San Judas Tadeo, the patron saint of desperate situations.

As usual, the train lurches hard from side to side. Enrique holds on with both hands. Occasionally, the train speeds up or slows down, smashing couplers together and jarring him backward or forward. The wheels rumble, screech, and clang. Sometimes each car rocks the other way from the ones ahead and behind. *El Gusano de Hierro,* some migrants call it. The Iron Worm.

In Chiapas, the tracks are twenty years old. Some of the ties sink, especially during the rainy season, when the roadbed turns soggy and soft. Grass grows over the rails, making them slippery.

When the cars round a bend, they feel as if they might overturn. Enrique's train runs only a few times a week, but it averages three derailments a month—seventeen accidents in a particularly bad month—by the count of Jorge Reinoso, chief of operations for Ferrocarriles Chiapas-Mayab, the railroad. One year before, a hopper like Enrique's overturned with a load of sand, burying three migrants alive. In another spot, six hoppers tumbled over. One migrant was crushed between the train car and a bridge the train was crossing. Another migrant was found dead downstream. The cars' rusty remains are scattered, upside down, next to the tracks. Enrique was once on a train that derailed. His car lurched so violently that he briefly thought of jumping off to save himself. Enrique rarely lets himself admit fear, but he is scared that his car might tip. *El Tren de la Muerte,* some migrants call it. The Train of Death.

Others cast the train in a more positive light. They believe it has a noble purpose. Sometimes, the train tops are packed with migrants. They face north, toward a new land, a neverending exodus. *El Tren Peregrino,* they call it. The Pilgrim's Train.

Enrique is struck by the magic of the train—its power and its ability to take him to his mother. To him, it is *El Caballo de Hierro.* The Iron Horse.

The train picks up speed. It passes a brown river that smells of sewage. Then a dark form emerges ahead. Migrants at the front of the train, nearest to the locomotive, call back a warning over the train's deafening din. They sound an alarm, migrant to migrant, car to car. *"¡Rama!"* the migrants yell. "Branch!" They duck.

Enrique grips the hopper. To avoid the branches, he sways from side to side. All of the riders sway in unison, ducking the same branches—left, then right. One moment of carelessness—a glance down at a watch, a look toward the back of the train at the wrong time—and the branches will hurl them into the air. Matilda de la Rosa, who lives by the tracks, recalls a migrant who came to her door with an eyeball hanging on his cheek. He cupped it near his face, in his right hand. He told her, "The train ripped out my eye."

A DREADED STOP

Each time the train slows, Enrique goes on high alert for *la migra*. Migrants wake one another and begin climbing down to prepare to jump. They lean outward, trying to glimpse what is causing the train to change pace. Is it another false alarm? Sometimes, an oncoming train forces the engineer to pull off onto a siding. A migrant, moving from car to car, can inadvertently step on the pressurized brake line that runs the length of the train. Other migrants, frustrated by the train's pace, disconnect the brake line on purpose. The conductor must stop to fix the problem. A bad curve can also cause a train to slow. If the train speeds up again, everyone climbs back up. The movement down and up the ladders looks like a strangely choreographed two-step.

But slowing down at Huixtla, with its red-and-yellow depot,

can mean only one thing: coming up is La Arrocera, one of the most dreaded immigration checkpoints in Mexico. Of the half-dozen checkpoints Enrique has eluded in southern Mexico, he fears La Arrocera most.

Immigration agents picked this place, named after two rice warehouses, because it is so isolated. There are acres of open cattle range and few houses or busy streets where migrants can hide. Usually, half of those aboard are caught by *migra* agents.

Enrique has defied La Arrocera before. On his last attempt, he lay flat on top of a hopper. It was night. *Migra* agents' flashlight beams danced over his car several times. Enrique held his breath. The train pushed forward.

This time, he arrives in the heat of noon. Tension builds. Some migrants stand on top of the train, straining to see the *migra* agents up ahead. The first migrants who spot twenty agents down the tracks scream a warning to the others: "*Bájense!* Get down!" As the train brakes, they jump.

The train lurches sideways. Enrique leaps from car to car, finally landing on a boxcar. The train stops. He lies flat, face-down, arms spread-eagle, hoping *la migra* won't see him. But several agents do.

"*¡Bájate, puto!* Get down, you whore!"

"No! I'm not coming down!"

There is no ladder all the way to the top. The only way up is to straddle their legs across two adjoining boxcars, using the horizontal ridges on the ends of the cars to inch higher. Maybe they won't come up after him.

"Get down!"

"No!"

The agents summon reinforcements. One starts to climb up. Enrique scrambles to his feet and races along the top of the train, soaring across the four-foot gaps between cars. As he runs, three agents follow on the ground, pelting him with rocks and sticks, an experience many migrants say they have here. Stones clang against the metal. Enrique flees from car to car, more than twenty in all, struggling to keep his footing each time he leaps from a hopper to a fuel tanker, which is lower and has a rounded top.

He is running out of train. He will have to go around La Arrocera alone. It may be suicidal, but he has no choice. More stones ping off the train. Enrique scurries down a ladder and sprints into the bushes.

"*¡Alto! ¡Alto!* Stop!" the agents shout.

As Enrique runs, he hears what he thinks are gunshots behind him.

Except in extraordinary circumstances, Mexican immigration agents are barred from carrying firearms. According to a retired agent, however, most have .38-caliber pistols. Some of the shelter workers tell of migrants hit by bullets. Others tell of torture. Before long, Enrique will meet a man whose chest is pockmarked with cigarette burns. The man tells him that a *migra* agent at La Arrocera branded him.

In the scrub brush, though, Enrique worries less about agents than about *madrinas* with machetes. The name for these men is a play on words: these civilians help the authorities, as a *madrina,* or godmother, would, and administer *madrizas,* or savage beatings. Human rights activists and some police agencies say the *madrinas* commit some of the worst atrocities—rapes and torture—and are allowed by authorities to keep a portion of what they steal.

Sometimes, a *madrina* rides the train and pretends to be a migrant. The *madrina* radios ahead to report how many migrants are aboard and where they are hidden so agents will know which cars to target when they stop the train. *Migra* agents wear green uniforms. Enrique can't distinguish *madrinas,* who wear plain clothes.

Enrique runs on. He crawls under a barbed-wire fence, then under a double strand of smooth wire. It is electrified. At night, Guillermina Gálvez López, whose wooden hut fronts the rails at La Arrocera, hears the trains and, not long afterward, the piercing screams of migrants, wet from the swampy grass, who run into the wire.

"Help me! Help me!" they wail.

Ten times in ten months, train riders have carried to her front door men and boys without arms, legs, or heads. Often they are injured as they try to outrun the agents and get onto and off of moving trains.

Migrants hide their money. Some stitch it into the seams of their pants. Others put a bit in their shoes, a bit in their shirts, and a coin or two in their mouths. Still others bag it in plastic and tuck it into intimate places. Some roll it up and slip it into their walking sticks. Others hollow out mangoes, drop their pesos inside, then pretend to be eating the fruit.

Enrique figures he doesn't have enough money to bother.

Enrique knows he has plunged deep into bandit territory. At least three, maybe five swarms of robbers, some with Uzis, some on drugs, patrol the three-mile dirt paths that migrants must use to go around La Arrocera, authorities say.

Migrants describe similar experiences. "Don't run, or we'll kill you," bandits yell. Strip off your clothes. Lay facedown on the ground. Bandits edge their machetes against migrants' throats or ears as they disrobe. Keep quiet, they are told. Don't look up. One bandit splits open waistbands, collars, and cuffs looking for hidden money. They keep belts, watches, and shoes. Migrants who resist are beaten or killed. Everyone gets a final warning: "If you say anything to the authorities, we will find you and kill you." Local residents see groups of migrants walking down dirt roads naked, stripped of everything.

There's El Cantil, a tall, skinny man named after a particularly agile and poisonous snake. El Cochero leads ten bandits. La Mano de Seda, the Hand of Silk, is known for his mastery at robbing people. La Mara Valiente lives in the nearby town of Buenos Aires and operates where the tracks cross Reforma Ranch.

After the day's robberies, bandits retire to the neighboring town of Huixtla to drink and visit prostitutes. At the Quinto Patio, with its hot pink façade, a sign beckons: LADIES DANCE. There are La Embajada nightclub, Los Piños, Las Brisas, and the Bar El Noa Noa, which advertises pole dancers.

The bandits are so well known and seem to operate with such impunity that Mario Campos Gutiérrez, a supervisor with Grupo Beta Sur, thinks the authorities collaborate. Many of the bandits, Campos says, are current or former police officers. If they are arrested, they pay bribes and are quickly released. Witness statements against them mysteriously disappear. Migrants can't wait around for months until the trial. Bandits long ago intimidated any La Arrocera residents who considered testifying.

"If you say anything, they kill you. Better to keep your mouth shut," says Antonio, a local elderly man, who is afraid to give his last name. An ice cream vendor near La Arrocera adds, "If you turn them in, they get out, and they come after you. They operate by light of day. There is no law here."

The last time Enrique sneaked past La Arrocera, he was

lucky because he was careful. He stuck with a band of street gangsters. Bandits try to avoid gangsters, who are probably armed, preferring easier prey. Enrique and the gangsters ran past a group of Mexican men standing by the tracks, machetes at their sides. The men looked at them intently but did not move or attack.

This time he is alone. He focuses on the thought that will make him run the fastest: "I cannot miss the train."

If he misses the one he just left, he knows he will be a sitting duck, waiting for days in the bushes and the tall grass until another one comes.

Enrique races so fast he feels the blood pounding at his temples. The ground is wet, slippery. The grass, growing in three-foot tentacles, lassos his feet. He stumbles, gets up, and keeps running. He passes an abandoned brick house. Half the roof is gone.

The house is notorious. Not long before, Grupo Beta found a bed of bricks inside, covered with emerald green leaves from a plant that looked like a bird-of-paradise—and two soiled pairs of panties crumpled on the dirt floor. Women are raped here, most recently a sixteen-year-old assaulted repeatedly over three days.

Many are gang-raped, including a Salvadoran woman, four months pregnant, who was assaulted at gunpoint by thirteen bandits along the railroad tracks to the south. They arrive at local hospitals with severe internal hemorrhaging and long scratch marks on their buttocks. Some get pregnant. A few go mad. In one Chiapas shelter, one raped woman paces, her arms tightly crossed in front of her, a blank stare on her face. At another shelter, a woman spends hours each day in the shower, trying to cleanse herself of the attack.

Nearly one in six migrant girls detained by authorities in Texas says she has been sexually assaulted during her journey, according to a 1997 University of Houston study. Some girls journeying north cut off their hair, strap their breasts, and try to pass for boys. Others scrawl on their chests, TENGO SIDA. "I have AIDS."

Enrique does not stop. He reaches the Cuil bridge, where the railroad spans a forty-foot stream of murky brown water. This, migrants and Grupo Beta Sur officers say, is the most dangerous spot. El Cantil's group of bandits often lays in wait here. Bandits haul mattresses up into nearby trees, eat lunch, and wait for their prey. They use local children as lookouts, who race forward on their bicycles to tell the bandits when migrants are drawing near. As migrants cross the bridge, the bandits drop out of the limbs and surround them. Other robbers hide along the tracks above and below the bridge, which is thick with bushes and vines. One fishes in the river or cuts grass with a machete, like a fieldworker, and whistles to the others to set a trap.

Just a month before, bandits ambushed five Salvadorans as they crossed the bridge at 4 A.M. They tried to run. The bandits shot one in the back. Four months later, three Salvadorans and a Mexican, all in their twenties, were killed. The Salvadorans, their hands tied behind them, were shot in the head. The Mexican was stabbed. All they had left was their underwear. A local resident counts forty migrants felled here by bandits, some hacked to death with a machete.

Enrique dashes across the bridge and keeps running. Mountains stand to his right. The ground is so wet that farmers grow rice between their rows of corn. He can feel heat and humidity rising from the loamy earth. It saps his energy, but he runs on. Finally, he stops, doubled over, panting.

He is not sure why, but he has survived La Arrocera. Maybe it was his extra caution, maybe it was his decision to run, maybe it was his attempt to lie flat and hide atop the boxcar, which delayed his getting off the train and gave the bandits an opportunity to target migrants ahead of him.

He is desperate for water. He spots a house.

The people inside are not likely to give him any. Chiapas is fed up with Central American migrants, says Hugo Ángeles Cruz, a professor and migration expert at El Colegio de la Frontera Sur in Tapachula. They are poorer than Mexicans, and they are seen as backward and ignorant. People think they bring disease, prostitution, and crime and take away jobs. At checkpoints, they bring gunfire, as well. Residents fear that the shots *migra* agents fire into the air to get migrants to surrender could fall on a child playing outside. Some migrants cannot be trusted. People in Chiapas talk of being robbed by migrants with guns and knives. They tell of an older woman who welcomed a migrant into her home and was beaten to death with an iron pipe. And of a man who sold chickens in a market and was kind to outsiders. He gave three Salvadorans a place to sleep and work killing and plucking birds. The Salvadorans robbed him and slit his throat.

Boys like Enrique are called "stinking undocumented." They are cursed, taunted. Dogs are set upon them. Barefoot children throw rocks at them. Some use slingshots. "Go to work!" "Get out! Get out!"

Drinking water can be impossible to come by. Migrants filter ditch sewage through T-shirts. Finding food can be just as difficult. Enrique is counting: in some places, people at seven of every ten houses turn him away.

"No," they say. "We haven't cooked today. We don't have any tortillas. Try somewhere else."

"No, boy, we don't have anything here."

Many La Arrocera residents lock themselves inside their homes when they hear the train coming. "I'm afraid," says local housewife Amelia López Gamboa, who corrals her family inside her one-room brick house and bars the door.

Sometimes it is worse: people in the houses turn the migrants in.

Enrique sees another migrant who has managed to make it around La Arrocera. He, too, needs water badly, but he doesn't dare ask. He is afraid of walking into a trap. To migrants, begging in Chiapas is like walking up to a loaded gun.

"I'll go," Enrique says. "If they catch someone, it will be me."

Enrique also knows he is less likely to frighten people if he begs alone.

He approaches a house and speaks softly, his head slightly bowed. "I'm hungry. Can you spare a taco? Some water?" The woman inside sees injuries from the train-top beating he took during his last attempt to go north. "What happened?" she asks. She gives him water, bread, and beans. The other migrant comes nearer. She gives him food, too.

A horn blows. Enrique runs to the tracks. He looks all around, trying to spot *migra* agents, who sometimes race ahead in their trucks to catch migrants as they reboard. Other migrants who have survived La Arrocera come out of the bushes. They sprint alongside the train and reach for the ladders on the freight cars.

Sometimes, train drivers back up the locomotive and get a running start. They accelerate to prevent migrants from reboarding up ahead. This time, though, the train isn't going full throttle.

Enrique climbs up onto a hopper. The train picks up speed. For the moment, he relaxes.

A DECISION

Back in Honduras, María Isabel is tense. She is bent on going to search for Enrique. Maybe she will find him along the way, in Mexico. If not, she will continue on to the United States. She and a friend have set a date to start the journey together.

Two days before the rendezvous, María Isabel confesses the plan to her aunt Gloria. She first gets Gloria's promise not to tell anyone, especially María Isabel's strict mother, Eva. "I'm going to the United States," María Isabel says.

Gloria finds a good-bye letter under María Isabel's mattress. "I'm leaving with a friend to find Enrique in Mexico," she writes. She bequeaths her stuffed toys to Gloria's fourteen-year-old daughter. The letter makes Gloria realize that María Isabel is serious.

That night, Gloria is so upset, her heart flutters. She can't sleep. The next morning, she confides in her daughter, Karla Yamileth Chávez. Karla immediately confronts María Isabel. "Are you crazy? You want to die along the way?" If you are pregnant, you could lose the child on the road, Karla says. She sends across town for María Isabel's mother.

Eva berates her daughter. "What are you thinking? If you have problems, come home. We'll manage."

María Isabel listens in silence. She is sorry she made the plan. When her travel companion arrives on the appointed day, María Isabel sends her away. But the reactions to her plan have only emphasized in her own mind how much danger Enrique is in.

STAYING AWAKE

The Iron Worm squeaks, groans, and clanks—black tankers, rust-colored boxcars, and gray hoppers winding north on a single track that parallels the Pacific coast. Off to the right are hillsides covered with coffee plants. Cornstalks grow up against the rails. The train moves through a sea of plantain trees, lush and tropical.

By early afternoon, it is 105 degrees. Enrique's palms burn when he holds on to the hopper. He risks riding no-hands. Finally, he strips off his shirt and sits on it. The locomotive blows warm diesel smoke. People burn trash by the rails, sending up more heat and a searing stench. Many migrants have had their caps stolen, so they wrap their heads in T-shirts. They gaze enviously at villagers cooling themselves in streams and washing off after a day of fieldwork and at others who doze in hammocks slung in shady spots near adobe and cinder-block homes. The train cars sway from side to side, up and down, like bobbing ice cubes.

Enrique's head throbs. The sun reflects off the metal. It stings his eyes, and his skin tingles. It drains the little energy he has left. He moves around the car, chasing patches of shade. For a while, he stands on a narrow ledge at the end of a fuel tanker. It is just inches above the wheels. He cannot let himself fall asleep; one good shake of the train, and he would tumble off.

Moreover, the Mara Salvatrucha street gangsters, some deported from Los Angeles, always prowl the train tops looking for sleepers. Many MS gangsters settle in Chiapas after committing crimes in the United States and being expelled to their home countries in Central America. The police in Chiapas are more forgiving of gangs than those in El Salvador or Honduras. "There, the police don't arrest you. They kill you," says José Eduardo Avilés, twenty-five, who was deported from Los Angeles to El Salvador and settled in Chiapas along the tracks.

The MS control the tops of freight trains operating north of the Río Suchiate, where many migrants going to the United States begin their trek through Mexico. They rob migrants riding the trains. Migrants, who are often afraid to press charges, make ideal victims.

About two hundred street gangsters in Chiapas share the rolling criminal enterprise. Father Flor María Rigoni, the priest at the Albergue Belén migrant shelter, counts nineteen groups. Each controls a specific part of the train route and certain stations. Periodically, the groups meet to decide who gets what.

"We ask for money to take people to the U.S. on top of our trains," says Jorge Mauricio Mendoza Pineda, twenty-four, describing what he and his Mara Salvatrucha gang do in Chiapas. "They give me their money. If people treat me well, I treat them well. If they don't, I don't. . . . If someone says, 'Please don't kill me,' I won't listen."

Before the train leaves, the gangsters roam the Tapachula depot, eyeing which migrants are buying food and where they stash their cash afterward. They try to get friendly with the migrants, telling them they have already done the train ride. Maybe they can offer tips? Many of the gangsters wear white plastic rosaries around their necks so the migrants will be less suspicious. They ask, "Where are you from? Where are you going? Do you have any money?"

Ten or twenty board the train, armed with machetes, knives, bats, lead pipes, and pistols. When the train gains speed, they surround a group of migrants. They tell them: hand over your money or die. Drugs embolden them. The gangsters carry marijuana and rocks of crack cocaine in the headbands of their baseball caps. A train engineer, Emilio Canteros Méndez, often sees the armed gangs through his rearview mirror. Fights erupt on top of the boxcars. Migrants who anger the gangsters because they don't have money or resist are regularly tossed off the moving train or left dead on the tops of the cars, to be discovered by train workers at the next stop.

Gangsters' warnings to migrants not to go to the police are ruthlessly enforced. Julio César Cancino Gálvez, with Grupo Beta Sur, recalls how a group of about thirty migrants at the Tapachula train station asked him why the authorities weren't clamping down on the gangsters. Cancino told them they needed witnesses. He urged the migrants to step forward and report abuses. One nineteen-year-old Honduran in the crowd spoke up. He described his assailant in detail.

Hours later, the Red Cross asked Cancino if he could help an injured migrant. It was the same Honduran teenager. His right ribs were broken. His entire chest and face were badly bruised. He spoke slowly, in a whisper, clasping his chest. Two gangsters had overheard his description and kicked him mercilessly. "Next time, we kill you," the gangsters told him. The teenager, afraid for his life, asked to be deported.

Many of the migrants on Enrique's train huddle together, hoping for safety in numbers. They watch for anyone with tattoos, especially gangsters who have skulls inked around their ankles—one skull, police say, for every person they have killed. Some wear black knit hats they can pull down over their faces. Their brutality is legendary. Migrants tell of nine gangsters who hurled a man off their train, then forced two boys to have sex together or be thrown off, too.

Enrique has heard of the most dangerous gangsters: El Indio, who claims the Guatemalan side of the Mexican border;

Blackie, a chubby Salvadoran with dark skin and MS tattooed on his forehead, whose territory stretches from the border to Arriaga in northern Chiapas; and El Yaga, Porkie, and Homeboy.

During his first attempts north, a chance meeting saved Enrique from the worst of the gangs. As he set out on his trip, he noticed another teenager, a gangster named El Brujo, at the bus station in Honduras waiting to go to the Mexican border. Enrique doesn't like gangs. But as the two spent hours traveling through Honduras and Guatemala together, they became friends. On their first train ride through Chiapas, El Brujo introduced Enrique to a dozen other MS members, among them Big Daddy, who is skinny and short; El Chino (the Chinaman), who has slanted eyes; and El Payaso (the Clown), who has a big mouth and eyes. On subsequent trips, when he was deported, he always stuck with one of these gang members to protect himself from any attacks.

On his seventh trip, the convenient relationship ends. He is on the train with El Brujo and two other MS gangsters, who are carrying machetes. One of them is upset because a member of the rival 18th Street gang has stolen his shirt during a train stop in Chiapas. The MS gangsters decide to retaliate and throw the gangster off the train. Enrique refuses to participate, creating a rift. "If you are MS, you have to kill 18th Streeters. And if you are 18th Street, you must kill MS. I wasn't like that," Enrique says.

After the fight with his friends, halfway through Chiapas, the gang members stop riding with Enrique. That night, without their protection, the six men beat him on top of the train. Now, for a second time, he is alone on a train. He must stay alert.

Some migrants, after days without sleep, nap on their feet,

using belts or shirts to strap themselves to posts at the ends of the hoppers. Others get off the train and stretch out across the rails, using one as a footrest and the other as a pillow. They believe it is the only way to catch sleep and not miss the next train—they trust that the vibrations from the locomotive will wake them. Some also believe, mistakenly, that snakes cannot slither over the rails, so they sleep there for protection. Exhausted, many sleep so soundly they do not hear the trains bearing down on them: the earsplitting horn, the screaming brakes. They lose limbs and are sometimes decapitated. By the time they see the migrants on the rails, train drivers know they don't have enough distance to stop the train. Many say they simply ask God for forgiveness and drive on.

Enrique allows himself to doze only on trains farther north, where the gangsters no longer control the tops of the trains. There, he jams his body into the crevice on top of a hopper, next to the trapdoors used to fill the car. Or he waits until the train rounds a curve, giving him a good view of all of the cars. He spots a boxcar with its door open. When the train slows, he jumps off and races to the boxcar, jumping inside for a quick nap.

In Chiapas, most train riders struggle to stay awake. Dagoberto Hernández Aguilar uses the memory of his first train ride to stay up. Two teenagers on top of a nearby boxcar dozed. The train suddenly lurched forward. The two slid off. He is not sure if they survived. He chants one sentence to himself, over and over, as he rides north: "It could have been me." Migrants take amphetamines, slap their own faces, do squats, talk to one another about how much money they'll make in the United States, tell jokes, pour drops of alcohol into their eyes, and sing. At 4 A.M. the train sounds like a chorus.

Today, Enrique is terrified of another beating. Every time

someone new jumps onto his car, he tenses. Fear, he realizes, helps to keep him awake, so he decides to induce it. He climbs to the top of the tank car and takes a running leap. With arms spread, as if he were flying, he jumps to one swaying boxcar, then to another. Some have four- to five-foot gaps. Others are nine feet apart.

The train passes into northern Chiapas. Enrique sees men with hoes tending their corn and women inside their kitchens patting tortillas into shape. Cowboys ride past and smile. Field-workers wave their machetes and cheer the migrants on: *"Qué bueno!"* Mountains draw closer. Plantain fields soften into cow pastures. Enrique's train slows to a crawl. Monarch butterflies flutter alongside, overtaking his car.

As the sun sets and the oppressive heat breaks, he hears crickets and frogs begin their music and join the migrant chorus. The moon rises. Thousands of fireflies flicker around the train. Stars come out to shine, so many they seem jammed together, brilliant points of light all across the sky.

The train nears San Ramón, close to the northern state line. It is past midnight now, and the judicial police are probably asleep. Train crews say this is where the police stage their biggest shakedowns. One conductor says the officers, fifteen at a time, stop the trains. They grab fleeing migrants by their shirts. The conductor has heard them say, "If you move, I'll kill you. I'll break you in two." Then, "Give us what you've got, or we send you back."

At nearby Arriaga, the chief of the judicial police, or Agencia Federal de Investigación, denies that his agents stop trains in San Ramón and rob migrants. The chief, Sixto Juárez, suggests that any robbing is done by gangsters or bandits who impersonate judicial officers.

Enrique has been caught here before. He had taken his

shoes off to dry blistered feet. Barefoot, he couldn't outrun the police. Today, his feet are still damp from his race around La Arrocera. But he has left his shoes on, ready to bolt.

Enrique greets the dawn without incident. The stars recede. The sky lightens behind the mountains to the east, and mist rises off the fields on both sides of the tracks. Men trot by on burros with tin milk containers strapped to their saddles, starting their morning deliveries.

Enrique figures that one in ten migrants makes it this far. Mario Campos Gutiérrez, supervisor of Grupo Beta Sur, estimates that half eventually get here—after repeated attempts. One migrant says, "I've done the most difficult part." Another: "When I get to this point, I begin to sing hallelujah."

Enrique puts Chiapas behind him. He still has far to go, but he has faced the beast eight times now, and he has lived through it. It is an achievement, and he is proud of it.

DEVOURED

Many migrants who first set out on the train with Enrique have been caught and deported. Others have fared worse; they are left broken by Chiapas. These migrants don't talk of The Pilgrim's Train, or of The Iron Horse. They have another name for the train: *El Tren Devorador.* The Train That Devours.

At the rate of nearly one every other day, the Red Cross estimates, U.S.-bound Central American migrants who ride freight trains lose arms, legs, hands, or feet. The estimate, offered by Martin Edwin Rabanales Luttman, chief of training for the Red Cross ambulance corps in Tapachula, is for the Mexican state of Chiapas alone. It does not count those who die instantly when they are cut in half or decapitated.

They fall from the trains for a variety of reasons. Some fall asleep and roll off; others are thrown by the street gangs who control the train tops. Because the migrants try to fool authorities and pass themselves off as Mexican, they carry no identification. If they die, their bodies are lowered, nameless, into common graves. In Tapachula, they end up down a hole in the cemetery with fetuses and stillborn babies.

At Arriaga, in northern Chiapas, snapshots of the dead are placed in a black book on Police Chief Reyder Cruz Toledo's desk. Some pictures are so new that he hasn't pasted them in yet.

In most photos, the eyes are open.

The chief keeps the book handy, hoping someone will identify the bodies. No one, he says, ever comes to look.

Carlos Roberto Díaz Osorto, seventeen, of Honduras, had almost crossed Chiapas. Carlos lies in bed number 1 of the trauma unit at Hospital Civil in the town of Arriaga in southern Mexico. Four days before he was brought in, Carlos had seen a man get both legs cut off by a freight train. But he had pushed fear out of his mind. He was going to the United States to find work.

At a curve near Arriaga, where the trains brake, Carlos raced alongside, asking himself, "Should I get on or not?" His cousins grabbed on to the sixth car from the end. Carlos panicked. Would he be left behind?

The train came to a bridge. Carlos did not give up. He crossed the span, jumping from one railroad tie to another. His shoelaces were loose. His left shoe flew off. Then his right shoe. He reached for a ladder on a fuel tanker, but the car was moving too fast, and he let go. He grabbed a railing.

The tanker jerked hard. Carlos held on, but he could feel air rushing beneath the car, sucking his legs in, close to the wheels. His fingers uncurled. He tried to bounce his feet off the wheels and push away. But as he let go, the air pulled him in. The wheels flattened his right foot, then sliced through his left leg above the knee.

"Help me! Help me! It hurts!" he screamed. He began to pant, to sweat, to ask for water, not sure anyone could hear him.

Paramedics from the Mexican Red Cross found him lying by the tracks. He had lost nearly a third of his blood, but the hot rails had cauterized many of his arteries. The medics applied two tourniquets. A doctor cut his bones, then sealed each artery and vein. He stretched skin over the openings and sutured them shut. Sometimes there are no drugs available to stave off infection, but Carlos was lucky. The Red Cross located some penicillin.

Many migrants who lose limbs to the train end up back in Tapachula, a dozen blocks from the depot where they first boarded the train, at the Shelter of Jesus the Good Shepherd. The shelter director, Olga Sánchez Martínez, tries to heal migrants left deeply wounded by the beast.

Olga is a petite middle-aged woman with silky black hair that touches her hips and a simple white rosary strung around her neck. She is always in motion, impatient to find solutions to problems. She buys blood and medicine so migrants won't die. She nurses them until they can be taken back home. "No one tells me something can't be done. Everything can be cured. Nothing is impossible," Olga says.

Says the hospital surgeon, José Luis Solórzano, "Without her, a lot of patients would have died."

At the hospital, almost all tell Olga they wish the beast would have killed them rather than leave them like this. They seethe. They curse God. Why didn't he protect them? They curse Olga. Their eyes speak fear. Who will ever marry them like this? How will they ever work, much less till a field again? "Let me die," they say, pushing Olga away. They tell her not to dress their stumps and wounds. They refuse to eat. Some try to hang themselves.

She perches on a corner of their hospital beds. She strokes their hair. She tells them that God has spared them for a reason. "If he wanted, he could have killed you. But he didn't. He left your eyes open," she says. When you are in this much pain and despair, she tells them, there is only one place to find strength. "God has a plan for you," she says. "You will learn to live—in a different way."

Then she tells them a story about herself.

When I was seven, she begins, I had an intestinal disease that went untreated for lack of money to buy medicine. It wrecked havoc on my insides. From then, off and on, I was gravely ill. At eighteen, I temporarily went blind and mute and had boils on my arms. My hair fell out. For thirty-eight days, I lay in a coma—sixty-six pounds of skin and bones. A year later, when I was well enough to work at a tortilla factory, a machine tore two fingertips off my left hand. She holds out her hand to the migrant. Plagued by constant stomach pain, so weak I couldn't get out of bed for months at a time, she tells them, I tried to slit my wrists.

In 1990, a doctor told me I had cancer and months left to live. I had two small children who would be left with my husband, who was once a womanizing alcoholic.

I was never very religious, but that day I went to church. I kneeled. I prayed. "They say there is a God. Why don't you cure me? Let me see my children grow, if only a little bit?" I made a pact: heal me, and I will help others.

The migrants listen.

She tells them she studied the Bible. It told her to help the weak, the hungry. She began visiting patients at a local public hospital. One year later, she saw a thirteen-year-old Salvadoran boy who had lost both legs trying to board a train. She walked home in tears. How, she asked God, could he be so cruel? The hospital pushed the penniless migrant out before he was healed. Olga brought the boy to recuperate at her humble home. Three days later, there was another young Salvadoran at the hospital who had lost both arms. "Don't feel alone. I will help you," she told him. She brought him home, too.

She taught herself, watching doctors, how to dress their wounds. Soon she had twenty-four migrants at home, so many she could barely open her front door. She moved the furniture outside so everyone could fit. Olga's husband helped dress and wash boys without arms. Olga begged money for food, medicine, and wheelchairs and to get migrants home. In 1999, she opened a shelter for injured migrants in a tiny former tortilla factory someone lent her.

As she finishes, she leans forward. She tells them she has never had a serious illness since she made her pledge in church that day. "God," she says, "has never left me alone."

She reaches out with her mangled hand. "God needs you. He doesn't need you with all your limbs. He needs your heart. You have much to give."

She confesses it has not been easy. Each day, at least one new wounded migrant passes through the shelter's lime green doors. They are logged into an intake book with their names and notations on which body parts they are missing or how they were otherwise injured. She has treated more than 1,500 wounded migrants since the shelter opened. It is a neverending stream. Those who don't fit in the four bedrooms' fifteen beds sleep in a long hallway on the floor.

She works for free, from dawn until late at night, seven days a week, to obtain money for food, units of blood, medicine, prostheses, and a scrap of land to build a permanent shelter. She sells tacos, pork rinds, cakes, chopped fruit, and donated bread in front of the hospital. Occasionally, a few churches in Chiapas let her solicit donations. She goes from car to car, begging, with a picture of a mutilated migrant she's trying to help and the prescription she must fill. People often tell her she's crazy to help foreigners who rob and murder and that she should help Mexicans instead.

Each Sunday she rises at 4 A.M. to head up into the mountains to a spot near an outdoor market. There, she sells used clothes people donate. It is still dark when she arrives. She dumps six big bags of used clothes onto the narrow sidewalk. She neatly lines up little bags of beans, sugar, and laundry soap—items a local grocery store donates because the packages are damaged and cannot be sold. When customers pause by the big pile of clothes, Olga madly paws through it, holding up items, hoping something will catch their fancy.

"Clothes for one, two pesos!" she yells.

A ragtag group helps her: the owner of a local hotel, a fertilizer salesman, a woman who sells children's clothing, a hardware store operator. A recovering alcoholic drives her around in his rickety truck. Together, they take injured migrants back to their hometowns in Central America when going by bus isn't feasible. A private doctor donates his time to reconstruct a boy's foot if Olga provides the materials for the operation. Olga and a church friend, Marilú Hernández Hernández, beg outside seven churches in five different towns. If a migrant is bleeding to death and there is no money to buy blood, they go to the tracks, even in the middle of the night, and plead for migrants to give theirs for free.

She's always running short on money. Medicine for one amputee costs $300. Sometimes there is no food for the migrants; she must ration antibiotics and not give patients a full dose; she runs out of gauze and must use boiled rags instead. Each pair of artificial legs costs at least $2,000. When she visits an orthopedic doctor, Jorge Luis Antonio Álvarez, who makes artificial limbs, she slides a few photos across his desk of the migrants she needs fitted, knowing she still owes him $4,500 for jobs he's already done. She pays little by little. Most migrants must leave the shelter before she can afford to buy them limbs. This is what pains her most.

Sometimes, she loses her patience with God. Some migrants, too battered by the beast, die. At times, Olga can't quickly come up with the money to buy the blood or medicine they need to fight for their lives. "What do you want me to do?" she asks God angrily. A thirteen-year-old girl was raped by the tracks and left with a broken neck and shattered hips. She could not move or talk. She buried that girl and thirty-nine others. She tries to buy them each a wooden coffin so they can be lowered into the ground with some dignity. But most slowly recuperate under Olga's care.

Each day, Olga begins at dawn at the city's drab public general hospital. Today, as she enters the emergency room, a social worker in a pink frock rushes up to Olga. The worker looks relieved.

"Señora Olguita, you have new clients," she says.

"Migrants?" Olga asks.

The social worker nods.

In room 2 she sees Andrea Razgado Pérez, a teenager, who has lost her right foot. Olga tells her she knows she fears her husband will see her as damaged goods and leave her. Olga says, "There's nothing you can't do if you have will." She describes a migrant who lost both legs but cooked for everyone in the shelter. She set up a chopping block across the armrests of her wheelchair. Andrea listens, sobbing. "Don't cry," Olga tells her. "This is the beginning of a new life. Nothing has been taken from you. God wants people who are useful. You must keep going forward. You have your hands. You must go forward and trust in God."

Olga heads to the shelter, which is full of people maimed by the train.

Tránsito Encarnación Martínes Hernández lost both feet. Olga has promised to get the young man prostheses, which cost $1,800. "You are going to walk again," she said. He has waited months at the shelter. He cannot bear the thought of going back to his small town in Honduras, where he won't be able to walk the hilly dirt paths, grow beans or corn or coffee, or play soccer with friends. He must start over, someplace new. "I ask God that I be able to walk, to learn a job that I can do this way." He waits, knowing that Olga is his best chance of ever being able to get the legs.

Leti Isabela Mejía Yanes sits on her bed. A single mother, she has an angular face and soft curly brown hair. She has lost both legs. In Honduras, Leti and her three children ate once a day—usually two pieces of bread with a watery cup of coffee. The youngest got only one piece of bread and breast milk. Sometimes, when her children cried with hunger, she scrounged together enough to buy a bit of tortilla dough and mixed it into a big glass of water to fill their bellies.

Her children begged her not to go. Her nine-year-old boy told her he would rather quit school and start working. "I already know how to write my name!" he pleaded. She left Marlon, eleven; Melvin, nine; and Daniel, one and a half, with relatives. When she walked away, Daniel still hadn't learned to talk. Olga, who found Leti at the hospital, brought her two liters of blood and antibiotics. At the shelter, she gave her painkillers and took out her stitches. At first Leti wanted to die. Now she wants to get better and see her children again. She sits in bed, embroidering a pillowcase with a drawing of Cinderella wearing a ballroom gown. She will wait here, sewing, until Olga can buy her legs, too.

Olga bathes people. She cooks. She gives them pills for pain. She cheerleads, watching with joy as they take their first steps with a prosthesis. She is impatient with those who wallow in pity. She coaxes them past the shelter's threshold to go to the ocean, which most have never seen. She places them on the sand, where waves can lap at their stumps.

Each day, she tends to their wounds. Each night, at 7 P.M., she races to church for Mass. She kneels before an altar with a bronze lamb, two winged angels, and a wooden carving of Jesus and his disciples at the Last Supper. She clasps her hands and closes her eyes. She prays. She tells God what she did that day. She thanks God for giving her strength to get through the day's travails. She asks him for ideas on how to make money to pay for medicines and prostheses. She asks for ten more years of life so she can build a permanent shelter for injured migrants. She ends each prayer the same way: "You are the one who makes this work possible."

Each night, when she hears the train whistle, she asks God to protect the migrants from the trains and the assaults. She prays that the beast not bring so many to her door.

Others who don't make it as far as Enrique are broken by Chiapas in a different way. They have been raped.

A bandit with a cobra tattoo marches Wendy into a cornfield. She is seventeen and the only woman among eleven Central Americans trying to sneak around a Mexican immigration checkpoint at Huehuetán in Chiapas. The man with the cobra tattoo and four other bandits have been lying in wait.

A Central American man tries to bolt. One of the bandits broadsides him three times with the flat blade of a machete. The bandits tell the nine other men, including Wendy's husband, to strip to their underwear, then lie facedown on the ground. A bandit searches their clothing for cash.

Then, say Wendy's husband and the other Central Americans, the man with the cobra tattoo on his arm orders Wendy to remove her pants. She refuses. He throws her to the ground and places the tip of his machete against her stomach.

She begins to cry. He puts the edge of the blade to her throat. She takes off her pants, and he checks them for money. "If you scream," he says, "we cut you to bits." Then he rapes her.

The other bandits curse the men on the ground, then curse their mothers and threaten to castrate them. "What the hell are you doing outside your country?" they say. One by one, during an hour and a half, each of the five bandits goes into the cornfield and rapes Wendy.

Her husband fills with rage. The bandits bring her back, crying. She cannot speak. She vomits, then faints. As they flee, her husband and the others carry Wendy to the checkpoint. She says, trembling, "I want to die." None of the bandits is arrested.

Wendy, from Honduras, is one of a large number of migrant girls who say they are raped as they travel north through

Mexico to get to the United States. A 1997 University of Houston study of U.S. Immigration and Naturalization Service detainees in Texas shows that nearly one in six says she was sexually assaulted.

The rapes are part of the general denigration and humiliation of Central Americans in Mexico, where the migrants are seen as inferior because they come from less developed countries, says Olivia Ruiz, a cultural anthropologist at El Colegio de la Frontera Norte in Tijuana. The targets, she says, can be either men or women.

OAXACA

Having avoided the fate of many other migrants, Enrique reaches Ixtepec, a southern crossroads in Oaxaca, the next state north, 285 miles into Mexico. As his train squeals to a stop around noon, migrants jump down and look for houses where they can beg for a drink and a bite to eat. *La bestia* might be behind them, but most are still afraid. In these small towns, strangers stick out. Migrants are easy to spot. They wear dirty clothes and smell bad after days or weeks without bathing. Often, they have no socks. Their shoes are battered. They have been bitten by mosquitoes. They look exhausted.

Most of the migrants want to stay on the grassy slope by the tracks where they catch outgoing trains, where they can hide in huisache or mesquite bushes if there is a *migra* raid. Two of them are too frightened to go into town. They offer Enrique 20 pesos and ask him to buy food. If he will bring it back, they will share it with him.

He takes off his yellow shirt, stained and smelling of diesel smoke. Underneath he wears a white one. He puts it on over the dirty one. Maybe he can pass for someone who lives here. He resolves not to panic if he sees a policeman and to walk as if he knows where he is going.

Blending in is critical. Migrants clip labels off clothes from Central America. Some buy Mexican clothes or ones sporting the name of a Mexican soccer team. Most ditch their back-packs shortly after entering Mexico.

Enrique tries to stay clean by finding bits of cardboard to sleep on. When he gets a bottle of water, he saves a little to wash his arms. If he is near a river or stream, he strips and slips into the water. He begs for clean clothes or scrubs the ones he is wearing and lays them on the riverbank to dry.

He takes the pesos the two migrants have given him and walks down the main street, past a bar, a store, a bank, and a pharmacy. He stops at a barbershop. His hair is curly and far too long. It is an easy tip-off. People here tend to have straighter hair.

He strides purposefully inside.

"¡Órale, jefe!" he says, using a phrase Oaxacans favor. "Hey, chief!" He mutes his flat Central American accent and speaks softly and singsongy, like a Oaxacan. He asks for a short crop, military style. He pays with the last of his own money, careful not to call it *pisto*, as they do back home. That means alcohol up here.

He is mindful about what else he says. *Migra* agents trip people up by asking if the Mexican flag has five stars (the Hon-duran flag has, but the Mexican flag has none) or by demand-ing the name of the mortar used to make salsa (*molcajete*, a uniquely Mexican word) or inquiring how much someone weighs. If he replies in pounds, he is from Central America. In Mexico, people use kilograms.

In Guatemala, soda is called *agua*. Here in Mexico, *agua* is water. A jacket is a *chamarra,* not a *chumpa.* A T-shirt is a *playera,* not a *blusa.*

Migra agents particularly like to test suspected migrants with words that have the same meaning in Mexico and in Central America and sound similar but are not exactly the same. A belt is a *cinto* or a *cincho.* Sideburns are *patillas* or *patitas.*

At one point, Enrique glances into a store window and sees his reflection. It is the first time he has looked at his face since he was beaten. He recoils from what he sees. Scars and bruises. Black and blue. One eyelid droops.

It stops him.

"They really screwed me up," he mutters.

He was five years old when his mother left him. Now he is almost another person. In the window glass, he sees a battered young man, scrawny and disfigured.

It angers him, and it steels his determination to push northward.

FOUR

Gifts and Faith

From the top of his rolling freight car, Enrique sees a figure of Christ.

In the fields of Veracruz, among farmers and their donkeys piled with sugarcane, rises a mountain. It towers over the train he is riding. At the summit stands a statue of Jesus. It is sixty feet tall, dressed in white, with a pink tunic. The statue stretches out both arms. They reach toward Enrique and his fellow way-farers on top of their rolling freight cars.

Some stare silently. Others whisper a prayer.

It is early April 2000, and they have made it nearly a third of the way up the length of Mexico, a handful of migrants rid-ing on boxcars, tank cars, and hoppers.

Many credit religious faith for their progress. They pray on top of the train cars. At stops, they kneel along the tracks, ask-ing God for help and guidance. They ask him to keep them alive until they reach *el Norte.* They ask him to protect them against bandits, who rob and beat them; police, who shake them down; and *la migra,* the Mexican immigration authorities, who deport them.

In exchange for his help, they make promises: to never drink another drop of alcohol, to make a difficult pilgrimage someday, to serve God forever.

Many carry small Bibles, wrapped in plastic bags to keep them dry when they ford rivers or when it rains. On the pages, in the margins, they scrawl the names and addresses of the people who help them. The police often check the bindings for money to steal, the migrants say, but usually hand the Bibles back.

Some pages are particularly worn. The one that offers the Twenty-third Psalm, for instance: "Yea, though I walk through the valley of the shadow of death, I will fear no evil: for thou art with me; thy rod and thy staff they comfort me."

Or the Ninety-first Psalm: "There shall no evil befall thee, neither shall any plague come nigh thy dwelling. For he shall give his angels charge over thee, to keep thee in all thy ways."

Some migrants rely on a special prayer, *La Oración a las Tres Divinas Personas*—a prayer to the Holy Trinity. It asks the saints to help them and to disarm any weapon raised against them. It has seven sentences—short enough to recite in a moment of danger. If they rush the words, God will not mind.

That night, Enrique climbs to the top of a boxcar. In the starlight, he sees a man on his knees, bending over his Bible, praying.

Enrique climbs back down.

He does not turn to God for help. With all the sins he has committed, he thinks he has no right to ask God for anything.

SMALL BUNDLES

What he receives are gifts.

Enrique expects the worst. Riding trains through the state of Chiapas has taught him that any upraised hand might hurl a stone. But here in the states of Oaxaca and Veracruz, he discovers that people are friendly. They wave hello and shout to signal if hostile police are lying in wait for them in an upcoming town. People living along the tracks are put out when migrants take clothing from laundry lines, a police chief says—but only because they don't ask first. "People in Oaxaca and Veracruz are more likely to help," says a train engineer. "It's just the way we are," says Jorge Zarif Zetuna Curioca, a legislator from Ixtepec.

Perhaps not everyone is that way, but there is a widespread generosity of spirit. Many residents say it is rooted in the Zapotec and Mixtec indigenous cultures. Besides, some say, giving is a good way to protest Mexico's policies against illegal immigration.

As one man who lives on the tracks in Veracruz puts it, "It's wrong for our government to send people back to Central America. If we don't want to be stopped from going into the United States, how can we stop Central Americans in our country?"

Not long after seeing the statue of Jesus, Enrique is alone on a hopper. Night has fallen, and as the train passes through a tiny town, it blows its soulful horn. He looks over the side. More than a dozen people, mostly women and children, are rushing out of their houses along the tracks, clutching small bundles.

Some of the migrants grow afraid. Will these people throw rocks? They lie low on top of the train. Enrique sees a woman and a boy run up alongside his hopper.

"*¡Órale, chavo!* Here, boy!" they shout. They toss up a roll of crackers. It is the first gift.

Enrique reaches out. He grabs with one hand but holds tightly to the hopper with the other. The roll of crackers flies several feet away, bounces off the car, and thumps to the ground.

Now women and children on both sides of the tracks are throwing bundles to the migrants on the tops of the cars. They run quickly and aim carefully, mostly in silence, trying hard not to miss.

"*¡Allí va uno!* There's one!"

Enrique looks down. There are the same woman and boy. They are heaving a blue plastic bag. This time the bundle lands squarely in his arms. "*¡Gracias! ¡Adiós!*" he calls into the darkness. He isn't sure the strangers, who pass by in a flash, even heard him.

He opens the bag. Inside are half a dozen rolls of bread.

Enrique is stunned by the generosity. In many places where the train slows in Veracruz—at a curve or to pass through a village—people give. Sometimes twenty or thirty people stream out of their homes along the rails and toward the train. They wave. They smile, they shout, and then they throw food.

The towns of Encinar, Fortín de las Flores, Cuichapa, and Presidio are particularly known for their kindness. A young Honduran migrant, Fernando Antonio Valle Recarte, points at the ground in Veracruz. "*Here,*" he says, "the people are good. *Here,* everyone gives." As migrant José Rodas Orellana readies to board a train in Veracruz, a man emerges from his house. Without a word, the man puts a large sandwich stuffed with scrambled eggs into Rodas's hands. The man turns back home. Rodas, his voice cracking with emotion, says, "We could never keep going forward without people like this. These people give you things. In Chiapas, they take things away."

Enrique and other migrants usually try to ride the trains under cover of darkness. Here, migrants hope to cross during daylight, because residents are likely to bring gifts to the tracks.

These are unlikely places for people to be giving food to strangers. A World Bank study in 2000 found that 42.5 percent of Mexico's 100 million people live on $2 or less a day. Here, in rural areas, 30 percent of children five years old and younger eat so little that their growth is stunted, and the people who live in humble houses along the rails are often the poorest.

Families throw sweaters, tortillas, bread, and plastic bottles filled with lemonade. A baker, his hands coated with flour, throws his extra loaves. A seamstress throws bags filled with sandwiches. A teenager throws bananas. A carpenter throws bean burritos. A store owner throws animal crackers, day-old pastries, and half-liter bottles of water. People who have watched migrants fall off the train from exhaustion bring plastic jugs filled with Coca-Cola or coffee.

A young man, Leovardo Santiago Flores, throws oranges in November, when they are plentiful, and watermelons and pineapples in July. A stooped woman, María Luisa Mora Martín, more than a hundred years old, who was reduced to eating the bark of her plantain tree during the Mexican Revolution, forces her knotted hands to fill bags with tortillas, beans, and salsa so her daughter, Soledad Vásquez, seventy, can run down a rocky slope and heave them onto a train.

"If I have one tortilla, I give half away," one of the food throwers says. "I know God will bring me more."

Another: "I don't like to feel that I have eaten and they haven't."

Still others: "When you see these people, it moves you. It moves you. Can you imagine how far they've come?"

"God says, when I saw you naked, I clothed you. When I saw you hungry, I gave you food. That is what God teaches."

"It feels good to give something that they need so badly."

"I figure when I die, I can't take anything with me. So why not give?"

"What if someday something bad happens to us? Maybe someone will extend a hand to us."

Many people in the area who give are from small towns where roughly one in five youngsters has left for the United States. In these places, residents understand that poor people leave their country out of a deep necessity, not because they want to. They have watched and worried as their own children struggled to reach the United States. They know it is harder still for the Central Americans to make it.

The son of retired schoolteacher Raquel Flores Lamora, who lives in the railside town of Santa Rosa, nearly died trying to cross into the United States. For three days he walked, until his feet were so raw and blistered he knew he would have to turn himself in to the INS to save his life. Instead, others in the group carried him the rest of the way.

Each night, Flores gets up from her threadbare sofa and heads to the tracks. There, she hands out food and clothing, often shirts and pants her children in California send for her to give.

Baltasar Bréniz Ávila's two sons walked for days to enter the United States, through searing heat and with little drinking water. They dodged snakes, as well as bandits trying to assault them. Now they work as car washers in Orange County, California. "When I help someone here, I feel like I'm giving food to my children," Bréniz says. "I bet people help them, too."

For some, the migrants' gratitude is enough reason to give. Migrants who haven't eaten in days sob when they are handed a bundle of food. Other times, thanks come in a small gesture: a smile, a firm handshake before they move on.

The impetus to help comes from the local bishop, Hipólito Reyes Larios. One of his favorite passages in the Bible is Matthew 25:35. People, it says, should welcome and show compassion and charity toward strangers. "One of the acts of mercy," the bishop says, "is to give shelter to a migrant."

In dozens of tiny local parishes throughout the archdiocese, priests preach and practice what Matthew said. At the Iglesia Rectoría de Beato Rafael Guizar y Valencia, a humble yellow brick church with forty pews, priest Ignacio Villanueva Arteaga's message to churchgoers on Sunday is straightforward: being a good Christian means being a good Samaritan. He describes why the Central American migrants felt forced to leave their lands and tells of the dangers and problems they faced along the way.

He tells of another refugee: the baby Jesus, whose family had to flee the land of Israel and go to Egypt after an angel told Joseph they were in danger. He leads a prayer and asks God to help migrants safely arrive at their destinations, find work, and be able to return to their countries someday.

Every couple of weeks, nearby, state and local police officers conduct sweeps to find migrants. Villanueva protects any migrant who runs inside the church. "They are migrants. We are going to feed them here," the balding priest tells the police, who, so far, haven't raided the church. He hauls some green mattresses piled outside into a small room used for studies and catechisms, where the migrants sleep.

When seven migrants ran from the train one evening and were arrested outside his church, Villanueva ran toward the commotion. "Why do you detain them? They aren't robbing anyone. They just want to go north," he told the officers. "Let them go." Soon eight police cars had arrived. More than fifty church members had gathered around their priest. Villanueva convinced the officers to release the migrants. He works hard, the priest says, to keep police officers on his side. Each Easter Sunday parade, he invites them to carry the cross.

The same goes on at a nearby church, the Parroquia San Isidro Labrador in Encinar. Each week the priest asks church members to feed migrants. If you are old or pregnant, or can't go to the tracks for some other reason, bring food to the church, he tells them. We will send someone to the tracks to hand it out for you.

No one recalls when the gift-giving started, probably in the 1980s, when Central Americans, fleeing war and poverty, began riding the rails north in large numbers. Wherever the trains stopped, the migrants went, gaunt and dirty, plagued by parasites they had picked up along the way, to front doors to beg. Occasionally one would fall off a train, weak with hunger.

Eventually people along the tracks, particularly in the state of Veracruz, began to bring food out to the trains, often where they slowed for curves or bad tracks. Those who had no food brought plastic bottles of tap water. Those with no bottles came out to the tracks to offer a prayer. As the procession of migrants has grown, so has the determination to help.

Along the tracks in Veracruz, residents mobilize at the first sign of a train.

Gladys González Hernández waits for the diesel horn. There it is, at last! The girl runs down the narrow aisles of her father's grocery, snatching crackers, water bottles, and pastries off the shelves. She dashes outside. Gladys and her father, Ciro

González Ramos, wave to the migrants on board the train. She is six years old.

They stand along the tracks at Fortín de las Flores and throw the crackers and the water and the pastries into the outstretched hands of the migrants.

Ciro González, thirty-five, taught Gladys to do this; he wants her to grow up right.

"Why do you give them food?" she asked him once. Her father said, "Because they have traveled far and haven't eaten."

Long ago, González's neighbor heard a migrant knock at his door. "Give me anything, *please*," he said anxiously, through parched lips. He had not eaten in two days. The man gulped down six bean tacos. Then, humbly, he said, "I hope God helps you someday. I was hungry. And you fed me well." The neighbor started throwing food to migrants as they rolled by on the train. González followed.

At 6 P.M. on a summer day, Jesús González Román, forty, and his sister, Magdalena González Román, thirty-one, sit outside their railside home in the town of Encinar. Neighbors come out to chat after long hours of work as bricklayers and field hands. Clouds float down between the steep green mountains. The evening cools. A neighbor gently urges his goats along as he guides them home along the tracks.

They hear a diesel horn.

Magdalena and her brother have two minutes. They run inside. Their mother, Esperanza Román González, seventy-eight, adjusts her pink apron and grabs her cane.

Jesús plucks three sweaters from a nylon bag, hand-me-downs from relatives. He ties them into a knot, so they will be easier to throw.

Magdalena puts tortillas into an orange-colored bag, then

snatches bread rolls and stuffs them into a blue bag. She ladles lemonade into a plastic bottle, spilling some in her haste.

The horn on the locomotive grows louder, more frequent.

At the stove, she scoops a bowl of stew into a plastic bag. "Ready?" she mutters. "We have bread, tortillas . . ." She dashes to the front room.

The horn blasts nearby.

Jesús and Magdalena race outside, where their mother is already hobbling past the wooden front gate, her long gray braids swinging.

It is dusk. Headlights glow on the train. It slows for a curve. The ground rumbles. Wheels pound. The engineer sounds the horn five times, warning the twenty-odd people who have come out with food, drink, and clothing to be very careful.

Jesús and Magdalena edge close to the tracks, dig in their heels, and brace each other, so the wind the train produces will not suck them under the wheels.

Jesús spots migrants on a hopper car. "Some are on top!" he yells. He waves the sweaters above his head.

A teenager in a green-and-white shirt edges down the ladder on the hopper. He holds on with his right hand and reaches out with his left.

Now seconds count. Magdalena hands Jesús her blue bag of bread. He thrusts it up, along with the sweaters. A moment later, Magdalena pushes up a bottle of lemonade. The youngster grabs everything.

"*¡Gracias!*" he yells above the din.

"*¡Que Dios los lleve!* May God watch over you!" Jesús shouts back, eyes smiling.

Esperanza stands silently, her hands stretched upward. She prays to the Virgin of Guadalupe, asking her to bring all the children on the train safely to their worried mothers in *el Norte*.

Some have decided that giving migrants food and prayers is not enough. One town opened its church to migrants. Some residents invite strangers to stay in their homes, sometimes for months at a time. Others protect migrants from the police, often at great risk, since they can be accused of immigrant smuggling.

The priest Salamón Lcmus Lemus chuckles as he looks out on the grounds of the María Auxiliadora church. "They have taken over my church," he says, smiling. Hundreds of migrants mill around in the courtyard. They sleep in every nook and cranny of the church: in three large rooms once used for sacraments, baptisms, and youth study groups; in the garage; in the hallways; on the dirt patio outside; in the former sacristy. Each picks out a bit of cardboard from a huge pile and lays it down anywhere he or she can find a spot to bed down. There are so many—up to 640 some nights—that migrants must move on after three days and make room for others.

For more than two decades, the church members have been led by priests who have fought for the rights of workers and the poor. The church members grew increasingly distressed as they watched groups of migrants huddle and sleep, wet and with the outdoor temperature sometimes dropping below zero, along the nearby tracks. They watched police officers haul migrants by the hair or twist their wrists behind their backs, the *"manita de puerco,"* before throwing them into the back of their pickup trucks. They saw many migrants injured as they tried to escape capture by the police. In two years, thirty-two migrants lost limbs to the train.

The municipal police, dressed in green and white, used

dogs. Municipal and state police would beat migrants, sometimes take their money, then throw them into the back of their trucks, says Julio César Trujillo Velásquez, a spokesman for the Diocese of Orizaba.

Church members organized teams that would rush out on a moment's notice to aid a migrant being abused by the police. "They aren't animals. They are human beings," says a church volunteer, Gloria Sánchez Romero. "You'd never want to be treated that way."

Police officers run into the church to arrest migrants hiding inside, sometimes with their guns drawn. One day, several *migra* officers came in, arrested four migrants, and put them into their truck.

The priest protested.

"Help us! They're going to hit us!" one migrant said.

"Shut up!" one of the officers said, hitting the migrant with a nightstick several times. The incensed priest, a crowd of a hundred around him, demanded that they let the migrants go. "This is a church. You have violated this place. Release them!" the priest said.

The police let the four go but kept six others they had grabbed outside the church.

Church members held public protests. About 150 gathered outside a local public hospital. They strung up a large banner that read, HOSPITAL, ENEMY OF MIGRANTS. They were angry that the hospital had allowed *la migra* to quickly deport a migrant who had lost a leg to the train. The migrant claimed that a police officer had pushed him toward the train, causing the accident. He had been deported quickly, before local officials could take his testimony. On a mile-long walk toward the hospital, they chanted, "We want justice!" and shut down the entrance to the local highway.

Church members decided they had to do more, says church volunteer Luis Hernández Osorio. They began to let a few migrants sleep and eat at the church. Word spread that the church was providing sanctuary. The police crackdowns mounted, and more and more migrants came to the church.

"You must help," Luis and a group of other churchgoers told the bishop. "They are our brothers. We must open the church's doors." An opposing group went to the bishop, saying he should keep migrants out of the church. These migrants are a threat to the security of our children and families, they said. They give the church a bad image. They hang underwear to dry on the church walls. They haven't bathed in weeks and smell. They spit and proposition our daughters. They are strangers, delinquents. They are turning the church's beautiful green lawn, where kids play after catechism classes, into a muddy brown lot.

The bishop sided with the migrants. He called the church's gray-haired priest, Lemus Lemus, and told him to help them. He promised to help raise funds to build a migrant shelter. "This is what I consider the mission of the church. It is fundamental," the bishop says. Half the church's eight hundred members quit in protest.

An informal truce was struck with the police and *la migra*. They no longer come into the church to hunt down migrants. Hundreds of migrants, mostly men, mill about the large courtyard of the yellow church with orange trim. They rest, play dominoes, wash laundry and hang it on lines that crisscross the courtyard. On one side of the courtyard is an open-air kitchen. Three times a day, they form a long line to be handed a meal. Usually it is rice and beans and whatever else has been donated, maybe a big bowl of soup. On the other side: a large outdoor basin where they wash their clothes. At 10 P.M., they lie down to sleep on the floor like canned sardines, one's feet next to another's head. There are no sheets.

All forty churches and eleven rectories that make up the diocese give food and money for the effort. On Ash Wednesday in February or March and the Day of the Migrant in September, all of the churches take up a collection. They pass around donation envelopes adorned with a drawing of a freight train. Each time, they raise about $3,300. The bishop goes to churches himself to preach about the need to help migrants.

Teams from the church go door-to-door, asking businesses to give. Four in five say yes, says volunteer Gregoria Sánchez Romero. Two bread store owners give extra loaves at the end of each day. A man with a chicken-sales company drops by every two or three weeks with fifty birds. On Saturday, a market in Córdoba hands over all the vegetables it hasn't sold that week. Another donor regularly brings two or three large gunnysacks of sugar. People arrive at the church with smaller bundles of beans, oil, rice, and lentils. Some cook a little extra for dinner— and bring the leftovers. A few bring bags of cement, to help build the migrant shelter.

Perhaps the greatest gift has come from the church's priest. Over his lifetime, he had saved $37,500 to live on during his retirement. He told church members, "These people will keep on coming, more and more. We must build." Then, when he was sixty-three years old, he quietly donated the entire amount to buy the land to build the migrant shelter.

Others give time. Luis Hernández Osorio, a small man with dark, intense eyes, puts in eight hours a day as an accountant and then another eight at the church. He confronts police problems and finds new donors. Each night, he picks up donated bread. Every eight days, he goes, a huge pot stowed in his car trunk, to a local fish store. The owner fills it with seafood. It feeds the migrants a main dish for two or three days. "Every day, I have to battle a lot of problems here. But I feel at peace," Hernández says. "I always wanted to do something with my life. I feel satisfied."

Alfonso Peña Valencia, an architect, volunteers six nights a week to work as a security guard at the church from 7 P.M. to 1 A.M. On the seventh night, Saturday, he guards until dawn. His wife, Rosita, administers first aid to migrants. Peña says, "I like it here. I want to help my brother."

For some, providing short-term shelter at the church is not enough. María del Carmen Ortega García, a barrel-chested woman with a big smile, lets migrants sleep in a room in her house. They remind Ortega of her son. In 1995, her eighteen-year-old, José Geronimo, in the United States illegally, was deported from California. She does not know what happened after he was driven across the border. She never heard from him again. She started small, offering migrants a cup of coffee, then a place to bathe.

One twenty-two-year-old Honduran, Israel Sierra Pavón, begged for money from Ortega along the tracks. She gave him 6 pesos and told him to go to her house, the one with a pig leashed on the patio, for dinner. He has stayed for nine months for free, working and saving money to continue his journey. Ortega has let seventeen migrants stay—some for days, some for months.

Francisca Aguirre Juárez's one-room home is so cramped that the three beds are all shoved together along the back wall. Aguirre, a middle-aged woman who is missing most of her front teeth and is dressed in a sweater full of holes, shares one bed with her daughter. Her son shares the middle bed with a migrant. Two migrants sleep in the third bed. In two years, eighty migrants have shared the room with her family. Most stay a week. Aguirre says she feeds the police occasionally, to keep them on good terms. Still, her landlord has threatened to kick her out for housing so many people.

Aguirre sells *memelitas,* a *masa* snack filled with black beans, from a street corner near the tracks. She barely has enough to feed her own children. Yet all four times the train rolls by between 6 A.M. and 10 P.M., she goes out to the tracks.

She signals the train conductor.

"Go slow, please, I'm going to give food!" she yells.

Some oblige, some don't. "*Muchachos! Comida!* Guys! Food!" she says. She gives water, apples, socks, and sandwiches stuffed with beans. Often, she says, she gets up to feed migrants on the 1:30 A.M. and 3 A.M. trains, too.

"A lot of people want to hoard money. Not me," says Aguirre, who started helping after she witnessed a twenty-five-year-old Honduran lose a leg trying to board a train. He screamed in pain for two hours until someone took him to a hospital. "I feel better if I help. They are suffering more than I do," she says.

Some residents offer protection from the police. When they see a police car coming or that officers are conducting a sweep, they unlatch their front gates and usher migrants in to hide in their gardens and backyards.

Baltasar Bréniz Ávila, who lives two blocks from the tracks in Encinar, had fed a twenty-five-year-old Honduran migrant some tacos. The man was on his porch, getting ready to leave, when a blue-and-white state police car cruised down the dirt road.

Bréniz whisked the migrant inside. The police knocked. "Turn him over! He's a migrant. We're going to arrest him. If you don't turn him over, we'll arrest you, too, for being a smuggler."

The police had pistols and machine guns. Bréniz knew that people charged with smuggling can spend years in jail. Bréniz, who sells rustic chairs door to door, tried to mask the terror he felt inside. He politely declined and said there was no reason to turn the man over. He told them the visitor was a relative from an outlying farm. The police retreated.

He let the migrant stay for an hour, until he was sure the coast was clear.

At María Auxiliadora, many church members, including its priest, have been intimidated by police officers for helping migrants. "If I see you doing this again, I'm taking you in," the officers warn. "It is a crime to help Central Americans."

Although humanitarian help is not against the law, this is not an idle threat, says Hernández, the church volunteer. Five church members have been arrested. None were charged, but that may have been due to their willingness to pay a bribe to buy their freedom, says Hernández. An entire family—a mother, father, and two sons—were taken in for giving three migrants a place to sleep. The police officers extorted 20,000 pesos from the family to set them free. Similarly, a church member, a taxi driver, gave five migrants a ride up the road. The state police freed him after he paid 30,000 pesos under the table, fearful that they might charge him with human trafficking.

Sometimes whole communities stand up to the police. Residents of El Campesino El Mirador, a railside hamlet nestled at the foot of a mountain, tell this story:

El Campesino El Mirador was policed by officers from nearby Nogales. One afternoon in late May 2000, a northbound freight train pulled onto a siding to let a southbound train pass. At that moment, police officers emerged from a bar by the tracks. Townspeople say the officers looked drunk. The police saw about fifty migrants on top of the stopped train and headed toward the freight cars to arrest them. Migrants jumped off and ran toward the mountain.

The police gave chase. Townspeople say the officers began to shoot. One bullet hit a Honduran girl, seventeen or eighteen years old, in the arm. She was eight months pregnant and said it was because she had been raped by a policeman in Chiapas.

The girl clawed her way up the mountain. After about one hundred yards, she reached a small concrete platform. On the platform stood a white cross. Panting and bleeding, she stopped, unable to go farther.

Three police officers caught up to her, grabbed her hair, kicked her, and beat her with their nightsticks.

"Leave me alone!" she cried. "You've already shot me. I'll lose this child."

María Enriqueta Reyes Márquez, thirty-eight, of El Campesino El Mirador, climbed up to the cross. She says she could see that a bullet had splintered a bone in the girl's arm. "It's as if they were hitting a dog," she recalls, her eyes brimming with tears. "They treat dogs better than that. They don't punish criminals, but they beat up these poor folks. Why? Why?"

Reyes says she demanded: "Stop hitting her." She and about fifty other people encircled the girl and the cross. They turned on the officers. "Cowards!" "Why are you hitting her?"

Two of the officers ran down the hillside, away from the angry mob. Someone kicked the third in the buttocks until he ran as well.

Afterward, the townspeople found a local man dead in a

ditch near the railroad tracks. They assumed that he had been killed when the officers began shooting. Now the people's rage boiled over.

The next day, five hundred residents of El Campesino El Mirador and two nearby towns marched to the city hall in Nogales, where all of the officers were from. They surrounded it. Some held rocks and sticks. They demanded the release of any migrants apprehended the day before—fifteen in all, some of whom were beaten.

Reyes, who had walked two and a half hours to Nogales, says she shouted at the mayor, "We are human. We should treat people in a humane way. It's okay to send people back. But they shouldn't shoot them, beat them this way."

The people of El Campesino El Mirador told the mayor of Nogales to keep his police out of their town.

Samuel Ramírez del Carmen, director of the Red Cross in nearby Mendoza, Veracruz, confirms that his paramedics were sent to treat a pregnant migrant who had been shot by Nogales police officers and that protests did run the police out of town.

Local news reporter Julián Ramos Hernández says that eight police officers were ultimately fired over the incident. "The police were firing at the migrants," Ramos says. "People were indignant."

For a month, Reyes says, other migrants from the train stayed on the mountain, afraid to come down. Three times each day, people trudged up to the palm-studded ridge of the hill to bring them food and water. The police, she says, have not been back.

NEW CARGO

Enrique is hungry, but he fears that the half-dozen rolls from the food throwers might be all there is to his good fortune, so he stashes them for later. In little more than an hour, the train nears a town: Córdoba.

The cargo is beginning to change. It is valuable and more easily damaged—Volkswagens, Fords, and Chryslers. Security guards check the freight cars, catch every rider they can, and hand them over to the authorities. More important, says Cuauhtemoc González Flores, an official of the Transportación Ferroviaria Mexicana railroad, is the fact that if a migrant falls and is injured or killed, it costs $8 a minute to stop the train, often for hours, until investigators arrive.

A sewage stream appears by the tracks. Córdoba is getting close. The migrants finish their water, because it is hard to run fast holding bottles. They tie sweaters or extra shirts around their waists. Enrique grabs his bag of bread. About 10 P.M., he smells a familiar cue: a coffee-roasting factory next to the red-brick station. As the train slows, he leaps and flees.

He eludes the station's security guards and eases to a walk. He sits on a sidewalk one block north of the station. Two police officers approach.

His odds are better if he does not bolt. He tucks his bread into a crevice. He swallows his fright and tries to look unconcerned.

The officers, in navy blue uniforms, walk straight up to him.

He does not move, even flinch. Cops can sense fear. They can tell if someone is illegal. You have to be calm, he says to himself. You can't look afraid or hide. You have to look right at them.

The police do not bear gifts. They pull out pistols. "If you run, I'll shoot you," one says, aiming at Enrique's chest. They take him and two younger boys, sitting nearby, to a cavernous railroad shed, where seven other officers are holding twenty migrants. It is a full-scale sweep.

They line up the migrants against a wall. "Take everything out of your pockets."

Only a bribe, Enrique knows, will keep him from being deported back to Central America. He has 30 pesos, about $3, that he earned lifting rocks and sweeping near the tracks in Tierra Blanca. He had briefly gotten off the train in Tierra Blanca, in part so he could earn enough to try to buy his freedom if he was caught by the police. Some officers will let you go for 20 pesos. Others demand 50—or more—and then turn you over to *la migra* to be deported anyway. Now he prays the coins he has will be enough.

One officer pats him down and says to empty his pockets.

Enrique drops his belt, a Raiders cap, and the 30 pesos. He glances at his fellow migrants. Each is standing behind a little pile of belongings.

"*¡Sálganse! ¡Váyanse, ya!* Get out! Leave!"

He will not be deported. But he pauses. He screws up his courage. "Can I get my things back, my money?"

"What money?" the officer replies. "Forget about it, unless you want to have your trip stop here."

Enrique turns his back and walks away.

Even in Veracruz, where strangers can be so kind, the authorities cannot be trusted. The chief of state police in nearby Fortín de las Flores will not comment on the incident.

Exhausted, Enrique retrieves his bag of bread, climbs onto a flatbed truck, and sleeps. At dawn, he hears a train. He trots alongside a freight car and clambers aboard, holding his bread.

THE MOUNTAINS

The tracks, smoother now, begin to climb. It grows cooler. The train passes sixty-foot-tall stalks of bamboo. It crosses a long bridge over a deep canyon. It rolls through putrid white smoke from a Kimberly-Clark factory that turns sugarcane pulp into Kleenex and toilet paper.

As he pushes north, Mexico changes. In Oaxaca, he rolled through cattle country. It was so hot, the tracks behind him looked like a squiggly line, warped by heat. It was so humid that green moss balls grew on the electrical wires by the tracks. Enrique passed a river that was a block wide. He was drenched in sweat. When the train slowed, the smell of perspiration washed over him.

In Veracruz, he rode through rows of silvery pineapple plants and lush fields of tall, thin sugarcane stalks that brushed up against the train. He saw sugar mill smokestacks and homes where people put day-old tortillas on their tin roofs to dry. All around him were swamps and mosquitoes. He had to watch closely for bees. He had heard that many are Africanized bees, and when smoke from the locomotive angers them, they swarm and attack migrants on top of the cars.

As he pushes north, the trains keep changing, too. Tracks are fastened to concrete ties, welded, and better maintained. The freight trains are longer and seem to glide more smoothly, roll more rapidly, and derail less frequently. Because there are more trains and because so many migrants have been hurt or detained back in Chiapas, fewer riders are on board. On some trains, Enrique sees only a dozen others.

In Orizaba, the train changes crews. Enrique asks a man standing near the tracks, "Can you give me one peso to buy some food?" The man inquires about his scars. They are from the beating he got on top of the train, a little more than a week ago now. He gives Enrique 15 pesos, about $1.50.

Enrique runs to buy soda and cheese to go with his bread. He looks north. Beyond a range of verdant mountains he sees the snow-covered Pico de Orizaba, the highest summit in Mexico. Now it will turn icy cold, especially at night, much different from the steamy lowlands. Enrique begs two sweaters. Before the train pulls out, he runs from car to car, looking into the hollows at the ends of the hoppers, where riders occasionally discard clothing. In one, he finds a blanket.

As the train starts, Enrique shares his cheese, soda, and rolls with two other boys, also headed for the United States. One is thirteen. The other is seventeen. Silently, Enrique thanks the food throwers again for the bread.

He relishes the camaraderie: how riders take care of one another, pass along what they know, divide what they have. Migrants will often designate one person to look out for trouble while the others rest. They give one another advice. In spots along the route where the train slows and migrants sprint from the shadows to board, reaching for the ladders, migrants riding atop the cars shout out if the train is going too fast.

"Don't do it! You'll get nailed!" they yell.

When Enrique lands an extra shirt or a tip about where to avoid the police, he shares. Other migrants have been generous with him. They have told him Mexican words they have learned. One offered a bit of soap when Enrique slipped into a shallow green river to bathe.

Enrique realizes that the friendships will be fleeting. Very few who set out together, including brothers, end up together. Often, migrants abandon an injured member of their group rather than risk being caught by the authorities. As he waits in

Veracruz for a train to leave, a thirty-one-year-old Salvadoran recalls how he recently watched a man get his right leg cut off as he was trying to elude *la migra* at a train stop. The Salvadoran stripped off his shirt and used it to wrap a tourniquet around the leg. Then he ran away, fearful *la migra* would arrest him.

"Don't leave me!" the injured man cried out. The authorities said the man died later that day.

Often, between train rides, Enrique prefers to sleep alone in a tall clump of grass, away from other migrants, knowing it will make him less of a target. Still, camaraderie often means survival. "I could get to the north faster alone," he figures, "but I might not make it."

The mountains close in. Enrique invites the two boys to share his blanket. Together they will be warmer. The three jam themselves between a grate and an opening on top of a hopper. Enrique stuffs rags under his head for a pillow. The car sways, and its wheels click-clack quietly. They sleep.

The train enters a tunnel, the first of thirty-two in the Cumbres de Acultzingo, the Peaks of Acultzingo. Each tunnel is named for a state in Mexico. Migrants tick off the states they have passed—and the many they still have to go. Outside is bright sun. Inside is darkness so black that riders cannot see their hands. They shout, *"¡Ay! ¡Ay! ¡Ay! ¡Ay! ¡Ay!"* and listen for the echo. Sometimes the tail of the train hasn't left one tunnel before the locomotive dives into another. The freight cars creak as they turn the curves. Enrique and his friends sleep on. Back in the daylight, the train hugs a hillside. Below, a valley is filled with fields of corn, radishes, and lettuce, each a different hue of green.

El Mexicano is the longest tunnel. For eight minutes, the

train vanishes inside. Black diesel smoke rises, hugging the tops of the cars.

It burns the lungs and stings the eyes. Some of the migrants bolt down the ladders, trying to escape the noxious haze. Enrique's eyes are closed, but his face and arms turn gray. His nose runs black soot. Engineers fear El Mexicano. If a locomotive overheats, they must stop. Riders spring for the arched exits, gasping for clean air.

Back outside, ice forms on the train cars. Migrants huddle between the cars or with strangers, seeking protection from the biting wind. Riders ache and shiver. Many don't have a blanket or a sweater. Some wear T-shirts. Their lips crack, and their eyes grow dull. They hug themselves. Three cram into the hole at the end of a hopper. To fit, they must sit on one another, hands across the chest, heads down. They pull their shirts over their mouths to warm themselves with their breath. When the train slows, they jog alongside to ward off the cold.

Some risk moving forward to the last of the train's three locomotives to press against the engine. Some stand in the warm plumes of diesel smoke. Others jump inside hoppers full of sand or grain, but only if they can find cars that are full enough that they will be able to crawl out. As night falls, some of the older migrants drink whiskey. Too much, and they tumble off. Others gather old clothing and trash and build fires on the ledges over the wheels of the hoppers. They hold their hands close to the fire, then press their palms to their frigid faces.

At dawn, the tracks straighten and level out. At one and a half miles above sea level, the train accelerates to 35 miles per hour. Enrique awakens. He sees cultivated cactus on both sides. Directly in front rise two huge pyramids—the pre-Aztec metropolis of Teotihuacán.

Then he sees switches and semaphores. Housing developments. A billboard for Paradise Spa. A sewage ditch. Taxis. The train slows for the station at Lechería. Enrique gets ready to run.

He is in Mexico City.

SUSPICION

The Veracruz hospitality has vanished. One Mexico City woman wrinkles her nose when she talks about migrants. She is hesitant to slide the dead bolt on the metal door of her tall stucco fence. "I'm afraid of them. They talk funny. They're dirty."

Enrique starts knocking on doors. He begs for food. In Mexico City, crime is rampant. In some churches, groups of bandits have entered during Mass and robbed all the parishioners at once. Churches hire armed guards to ensure peaceful services. In Mexico City, people are edgy and often hostile. "We don't have anything," they say at house after house, usually through locked doors.

In Lechería, one resident, Olivia Rodríguez Morales, the wife of a retired railroad mechanic, lives just one block south of the station in a rust-colored boxcar she's converted into a home. Rodríguez is a soft-spoken woman with silver-rimmed spectacles and a gold cross on a chain around her neck. Yet when she is asked about migrants, she stops knitting a blue shawl and stiffens; her demeanor turns cold.

One afternoon, Rodríguez recalls, six migrants along the tracks asked a young man from the neighborhood for some money. He said no. That night, as he was walking home, the same migrants grabbed him near the station. They tied his hands with barbed wire. They took his money, his watch, and his clothes. They beat him over the head with a machete. They left him naked.

It rained that night. Slowly, the young man dragged himself to his door. He was in critical condition and spent three months in the hospital. Although he never spoke of it, Rodríguez and other neighbors heard that he had been raped by the migrants. In the close-knit railroad employee community, most had known the man since he was a boy.

Before, she had felt pity for migrants. She had offered them food and help. Now, when migrants ask her, several times a day, for help—a taco, a coffee, a shirt, or a pair of socks—she always turns them down flat. "We don't trust them," she says. "After that, people closed their doors."

Each dawn, when residents head out for their jobs, they worry. Are the migrants hiding in clumps of yellow flowers between the tracks innocents traveling north or dangerous men who are running from the law in their own countries? "You don't know who they are. Some come out of necessity. Some may be fleeing some problem," Rodríguez says.

Her neighbor Oscar Aereola Peregrino, agrees. "*Por uno pagan todos*. One sins, and everyone pays," he says.

Enrique goes house to house, hoping for mercy. Finally, at one house, another gift: a woman offers him tortillas, beans, and lemonade.

Now he must hide from the state police, who guard the depot at Lechería, a gritty industrial neighborhood on the northwestern outskirts of Mexico City. Enrique is surrounded by smokestacks. There is a scrap metal recycling plant, a sprawling Goodyear tire factory, and a plastics factory. The railroad tracks are littered with broken dolls, old tires, dead dogs, and worn shoes. He must avoid *la migra*, which sometimes shows up at the station in unmarked cars. Most migrants at the station hide between or inside boxcars or in the grass.

Enrique crawls into a three-foot-wide concrete culvert, one of several in a field north of the station. The field is filled with cows and sheep and bursting with yellow and purple flowers. Before, when he made it this far, he spent the night curled up in the culvert with other migrants. The police never saw him. Barring bad luck, he tells himself, he might make it to the border.

Enrique is thirteen miles from the heart of Mexico's rail system. Still, the station here, separated into two staging areas and six tracks, bustles with activity. Trains heading into Mexico City stop first in Lechería to leave any cars with combustible contents. On their way north, they stop to pick the cars back up. Fifteen trains leave Lechería every twenty-four hours, says José Patricio Sánchez Arellano, who handles human resources for Lechería and other stations for Ferrocarril y Terminal del Valle de México.

Outside the culvert where Enrique hides, trains clang and crash as they add and subtract cars, forming trains that are nearly a mile long.

Enrique must pick wisely. Not all of the trains go all the way to the border. Many migrants look for trains operated by Ferrosur, one of three train companies that operate out of the station. Ferrosur has fewer security guards. Another company, Transportación Ferroviaria Mexicana, sometimes puts guards on its trains to prevent anyone from using wire cutters to open sealed boxcars and steal merchandise.

At 10:30 P.M., a northbound train arrives. This is the train Enrique prefers. It travels all the way to the Texas border, mostly at night, when the dark will make it harder for him to be detected. From Mexico City onward, the rail system is more modern, and trains run so fast that few migrants ride on top.

Enrique notices a few train cars that are unusual. In Lechería, train companies sometimes load a large closed container the size of a boxcar into a slightly larger, open container—a box inside a half box. Some migrants slide into a small spot between the two containers. But if the train suddenly brakes and the inside container shifts, it can press them against the other container and kill them.

Enrique and his two friends pick a boxcar. He braces the door open with a rock. If they are caught inside, it will be hard to escape, but they count on the scarcity of *migra* checkpoints in northern Mexico. Four of five times along this part of the route, one rail official estimates, authorities don't stop the train. The boys load cardboard to lie on and stay clean.

Enrique notices a blanket on a nearby hopper. He climbs a ladder to get it and hears a loud buzz from overhead. Live wires carry electricity above the trains for 143 miles north. Once used for locomotives that no longer operate, the wires still carry 25,000 volts to prevent vandalism. Signs warn: DANGER—HIGH VOLTAGE. But many of the migrants cannot read.

They do not even need to touch the lines to be killed. The electricity arcs up to twenty inches. Only thirty-six inches separates the wires from the tallest freight cars, the auto carriers. In railroad offices in Mexico City, in a large control room, computers plot train routes with blue and green lines, and at least once every six months the screens flicker, then black out. That means a migrant has crawled on top of a car, been hit by electricity, and short-circuited the system. When the computers reboot, the screens flash red where it happened.

Enrique climbs the hopper car. Carefully, he snatches a corner of the blanket and yanks it down. Then he scrambles back to his boxcar and settles into a bed that he and his friends have fashioned out of straw they found inside.

The boys share a bottle of water and one of juice. The modern locomotives glide past the outer reaches of Mexico City. The landscape turns more and more desolate—sand and scrub brush, jackrabbits and snakes. They cross boulders, dry riverbeds, and canyons with sheer rock walls. They plow through a heavy fog, and Enrique sleeps soundly—too soundly.

He does not sense when police stop their train in the middle of the central Mexican desert. Officers dressed in black find the boys curled under their blanket in the straw. Enrique is afraid. The last time he was stopped here, he jumped down, grabbed two fistfuls of rocks, and barely eluded capture. Now, there is no place to run. These officers take them to their *jefe*, who is cooking a pot of stew over a campfire. He pats them down to check for drugs. Then, instead of arresting them, he gives all three tortillas and water—and toothpaste to clean up.

Enrique is astonished. The *jefe* lets them reboard the boxcar and tells them to get off the train before San Luis Potosí, where sixty-four railroad security officers guard the station. When the train gets to within four blocks of the station, the guards drive alongside, arresting migrants as they jump off and turning them over to *la migra*. At midmorning, Enrique sees two flashing red antennas. The boys jump off the train half a mile south of town.

His friends pay for a taxi to the north side. Enrique goes in search of food. "We don't have any," people say. Finally, one person gives him an orange. Another gives him three tacos. He shares them with his friends.

Until now, Enrique has opted to keep moving. In the South, in a pinch, he could pick mangoes that grow along the tracks. Once, in Chiapas, he survived on mangoes for three days. But here the countryside is too desolate and dry to live off the land, and begging is too chancy. There are no agricultural fields in sight, just factories that make glass and furniture. He needs to work if he is going to survive. Besides, he does not want to reach the border penniless. He has heard that U.S. ranchers shoot migrants who come to beg.

He trudges up a hill to the small home of a brick maker. Politely, Enrique asks for food. The brick maker offers yet another kindness: if Enrique will work, he will get both food and a place to sleep. Happily, Enrique accepts.

Some migrants say Mexicans exploit illegals by stiffing them after a day's work. Or they pay only a fraction of the going wage, which is 50 pesos, or about $5, a day. But the brick maker does better than that: 80 pesos. And he gives Enrique shoes and clothing.

For a day and a half, Enrique works at the brickyard, one of three hundred that straddle the tracks on the northern edge of San Luis Potosí. Workers pour clay, water, and dried cow manure into large pits. They roll up their pants and stomp on the sloppy concoction, as if pressing grapes to make wine. When the slop becomes a firm brown paste, they slap it into wooden molds. Then they empty the molds on flat ground and let the bricks dry.

The bricks are stacked into pyramids inside ovens as big as rooms. Under the ovens, the fires are stoked with sawdust. Each batch of bricks bakes for fifteen hours, sending clouds of black smoke into the sky.

Enrique's job is to shovel the clay. At the end of the day,

covered in clay and manure dust, he bathes in a cattle trough. At night, he sleeps in a shed on a dirt floor he shares with one of his friends from the train.

"I have to get to the border," Enrique tells him.

Should he take another train? In all of his attempts, he has survived more than thirty train rides. This time, freight cars have brought him 990 miles from Tapachula near Guatemala. Is he pushing his luck?

His employer says he should ride a Volkswagen van called a *combi* through a checkpoint about forty minutes north of town. The authorities won't stop a *combi*, the brick maker says. Then he should take a bus to Matehuala, and he might be able to get a ride on a truck all the way to Nuevo Laredo on the Rio Grande.

THE TRUCKER

Enrique collects his pay, 120 pesos. He spends a few on a tooth-brush.

He hails a *combi*. It breezes through the checkpoint. He pays 83 pesos to board a bus to Matehuala. The desert is dotted with tall, crooked Joshua trees. A few people on the side of the road hawk snakeskins. Three hours later, a pink archway welcomes him to Matehuala.

Outside the bus station, he sees a kind-looking man. "Can you help me?" Enrique asks.

The man gives him a place to sleep. The next morning, Enrique walks to a truck stop. Matehuala is on a principal route for truckers headed to the United States. A convoy of trucks rolls by. Some truckers stop to eat or to gas up.

"I don't have any money," he tells every driver he sees. "Can you give me a ride however far north you are going?"

One after another, they turn him down. Many, having made the lonely haul from Mexico City, would welcome company for the remaining 380 miles to the border. Still, at least nine in ten truckers here, one trucker at the stop says, refuse migrants. If they said yes, police might accuse them of smuggling. Drivers say it is enough to worry about officers planting drugs on their trucks and demanding bribes. Moreover, some of the truckers fear that migrants might assault them.

Finally, at 10 A.M., one driver takes the risk. Enrique pulls himself up into the cab of an eighteen-wheeler hauling beer.

"Where are you from?" the driver asks.

Honduras.

"Where are you going?" The driver has seen boys like Enrique before. "Do you have a mom or dad in the United States?"

Enrique tells him about his mother.

A sign at Los Pocitos says, CHECKPOINT IN 100 METERS. The truck idles in line. Then it inches forward. Judicial police officers ask the driver what he is carrying. They want his papers. They peer at Enrique.

The driver is ready: my assistant. But the officers do not ask.

A few feet farther on, soldiers stop each vehicle to search for drugs and guns. Two fresh-faced recruits wave them through.

Oblivious to the chatter on the trucker's two-way radio, Enrique falls asleep. The scenery changes again. Joshua trees give way to low-lying scrub brush. The driver clears two more checkpoints. As he nears the Rio Grande, he stops to eat. He buys Enrique a plate of eggs and refried beans and a soda, another gift. Riding a truck, Enrique figures, is a dream.

Sixteen miles before the border, he sees a sign: REDUCE YOUR SPEED. NUEVO LAREDO CUSTOMS.

Don't worry, the driver says, *la migra* check only the buses.

A sign says, BIENVENIDOS A NUEVO LAREDO. Welcome to Nuevo Laredo.

The driver drops him off outside the city, near its airport, just past the Motel California. With the 30 pesos he has left, he takes a bus that winds into the city.

Often, as he struggled to get through central and northern Mexico, Enrique came close to getting caught and deported. Time after time, his luck held.

In Matías Romero, Oaxaca, *migra* agents surrounded his train and caught many of the riders. Enrique jumped off and dashed to some bushes. He lay in the thicket, afraid to breathe. After what seemed like an hour, when the train began to roll, he sprinted alongside one of the cars and jumped back on.

When the train reached Medias Aguas, Veracruz, and stopped briefly, Enrique climbed down and sat next to the track, talking to other migrants. But for the locomotive idling and a compressor cycling to feed the brakes, the night was ghostly still.

"Don't you dare run!" two men in green fatigues said as they pinned him in the beams of their flashlights. A small army unit, based next to the train station, was out catching migrants.

Enrique bolted. The soldiers chased him relentlessly. Though exhausted after nearly two days without sleep, Enrique outran both of them. He darted two blocks along the tracks toward the north edge of town to a dirt road called Miguel Hidalgo. Facing the rails was the backyard of a house. It looked empty. The house was built on three-foot concrete pilings, to keep it from flooding. He ran through the yard, fell to his stomach, and crawled under it. He waited. Nothing.

It was midnight. Enrique ached with fatigue. He gathered some boards scattered beneath the house, stood them on their sides so no one could see him, and lay in the dirt. In seconds, he was asleep.

The train coupled and uncoupled cars. It split the night with clanging and crashing. Then, slowly, it pulled out, rumbling the ground as it passed behind Enrique and the house.

Enrique heard nothing. He was safe. Surrounded by dirt, he slept.

Now, as he winds his way into Nuevo Laredo, he has one more piece of good fortune. His bus stops at the Plaza Hidalgo, in the heart of Nuevo Laredo. It is a city park the size of a square block. There, under palm trees, the park is full of people. Some are migrants, who sit on the steps of the big clock tower. Others are smugglers, who circulate, offering, in a whisper, to take people over to the United States for a good price.

Enrique has no money. But he sees a man from Honduras whom he met on the train. The man takes him to an encampment along the Rio Grande. Enrique likes it. He decides to stay until he can cross.

That night, as the sun sets, Enrique stares across the Rio Grande and gazes at the United States. It looms as a mystery.

Somewhere over there lives his mother. She has become a mystery, too. He was so young when she left that he can barely remember what she looks like: curly hair, eyes like chocolate. Her voice is a distant sound on the phone.

Enrique has spent forty-seven days bent on nothing but surviving. Now, as he thinks about her, he is overwhelmed.

FIVE

On the Border

"You are in American territory," a Border Patrol agent shouts into a bullhorn. "Turn back."

Sometimes Enrique strips and wades into the Rio Grande to cool off. But the bullhorn always stops him. He goes back.

"Thank you for returning to your country."

He is stymied. For days, Enrique has been stuck in Nuevo Laredo, on the southern bank of the Río Bravo, as it is called here. He has been watching, listening, and trying to plan. Somewhere across this milky green ribbon of water is his mother.

Enrique is challenging the unknown to find her. During her most recent telephone call, she said she was in North Carolina. He has no idea if she is still there, where that is, or how to reach it. He no longer has her phone number. He did not think to memorize it.

Many of the youngsters from Central America and Mexico who go north on their own do not memorize telephone numbers or addresses. They wrap them in plastic and tuck them into a shoe or slip them under a waistband. Occasionally kidnappers snatch the children, find the numbers, and call the mothers for ransom.

Stripped of phone numbers and destinations, many of the children become stranded at the river. Defeat drives them to the worst this border world has to offer: drugs, despair, and death.

It is almost May 2000, nearly two months since Enrique left home the last time. He is a hardened veteran of seven attempts to reach *el Norte*. This is his eighth; he has pushed forward 1,800 miles. By now, his mother must have called Honduras again, and the family must have told her that he was gone. His mother must be worrying.

He has to telephone her. Besides, she might have saved enough money to hire a coyote who can take him across the river.

He remembers one number back home—at a tire store where he worked. He will call and ask his old employer to find Aunt Rosa Amalia or Uncle Carlos Orlando Turcios Ramos, who had arranged his job, and ask them for his mother's number. Then he will call back and get it from his boss.

For the two calls, he needs two telephone cards: Fifty pesos apiece. When he phones his mother, he'll call collect. He cannot beg 100 pesos. People in Nuevo Laredo won't give. Mexicans along the border, he notices, are quick to proclaim their right to immigrate to the United States. "Jesus was an immigrant," he hears them say. But most won't give Central Americans food, money, or jobs.

So he will work by himself. For migrant children, there are few options: shining shoes, selling gum or candy on the sidewalk, or washing cars. He'll wash cars.

A REFUGE

The encampment he has joined is a haven for migrants, coyotes, junkies, and criminals, but it is safer for him than anywhere else in Nuevo Laredo, a city of half a million and swarming with *la migra* and all kinds of police, who might catch him and deport him. Worse than stuck, he would be back at the beginning.

The camp is at the bottom of a narrow, winding path that slopes to the river. A clump of reeds hides it from constant surveillance by the U.S. immigration authorities. They watch with cameras and agents in white sport-utility vehicles who patrol back and forth along a dirt road on top of a steep embankment along the far side.

Enrique shares one of five soiled, soggy mattresses with three other migrants. Still others lie on pieces of cardboard. For their clothing, they use "the closet"—a wire spring standing upright, from a mattress stripped of its ticking. Each resident of the camp has a space on one of the bare coils on which to hang his shirt and pants.

Enrique smells excrement from goats and his fellow campers, whose bathroom is the surrounding grass. The camp is strewn with trash. Red ants cover the ground, and millions of gnats hover over the river. In the daytime, it is scorching hot. Each day, he strips and wades in knee-deep to scrub away sweat and grime. When he is too afraid to venture into Nuevo Laredo to drink from a faucet in a park, he takes water from the river, which carries raw sewage from scores of towns. People tell him of a superstition: Drink from the Río Bravo, and he'll be stuck in Nuevo Laredo forever. He risks it anyway. The water tastes heavy, but it does not make him sick.

The camp is a hard place for Enrique to sleep in. It is noisy all night with the sound of migrants coming and going as they try to cross the river. They swim or ride inner tubes to a tiny, lush island in midstream, then rest and hide until they see a chance to make it the rest of the way. INS bullhorns bark, warning them back. Enrique can hear cars at a U.S. entry checkpoint a few blocks away.

He knows he will have to cross if he ever wants to see his mother again. As he looks across the river, he can see a church steeple, train tracks, and three antennas with blinking red lights. He tries to summon his mother's calm voice.

If only he could call her.

Each evening, without fail, he summons his courage and goes to the Nuevo Laredo city hall with a large plastic paint bucket and two rags. From a spigot on the side of the building, he fills the bucket. Then he goes to parking places across the street from a bustling taco stand. Unlike at other businesses, the workers at the taco stand do not run him off. One of his rags is red. Each time someone arrives to eat dinner, he waves the red rag to guide the customer into a parking space, like a ground crew member ushering a jetliner to a gate.

Usually there is competition. Two or three other migrants set up their buckets along the same sidewalk.

Enrique approaches a woman driving a yellow Chevrolet Impala with chrome-spoke wheels. She is talking on her cell phone. May he wash her car? She ends the call and declines.

A man and his young daughter drive up. "May I clean your car?"

"No, son."

The woman with the Impala returns with her tacos. Enrique waits until traffic is clear, then waves his red rag and guides her out. Suddenly, she reaches out her car window and presses 3 pesos into his hand.

Enrique approaches dozens of people, but just one or two say yes. By 4 A.M., when the stand closes, he has eked out 30 pesos, or $3.

A LIFELINE

The air around the taco stand fills with the aroma of barbecue. Enrique watches workers pull strips of meat from a vat, put them on large chopping blocks, and cut them up. Customers sit at long stainless-steel tables and eat. Sometimes, when the stand closes, the servers slip him a couple of tacos.

Otherwise, for his only meal every day, he depends upon the Parroquia de San José, or St. Joseph's Parish, and another church, the Parroquia del Santo Niño, the Parish of the Holy Child. Each gives food cards to migrants. One is good for ten meals and the other for five. Enrique can count on one meal a day for fifteen days. The cards are like gold. Sometimes they are stolen and turn up on a meal-card black market. Migrants who bathe in the river leave their cards on the bank and carry rocks into the water to throw at anyone who tries to take them.

Each day, Enrique goes to one church or the other to eat. It is safe; the police stay away. Like clockwork, Leti Limón, a volunteer, swings open the double yellow doors at San José and shouts, "Who's new?"

"Me! Me!" men and boys cry out from the courtyard. They rush to the door and jostle against it.

"Get in line! Get in line!" Limón is poor herself; she cleans houses across the river in Laredo, Texas, for $20 apiece. But she has helped to feed these migrants for a year and a half, figuring that Jesus would approve. She issues the newcomers beige cards and punches the cards of those who enter. A parish priest counts 6 percent children.

One by one, the migrants stand behind chairs at a long table. At the head is a mural of Jesus, his hands extended toward plates of tacos, tomatoes, and beans. Above him are his words: COME TO ME, ALL YOU WHO ARE WEARY AND FIND LIFE BURDENSOME.

The lights dim, and two big fans spin to a stop, so everyone can hear grace. In the still air, the room turns hot, nearly suffocating; perspiration trickles down the migrants' faces and soaks their shirts. A volunteer or one of the migrants begins the short prayer. Some who have not eaten in two or three days cannot wait; from behind their chairs, they grab at the tacos with one hand, at bread with the other.

A volunteer asks everyone to remove their hats, to please eat everything on their trays or give it to someone near them.

Chairs screech as everyone pulls them out at once. Spoons of stew touch lips before bottoms hit the seats. There are more migrants than chairs. Some eat standing. Others squat on the floor, plates balanced on their knees. They eat in quiet desperation. In a clatter of forks against plates, beans, stew, tomatoes, rice, and doughnuts disappear.

Afterward, opposite a portrait of the Virgin of Guadalupe, about a dozen of the migrants always gather around a map of

Texas. It is covered in plastic, but fingerprints have blackened parts of it anyway. They tell how they will get there, and they discuss the state of the river. Is it high? Low? Then they sneak out an apple or a banana to give to a friend.

At church dinners Enrique meets other children who hope to reach their mothers in the United States. A sixteen-year-old boy, Ermis Galeano, is stuck, too. He and Enrique compare stories. Both are from Honduras.

Both have been robbed. As with Enrique, bandits on top of a train struck Ermis in the face with a board. It tore out his front teeth, leaving two black holes. As with Enrique, the bandits left him in his underwear, sobbing and bloody. They ripped up his scrap of paper with his mother's phone number on it, too, and tossed it to the wind.

Ermis's mother, María, left him for North Carolina when he was ten. She sent money, five letters, and fifteen photos. She called every two weeks. It was not enough. Ermis missed the occasional three-hour bus rides they had taken to Tegucigalpa to buy things, his mom's spaghetti, how they would go to the tortilla store together. He missed his mother's smell. After she left, he would put on her deodorant, stare at her picture, and cry. He slept in her bed, hoping to feel near her. Being raised by his aunt wasn't the same. "My mom told me she loves me. No one else ever told me that," Ermis says. This is his third attempt to go to her.

A fifteen-year-old girl, Mery Gabriela Posas Izaguirre, or Gabi, as she prefers, tells Enrique her story.

She had reason to leave Honduras. Her mother, who was divorced, had sold the dining room table, the refrigerator, and the pots and pans to send Gabi to school. Finally, her mother had sold some of the beds. Gabi slept on the floor.

Early one morning in July 1999, Gabi says, her mother

snuggled next to her and hugged her. She had already spent half the night curled up next to her sons. When Gabi came home from school that afternoon, there was a note: "I'm going for a little while. I'm going to work very hard." Her mother left Gabi's older brother in charge and asked the children to pray three times a day: before they ate, slept, or went outside.

Gabi and her two brothers ached for her. They began sleeping in her bed to feel near her. Gabi would drift off smelling her mother's scent on the pillow. She dreamed that her mother was at home, scolding her in the morning, telling her to get to school on time. She imagined that they were going to the park. She missed teasing her for playing "old-fogy music"—Beethoven.

"The house felt sad, empty," Gabi says.

Every time the telephone rang, Gabi raced to answer it. "When are you coming home?" she begged her mother. Then she turned harsh: "Why did you bring us into the world, if you were going to leave us?" Of forty-eight children in her class, thirty-six had a parent in the United States, most often a mother.

At her new home in the northeastern United States, her mother cleaned house and babysat two toddlers. One day, she sent Gabi a Barbie doll. The toddlers had already torn open the box. Gabi seethed. She sat alone, envisioning her mother playing with her new charges.

"How are the beaches?" she asked, snidely.

They argued.

"I'm taking care of other kids instead of you. Can you imagine what that's like?" her mother demanded. "You don't know what I've suffered."

Gabi didn't believe her. All she wanted was to be with her.

Winter came. Her mother called, crying. She was sick, lonely, and out of a job.

"I knew I had to go," Gabi said. "I thought: 'I'm young. I want to help her, so she can come home.'"

By Christmas of 1999, going had become an obsession.

Her mother was terrified that Gabi would make the trip alone and be raped. She asked Gabi's aunt Lourdes, twenty-six, to go with her. A smuggler promised to deliver them for $2,000 up front, but he robbed and abandoned them in Tapachula, just inside the southern border of Mexico. They were deported to Guatemala.

Gabi resolved to try again, this time through the Lacandón jungle in the Mexican state of Chiapas. She and Lourdes spent days washing clothes along the Usumacinta River in exchange for food, asking every smuggler who went by if he would take them through the mountain pass.

"If you can't pay with cash," one said, "you know how women pay."

Angrily, Gabi refused.

Finally, four smugglers let them tag along with eighty migrants who Gabi learned had paid between $5,000 and $8,000 apiece. They put her up front to help cut a path in the dense vegetation. She rebuffed constant demands for sex. She tried to look as ugly as possible. She hardly slept, never smiled or combed her hair. Her legs turned black with ticks. She felt as though bugs were eating her alive, but she dared not lift her skirt to remove them. She kept repeating to herself, "I have to get to my mother."

She and Lourdes switched to hitchhiking. But a *migra* agent caught them trying to walk around a checkpoint. The agent was a woman, Gabi says, who ordered her to strip and checked her clothing for hidden cash, then scolded her for having so little money that there was no way for her to release them.

"Please let us go," Gabriela begged. "I'm going to help my mother."

"*Váyanse.* Go!" the agent said.

Finally, Gabi and Lourdes made it to Nuevo Laredo. She tells Enrique she feels stuck here, too. Sometimes, she says, she wants to kill herself.

Another Honduran teenager at church dinners is Kelvin Maradiaga. He, too, lost the phone number and address of his mother, Adalinda, in New York during his journey. Running from Mexican officials in southern Mexico, he fell into a puddle. His mother's phone number, jotted down with a felt-tip pen, blurred into oblivion.

A man at a taco stand gave him a job washing dishes. He was able to buy a phone card to call Honduras to try to get his mother's phone number again. But the only phone in his small southern Honduran town, which belongs to an agricultural co-operative, had been disconnected.

After months of travel, Kelvin fears he has only one choice: to go back to Honduras, get his mother's phone number, and attempt the journey all over again. "She would tell me about her problems. I would tell her about mine. I need to see her. I want to see her," says Kelvin.

Outside the church after dinner, many migrants engage in a crude kind of street therapy: Who has endured the worst riding the trains? They measure trips not in days but in shoes lost, beatings taken, belongings robbed. They show off scars. "I walked four days." "I walked twenty-eight days!" They air feet covered in large blisters, toenails that have turned up from walking.

A young man sits on a green metal bench outside the church. He has been stuck here for weeks, and he trumps everyone. He slides up a leg of his black jeans and takes off a black, high-topped sneaker, then a prosthesis. His right calf tapers into a pink stump.

A SMUGGLER

For permission to stay in the relative safety of the river encampment, the leader, El Tiríndaro, who is addicted to heroin, usually wants drugs or beer. But he has not asked Enrique for anything. El Tiríndaro is a subspecies of coyote known as a *patero,* because he smuggles people into the United States by pushing them across the river on inner tubes while paddling like a *pato,* or duck. Others in the business keep clients in rented houses or hotel rooms. El Tiríndaro is small-time; he uses the camp. Enrique is a likely client.

In addition to smuggling, El Tiríndaro finances his heroin habit by tattooing people and selling clothing that migrants have left on the riverbank. In a pinch, he reverts to his previous profession, petty theft. One day, Enrique bumps into El Tiríndaro on the street. He has his arms around a live turkey he has stolen out of someone's yard.

The smuggler has a short fuse when he needs a fix. He shoots up constantly. Enrique stares as El Tiríndaro lies on a mattress, mixes Mexican black tar heroin with water in a spoon, warms it over a cigarette lighter, draws it into a syringe, and stabs the needle straight into a vein.

When the drugs take hold, El Tiríndaro hallucinates. He hears imaginary voices, crowds of people descending on the camp. Sometimes he is so slowed by heroin that he can barely get up or move. He can earn $2,000 to $3,000 in a single large smuggling operation but blow it in a day on heroin, which he likes to mix with cocaine. He shares his drugs with friends in a local mob called Los Osos, named after a billiard cantina where they drink.

Besides migrants, the camp has ten perpetual residents. Seven are addicts. They call heroin *la cura,* the cure.

A few at the campsite are Mexican criminals who have

been deported by the United States. One is called El Lágrima, the Tear. He is tattooed with TJ, a symbol of the Mexican mafia; a teardrop, signifying a dead gang friend; and a spider-web, tucked next to his right eye.

Also among the permanent campers are several migrants who are stuck. One, a fellow Honduran, has lived on the river for seven months. He has tried to enter the United States three times. Every time, he has been caught. He has descended into depression and a life of glue sniffing. Each time he tried to cross, he says, he went alone. Enrique listens. They call Enrique El Hongo, the Mushroom, because he is quiet, soaking everything in.

Enrique clings to the camp, where he is protected. Staying with El Tiríndaro means the Los Osos bandits, who rob people under a nearby bridge and along the river, won't target him.

Los Osos, once a group of neighborhood children who played along the river, became a band of forty men who move drugs and people across the Rio Grande. They began as *pateros*. Then they armed themselves with revolvers and knives. Anyone who wanted to cross this stretch of river had to pay Los Osos. Other *pateros* were threatened with death when they tried to cross clients in the area. Half of all migrants found "drowned," autopsies reveal, died before ever entering the water, says Nuevo Laredo human rights activist Raymundo Ramos Vásquez.

Other smugglers undercut Los Osos's business in the 1990s by using different spots to cross migrants along the river. Los Osos turned to smuggling bales of marijuana. Turf gunfights broke out on the river with other local gangs—the Hommies, the Parque Morelos, Los Perros, the Chiquillos Boys, and Cuatro Vientos.

El Tiríndaro stuck with the less dangerous job of *patero*. Each week, he gives police officers who patrol the river a 10 percent cut of his earnings as a smuggler. The police show leniency toward anyone at the camp.

When the police arrive at the river, they ask Enrique for identification papers. They check his pockets for drugs. They help themselves to whatever change is there. Still, Enrique is spared the more severe shakedowns other migrants face. Leonicio Alejandro Hernández, thirty-three, says that four municipal officers approached him on the banks of the Rio Grande and said, "We charge a thousand pesos [$100] to cross this river."

Hernández balked, and the officers lowered their price. "If you don't give us five hundred pesos, ten days in jail!" he says one yelled.

He says another warned, "Throw yourself into the river, and I'll kill you."

Hernández says he paid them and swam away.

Octavio Lozano Gámez, the municipal police chief in Nuevo Laredo, acknowledges that of his 720 employees, "a small minority of police officers in the city have this problem of robbing people." Lozano doubts, however, that even his corrupt officers would pick poor migrants to rob. "Any smart police would seek out someone with more money, gold chains, wristwatches."

Because he is so young, everyone at the camp looks after Enrique. When he goes at night to wash cars, someone walks him through the brush to the road. When he leaves during the day, someone always yells, "Be careful." They warn him against heroin. They offer tips on which parts of the city are thick with police, places he should not go. But leaving the camp scares him, and they give him marijuana to calm him down.

Car washing goes poorly. One night, he earns almost nothing.

At 9:15 P.M., Enrique receives 2½ pesos for helping a woman in a small station wagon back up. Five minutes later, a woman in a blue dress arrives in a white Pontiac Bonneville.

"May I wash your windows?" She nods and walks toward the taco stand. Enrique wipes the front of the car, then the side windows, moving his hand, with its fingers splayed across the back of a rag, in quick, ever-growing circles. He walks around the car, wiping and wiping, first clockwise, then counterclockwise. He cleans inside, even the floorboards. The moon is out, but it is 90 degrees. Sweat trickles down his face. He must finish before the woman's tacos are ready. In minutes, he is done.

She returns, fumbles for her car keys, gets in, then puts two coins—3½ pesos—in his hand. *"Gracias,"* he says.

A man tips him for guiding him backward out of a parking spot. "I hope this helps you, boy."

Enrique thanks everyone.

By 10 P.M. he has accumulated only 10 pesos, about $1. He sits over the open top of his water-filled bucket to cool off. Between then and 4 A.M., he scrambles after every car that pulls in. In eight hours, he makes 20 pesos.

The fifteen days on his meal cards pass quickly. Now he needs part of his money to eat. Every peso he spends on food cannot go toward the phone cards. He begins to eat as little as possible: crackers and soda.

Sometimes Enrique does not eat at all. He feels weak. Occasionally, local fishermen give him a fish they have caught. Friends at the camp share their meals. They offer scrambled eggs or a bowl of chicken soup. One teaches him to fish with a line coiled on a shampoo bottle. The line, fitted with a hook, has three spark plugs at the end to sink it. Enrique swings the spark plugs around his head, then casts toward the middle of the Rio Grande. The line whirs as it spools off the bottle. He hauls in three catfish.

Even El Tiríndaro is generous; the sooner Enrique can buy a phone card and call his mother, the sooner Enrique will need his services. When one of Enrique's meal cards is stolen, El Tiríndaro gives him the unexpired card of a migrant who has crossed the river successfully.

He knows that Enrique cannot swim, so he paddles him back and forth on the water in an inner tube to quiet his fears. When the river level drops, it exposes the lower branches of willows lining the banks. They are festooned with clothing that the migrants discard as they begin to wade out. Plastic bags, shorts, and underwear hang from the boughs like tattered Christmas ornaments. El Tiríndaro takes Enrique on the inner tube along the bank as he collects the clothing. They wash the clothes in the river, then sell them near the taco stand and hawk any inner tubes they find for 15 pesos apiece at a tire store. El Tiríndaro lets Enrique keep a T-shirt they find.

Enrique learns that El Tiríndaro is part of a smuggling network. He has partners in three safe houses on the U.S. side of the river, people who will hide migrants if Border Patrol agents are in pursuit. A middle-aged man and a young woman, both Latinos, meet him and his clients after they cross the river. Then they all drive north together, and El Tiríndaro walks his clients around Border Patrol checkpoints, giving wide berth to the agents. After the last checkpoint, El Tiríndaro returns to Nuevo Laredo, and the couple and others in the network deliver the clients to their destinations. The price is $1,200.

El Hongo listens as his campmates talk about dos and

don'ts: Find an inner tube. Take along a gallon of water. Learn where to get into the river, where not. They talk about the poverty they came from; they would rather die than go back. Enrique tells them about María Isabel, his girlfriend, and that she might be expecting.

Enrique talks about his mother. He says he is extremely depressed. "I want to be with her," he says, "to know her."

"If you talk, it's better," a friend says.

But it gets worse. He fears being attacked by bandits outside his circle of friends. He hears of atrocities: knives, a rifle to the chest, beatings with tree limbs, demands for shoes and money.

Migrants huddle around the San José church like cattle pressed up against a barn seeking protection from a cold winter chill. They share experiences. Gonzalo Rodríguez Toledo, twenty-three, from Nicaragua, was approached by two middle-aged men on the river by Enrique's camp. They put a knife to his chest and robbed him. Oscar Vega Ortiz, twenty-six, saw a man on a mule appear as he and four other migrants got ready to cross the river. The man pointed a rifle at his chest. "Your money or your life," he told Vega.

Manuel Gallegos prepares to have his last meal at the church before returning home to Mexico City. That morning, he took most of his clothes and shoes off to cross the river. Bandits spotted him. Gallegos ran, but the bandits, cursing, caught up to him and beat him with a small tree trunk. Gallegos's breathing is labored. He hikes up his shirt. His back is red and raw. Several ribs are broken. He will not try to cross again.

One gang, Enrique knows, wants to harm him. Salvadorans with MS tattooed on their foreheads, the sign of the Mara Salvatrucha, hang out like dogs at the San José church, sniffing out robbery prospects. Unlike migrants, they wear new black

Nikes. "I'll pass you across the river. Give me two hundred pesos," they say to the unwary; then they take their clients to the riverbank and assault them. After robbing them, they tell the migrants to keep mum about what has happened or they will hunt them down and rape them.

The glue sniffer at camp tangles with them, and Enrique steps in. One Salvadoran covered in tattoos threatens to thrash Enrique. He is spared only by the intervention of a migrant MS from his old neighborhood back home.

But his luck with the authorities runs out. One afternoon *migra* agents come to the camp. They ask Enrique where he is from.

"I'm from Oaxaca," Enrique says in the accent he learned as he passed through.

The agents pause. "What are you doing here?"

"Fishing," Enrique says, trying to stay calm.

"You can't fish here. You have to leave. Get out of here."

He leaves, only to be arrested in town—twice, both times for loitering. Where is he from?

"Veracruz," Enrique says.

"Get in," the officers yell, pointing to their squad car. They call him a street bum and lock him up with three drunks who are singing. The toilet is running over, the drunks have smeared some of its contents on a wall, and the stench is overpowering. Both times, Enrique wins his release by sweeping and mopping.

One night, as he walks twenty blocks back to the river from washing cars, it rains. El Tiríndaro doesn't usually sleep at the river when it rains. The camp, Enrique fears, will be too dangerous without El Tiríndaro there. He ducks into an abandoned house. It has gaping holes in the roof. He finds some cardboard and places it on a dry spot. He removes his sneakers and puts them and his bucket near his head. He has no socks, blanket, or pillow. He pulls his shirt up around his ears and breathes into it to stay warm. Then he lies down, curls up, and tucks his hands across his chest.

Lightning flashes. Thunder rumbles. Wind wails around the corners of the house. The rain falls steadily. On the highway, trucks hiss their brakes, stopping at the border before entering the United States. Across the river, the Border Patrol shines lights on the water, looking for migrants trying to cross.

With his bare feet touching a cold wall, Enrique sleeps.

MOTHER'S DAY

It is May 14, 2000, a Sunday when many churches in Mexico celebrate Mother's Day.

Finally, Enrique has saved 50 pesos. Eagerly, he buys a phone card. He gives it to one of El Tiríndaro's friends for safekeeping. That way, if the police catch him again, they cannot steal it.

"I just need one more," he says. "Then I can call her."

Every time he goes to Parroquia de San José, it makes him think about his mother, especially on this Mother's Day. In addition to the refectory, on the second floor are two small rooms where up to ten women share four beds. They have left their children behind in Central America and Mexico to find work in *el Norte*, and they have found this place to sleep. Many of the single mothers pause at the 2,000-mile-long U.S.-Mexico border before making their final push into *el Norte*. Each could be his mother eleven years ago.

They try to ignore a Mother's Day party downstairs, where

150 women from Nuevo Laredo laugh, shout, and whistle as their sons dance, pillows stuffed under their shirts to make them look pregnant. Upstairs, the women weep. Like Enrique's mother, these women feel sadness, guilt, and hope. One has a daughter, eight years old, who begged her not to go. The girl asked her mother to send back just one thing for her birthday: a doll that cries. Another cannot shake a nightmare: back home, her little girl is killed, and her little boy runs away in tears. Daily she prays, "Don't let me die on this trip. If I die, they will live on the street."

Lourdes Izaguirre, Gabi's aunt, arrives at the Rio Grande exhausted, worried, and crying. It has taken Izaguirre three months to get here. She cannot call home; her family has no phone.

She has walked away from Byron, five, and Melissa, ten, as well as her ten-year-old sister and eleven-year-old brother, whom she had been raising for her ailing mother. She is heading north to find work in the United States.

"We try to keep each other from going crazy," says Águeda Navarro, thirty-four, who left behind her children, fourteen and four, a few weeks earlier.

Another mother, Belinda Cáceres, twenty-nine, prays that her children, ages twelve, nine, and two, will have enough to eat and will not get sick while she is gone.

The mothers share the same fears: Will their children forget them? Will they see their children again?

Back home, Izaguirre says, making Tommy Hilfiger–labeled shirts netted her $30 a week. It was not enough to feed her son and daughter each night, even when her ex-husband helped with the light and water bills.

Byron, her son, went to a birthday party and saw a piñata.

He asked why he could not have a party, too. Melissa, her daughter, needed books and school supplies. She asked why she could not have them. Izaguirre told them she would go to the United States and send money for piñatas and books. Melissa offered to quit school and go to work so their mother would not leave.

"I'm going to work so you can study," Izaguirre told them. "I will never forget you." Now she fears that something will happen to them and she will be too far away to comfort or help. Worse, she fears that the separation will last too long and her children will give her the same icy reception she has watched other mothers endure. "You lose the love of your child," she says.

She begins to cry. "I feel bad for doing this. It wasn't worth it. I'd rather starve with my children. But I've come this far. I can't go back." She mortgaged her property and borrowed money from a neighbor for her journey. Her voice turns firm again. "I can't go back empty-handed."

"I worry about dying along the way. I know going into another country is wrong. I know God would be against this. But I hope he understands."

Many of the women in the room became single mothers because they were unwilling to endure the more difficult parts of their relationships with men: drunkenness, beatings, mistresses. Alone, most found supporting their children difficult. Father Ovidio Nery Rodríguez, a priest in Tegucigalpa, explains, "To not prostitute themselves, to feed their children, they leave."

Though many mothers expect the separations to be short, typically they last six to eight years, says Analuisa Espinoza, a Los Angeles Unified School District social worker who specializes in immigrants. By then, they are strangers. Some mothers, picking up children from smugglers, hug the wrong ones.

Enrique wonders: What does his mother look like now?

"It's okay for a mother to leave," he tells a friend, "but just for two or four years, not longer." He recalls her promises to return for Christmas and how she never did. He remembers how he longed to have his mother with him each time his grandmother scolded him. "I've felt alone all my life." One thing, though: she always told him she loved him. "I don't know what it will be like to see her. She will be happy. Me too. I want to tell her how much I love her. I will tell her I need her."

Across the Rio Grande on Mother's Day, his mother, Lourdes, thinks about Enrique. She has, indeed, learned that he is gone. But in her phone calls home, she never finds out where he went. She tries to convince herself that he is living with a friend, but she remembers their last telephone conversation: "I'll be there soon," he said. "Before you know it, on your doorstep." Day after day, she waits for him to call. Night after night, she cannot sleep more than three hours. She watches TV: migrants drowning in the Rio Grande, dying in the desert, ranchers who shoot them.

Enrique's disappearance stirs up a bad memory: Lourdes's ex-boyfriend and Diana's father, Santos, tried to make his way back to the United States after being deported to Honduras. He never arrived. Lourdes is convinced he was killed in Mexico or drowned in the Rio Grande.

One of Lourdes's roommates has a relative who arrives at their apartment. He lies on the couch, recovering from the traumatic trip through Mexico. His smuggler loaded 150 migrants inside the tank of a truck that normally hauled gasoline. By the time the truck stopped, he tells Lourdes, several men had died of asphyxiation. Their tongues were hanging out.

She imagines the worst and becomes terrified that she might never see Enrique again. She is utterly helpless. She asks God to watch over him, guide him.

On the afternoon of the Mother's Day celebration, three municipal police visit the camp. Enrique does not try to run, but he is jittery. They ignore him. Instead, they take away one of his friends.

Enrique has no money for food, not even for crackers. He takes a hit of glue. It makes him sleepy, takes him to another world, eases his hunger, and helps him forget about his family. He lies on a mattress and talks to the trees. He cries. He talks about his mother. "I want to be near my mom. I want to be near to her," he says over and over again until the fog in his mind lifts.

A friend catches six tiny catfish. He builds a fire out of trash. It grows dark. He cuts the fish with a lid from an aluminum can.

Enrique hovers nearby. "You know, Hernán, I haven't eaten all day."

Hernán guts the fish.

Enrique stands silently, waiting.

A SETBACK

It is May 15. Enrique has had a good night washing cars: he made 60 pesos. At midnight, he rushes to buy his second phone card. He puts only 30 pesos on it, gambling that his second call will be short. If his old employer finds Aunt Rosa Amalia and Uncle Carlos and gets his mother's number, it won't take many minutes to call his boss a second time and pick it up.

Enrique saves his other 30 pesos for food.

He and his friends celebrate. Enrique drinks and smokes some marijuana. He wants a tattoo. "A memory of my journey," he says.

El Tiríndaro offers to do it for free. He takes Enrique to a two-bedroom house near the river, a Los Osos hangout where El Tiríndaro sleeps when it rains. Two drug addicts who live in the house use it to cook crack cocaine. Four wealthier teenagers from Nuevo Laredo are sitting on couches in the living room, smoking crack they have just bought.

El Tiríndaro shoots up to steady his hand.

Enrique wants black ink, but all El Tiríndaro has is green. Enrique pushes out his chest and asks for two names, so close together they are almost one. For three hours, El Tiríndaro digs into Enrique's skin. In gothic script, the words emerge:

EnriqueLourdes.

His mom, he thinks happily, will scold him.

The next day just before noon, he stirs from his dirty mattress. He borrows some toothpaste, squats at the river, dips his toothbrush into the murky water, and cleans his broken teeth. They still ache from the beating he took on top of the train a few weeks ago. So does his head, which throbs constantly. A dark pink welt an inch long scars his left forehead like a cross. He still cannot see well with his left eye, and the lid sags. His arms and legs are mottled with bruises, and he has been wearing the same clothes for days. He brushes gently, methodically, then cups water into his mouth with his hands and gargles. He washes his face, tosses water on his hair. He stores the toothbrush on his portion of the upright mattress coil.

He is hungry. Hours pass. His hunger grows. Finally, he cannot stand it. He retrieves the first phone card from the friend who is holding it, and he sells it for food.

Worse, he is so desperate that he sacrifices it at a discount, for 40 pesos. He saves a few pesos for the next day and uses all of his money to buy crackers, the cheapest thing that will fill his stomach.

Now he has gone from two phone cards to one, worth only 30 pesos. He regrets surrendering to his hunger. If only he can earn 20 pesos more. Then he will go ahead and phone his old boss and hope that his aunt or uncle will call back, so he won't need a second card.

But someone has stolen his bucket. Without it, he is lost: he used it for sitting, chopping food, washing his feet, and earning a living.

When he thinks about giving up, he tries to reassure himself: "I know my day will come. I know I shouldn't get desperate." After his crackers, he lies on his mattress, stone quiet, and looks at the sky. His friend can see that he is depressed. Since Enrique has been at the river, he has watched thirty other men and boys sleep at the camp, pay a smuggler, then cross the river into the United States.

The friend tries to cheer him up. He urges him not to despair. There is nothing left to do, the friend says, but to risk the cops, go downtown and beg. They will do it together.

They go to Avenida Guerrero. It is filled with tourists who spill across the border to shop, drink, dance, and hire prostitutes. Poor Mexicans flock there to beg. Five-year-olds tap the tourists on the arm and ask them to buy tiny packs of gum. Old women sit on sidewalks and extend their weathered hands, seeking a coin or two. Avenida Guerrero is thick with police. For Enrique, a Central American without papers, it is treacherous ground.

But he is desperate. His friend leans on his arm, drags a

foot, and pretends to be lame. They approach every tourist they see. "Want me to show you where the train hit me?" the friend offers. Slowly, he lifts his cuff.

People recoil. "No, no. Here!" They give a peso and scurry away.

Enrique and his friend quickly lose their nerve. They retreat to the river before the police can catch them, with only enough to buy more crackers.

A friend at camp lends him a bucket. He trudges back out to the car wash across from the taco stand. He sits on the bucket. Carefully, he pulls up his T-shirt. There, in an arch just above his belly button, is his tattoo, painfully raw.

EnriqueLourdes. Now the words mock him. For the first time, he is ready to go back home. But he holds back his tears and lowers his shirt. He refuses to give up.

THE MOMENT

He considers crossing the Rio Grande by himself. But his friends at camp warn him against it.

They tell him the trek is treacherous from the moment you step into the river. A month ago, one of the camp dwellers saw a man's body float past. It was bloated. Sometimes, friends say, migrants are killed when whirlpools suck them under. Other times, whirlpools smash their heads against rocks. Sometimes their legs cramp and they sink. Other times INS helicopters fly too low, whip up waves, and swamp inner tubes, riders and all. They call the helicopters mosquitoes; they come down and bite.

Migrants at the car wash tell him about the trains. Eight to ten leave for *el Norte* every day. Security guards stand on a platform over the freight cars, watch for migrants, and pull them off before they cross the bridge. As soon as the trains reach the U.S. side, the cars are inspected again.

Then, at Milla 12, the first INS checkpoint north of Laredo, the trains stop inside a fence. It is impossible to run. Agents scan the cars with an infrared telescope to pick up body heat. And then come the dogs. The INS uses them at its second checkpoint, some eighty miles north, near Cotulla. The trains carry new Fords and Chryslers. Migrants like to hide in the cars or among them, and the dogs sniff them out.

One of the dogs is a Malinois, imported from Belgium for her keen ability to smell human sweat and saliva, even from outside closed cars with their windows rolled up. Her name is Franca. She takes commands in German.

Immigrants smear themselves with garlic to throw her off. She begins upwind of the train and runs alongside its length, straining at the leash until she gets a hit. She jumps up and down when she suspects that they are there, and she rarely misses. Agents open and inspect the double-decker boxcars. "Ten-four! We have bodies up here!" they announce. Agents praise the dog and let her play with a rubber toy.

Enrique decides that walking across Texas is out. Without a guide, his campmates say, it is easy to get lost and wander in circles in the sameness of the brush lands. The trek to San Antonio takes seven or eight days, in desert heat of up to 120 degrees, with diamondback rattlers, lacerating cactus needles, water slimy with cattle spit, saucer-sized tarantulas, and wild hogs with tusks. Some migrants, dehydrated and delirious, kill themselves. Their leathery corpses sway from belts around their necks on whatever is sturdy and tall. Water jugs lie empty at their feet.

Some are shot by ranchers as they try to beg or steal food or drink. A few weeks after Enrique arrived in Nuevo Laredo, Mexican immigrant Eusebio de Haro Espinosa, twenty-three, went up to a rancher in Bracketville, Texas, forty miles from the border, and asked for water. The rancher, Samuel Blackwood, seventy-five, shot him in the leg with a .357 Magnum. He didn't seek medical help. Espinosa bled to death.

Texas ranchers have become increasingly riled by immigrants who trespass. "There are two kinds of wets," says retired trucker Jake Smith, who lives in a trailer on a ramshackle ranch in Martinez, near Cotulla, Texas. "Good wets. And bad wets." When immigrants are near, the dogs bark. Smith sits on the front porch with a pistol in his lap.

Bad immigrants pack drugs, break into your place, and steal things, he says. Even the good ones, who are in search of honest work, leave the gates open, let the cattle out, or break into your place looking for food and water, says Smith, a crusty, white-haired man who occasionally gets his glass eye cleaned by a nearby large-animal veterinarian.

Ranch owner Joe Crisp has installed three locks on each window of his home. Immigrants have broken in eight times. Once they rammed a hole in his wall to get inside. Another time, they broke through the roof. Such intrusions are so common that Border Patrol agents advise ranchers to leave water and food outside, beside their doors. Every rancher near the Crisp and Smith homes has heard about the incident when a rancher turned down an immigrant who asked to use his telephone. The immigrant tied the rancher to a chair and stole his pickup truck.

Some of Enrique's campmates say they were apprehended when a rancher pointed a pistol at them, told them to freeze, and then dialed the U.S. immigration agents on his cell phone. Many migrants trying to enter are caught by the INS: 108,973 near Laredo in 2000, the year Enrique is trying.

Enrique will have to outsmart Border Patrol agents on the other side who are skilled and dogged.

Tracker Charles Grout can spot a footprint from a moving Ford Bronco. His partner, Manuel Sauceda, can tell, within a range of a few hours, how old it is.

They are agents for the U.S. Immigration and Naturalization Service based in Cotulla, halfway along a seven- to eight-day walk between the Rio Grande at Nuevo Laredo and San Antonio. Their job is to arrest immigrants who enter Texas illegally.

Salary increases for Grout and Sauceda are based partly on how many migrants they catch. They work together, along railroads and in the desert, taking turns tracking on foot and driving ahead in the Bronco, sometimes for days.

One Thursday in September 2000, Sauceda discovers footprints near a cattle trough southwest of Encinal. He knows immigrants drink from the trough, although the water smells like rotten eggs and is laced with green scum. He circles the footprints and draws closer.

If footprints are not windblown or caved in, they are recent. If no animals, such as centipedes, snails, birds, or snakes, have crossed them, they are fresh. If there are discarded food wrappers nearby and if the wrappers are not covered with ants, the tracks are brand-new.

Sauceda circles the water trough, sweat trickling down his face, searching among piles of cow manure for clues. He faces the sun and looks for tiny shadows.

Then he finds more tracks. They have been made that

morning. He detects patterns: one track is waffled, another has fine lines, and another is shaped like the pointed toe of a boot. "I see at least four here," he says. He smiles. Like a bloodhound, he leans over and picks up his pace.

Changes at the Cotulla office show how much harder it has become to sneak past agents like Grout and Sauceda.

In 1994, Cotulla had 20 agents. Now, in Cotulla alone, Enrique will face 70 agents. Cotulla is one of eight INS stations north of Nuevo Laredo. In all, the INS has hired more than 5,600 additional agents since 1993 to expand its forces along the southern U.S. border.

In addition, agents use a growing arsenal of technology: helicopters, night-vision goggles, thermal imaging that picks up body heat, and seismic sensors that detect footsteps along immigrant trails. One INS officer's only job is to move the sensors to outsmart smugglers who try to plot their locations.

Earlier on this day, alerted by sensor 53, agents caught eleven Mexican men who had been walking across the desert for four days.

Grout and Sauceda are particularly dogged, partly because it means saving lives. Every two weeks or so, Sauceda says, he has to call an ambulance for an immigrant who has been bitten by a rattlesnake or hit by a train or has grown so dehydrated in the Texas desert that he is nearing collapse.

Sauceda follows the footprints at the water trough. He comes to a trail, climbs into the Bronco, and drives, opening and closing gates with keys from a ring that holds scores, given to the agents by ranchers.

The temperature climbs to 100 degrees—cool compared with the highs of 112 to 118 the week before, which had partially melted the asphalt on Interstate 35. The Bronco has a range-fire-prevention reminder on the dashboard: DO NOT OPERATE OFF THE ROAD IN DRY GRASS OR BRUSH. Sauceda ignores it.

By 2 P.M., Grout and Sauceda have lost and found the tracks several times.

Whoever is leaving them seems to be angling toward a tower with an antenna. The two trackers search every big tree and water source. They come to a barbed-wire fence. Marks in the dirt show that their quarry has crawled under it. Grout picks up the tracks on the other side. "There they are, the same ones," he says. "Bigger than Dallas."

The track makers are headed for Encinal. If they reach town, it will be virtually impossible to find them, and the agents' half day spent in the cactus and the searing heat will be wasted.

Sauceda, dripping sweat, trots alongside the footprints. Grout drives ahead, to the edge of town. He spots an odd-looking dirt driveway. The right side has been dragged clean. It leads to a ramshackle house.

He parks. There, in soil leading to the driveway, are the footprints: waffle, fine lines, the point of a boot . . .

"I got 'em!" he says into a walkie-talkie.

"Where?" Sauceda asks.

"Same place as the last time."

Grout takes three paces toward the house. A rottweiler lunges from behind a tree. Grout reaches for his .40-caliber Beretta. A chain stops the dog a few feet in front of him.

Carefully, Grout presses forward seven more paces, then swings open the door to a yellow shed. Jammed inside are five surprised immigrants. He handcuffs them.

Back at the Bronco, he inspects their footwear. Waffle, fine lines, pointed boot. He smiles.

A Central American youth rides a freight train through Mexico toward the United States. Each year, thousands of children cling to the tops and sides of trains as they journey north in search of their parents. Some say they need to find out whether their mothers still love them.

The view through a fence at the home where Enrique lived with his paternal grandmother. Across the valley were his sister and the phone on which
they occasionally talked to their mother. Enrique ended the strained calls
by saying, "I want to be with you."

María Marcos looks at photos of her grandson Enrique. As he began to rebel, she asked him: "Don't you love me? I am going to send you away." "Send me!" he said. "No one loves me."

Buzzards and children are competitors for trash at the dump in Tegucigalpa. The same fate might have awaited Enrique without the money that arrived from the United States. Still, he began to grow angry and rebellious. "I see so many children with mothers," he told his sister. "I want that."

Central American migrants headed for the United States ride in railroad cars through southern Mexico.

Migrants flatten themselves to avoid being hit by tree branches as their freight train rolls through Chiapas in southern Mexico. Enrique learned several lessons about the state known to immigrants as "the beast." Among them: Trust no one in authority, and never ride alone.

One migrant watches as another leaps from freight car to freight car during a train's brief stop in Mapastepec.

Thirteen-year-old David Velásquez, left, and seventeen-year-old Roberto Gaytán wait to be jailed after being caught in Tapachula, Mexico. The Guatemalans were headed for Los Angeles and North Carolina.

Migrants arrested in a dawn sweep at the Tapachula rail yard are behind bars before their probable deportation. Central Americans are sent back to the Guatemalan border on *el bus de lágrimas*, the bus of tears. Making as many as eight runs a day, the buses deport more than 100,000 passengers a year.

Oscar Omar Valle of Honduras reboards a train after a stop in Cordoba, Mexico, where he sought food. Like Enrique, he is unprepared for the cold ahead. A migrant knows that if he doesn't run fast enough while grabbing onto a moving train, he can be jerked forward, lose his grip, and be pulled under the wheels.

Santo Antonio Gamay, hoping to make it to Toronto, shows the fatigue and tension from fifteen hours of riding a train. He has been arrested and deported three times before. In minutes, he will jump off to again try to outrun law enforcement officers.

Riders sit atop a northbound freight train as it rolls through lush Veracruz state in Mexico. Enrique's experiences in Chiapas taught him to fear the worst from people, but here he was stunned by kindness. People in many villages streamed toward the tracks with gifts.

The hands of migrants and food givers meet as a train passes through Fortín de las Flores in Veracruz. A World Bank study found that 42.5 percent of Mexicans live on two dollars or less a day. In rural areas, the people who live along the tracks are often the poorest.

Enrique washes a car in Nuevo Laredo, Mexico. He needed to earn one hundred pesos to call Honduras to get his mother's phone number, which he had lost during a beating by train bandits.

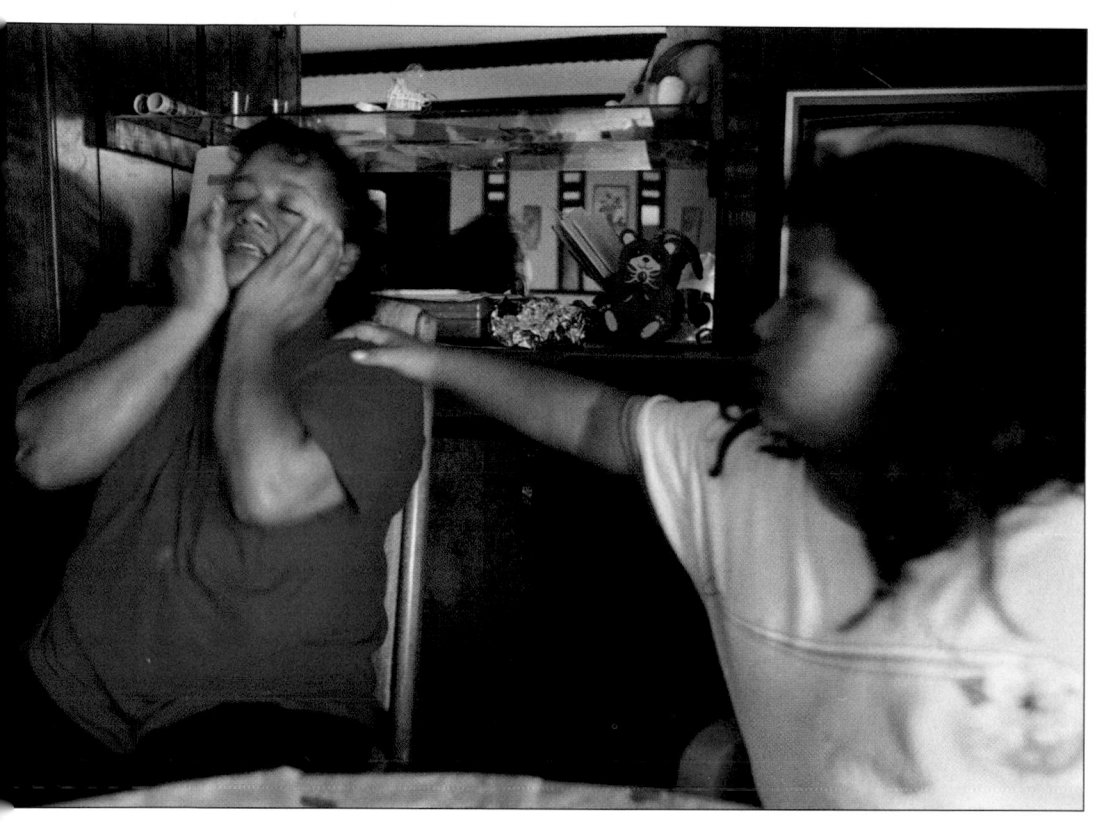

Lourdes breaks down as she talks about her life and her separation from her son. Her nine-year-old daughter, Diana, who was born in the United States, offers comfort.

Central Americans emerge from the Rio Grande in Texas after wading across. In the plastic bags are dry clothes. Before Enrique entered the water, he tore up a scrap of paper with his mother's phone number on it and scattered it on the bank. This time, he had memorized the number.

Many immigrants are glad to be tracked down. Isaías Guerra, from Veracruz, Mexico, looked relieved when Grout found him. Guerra had been lost in the wilderness for two days. He had survived by eating cactus. The first day, five coyotes had followed him. The animals got so close that Guerra hit two of them with a stick to force them to back off. That night, he slept in a tree. The next day, a large mound a dozen feet away from him that at first looked like cow dung started moving. A rattlesnake, coiled, as thick as his upper arm, prepared to strike. He saw three more snakes. At dusk, he spotted a bobcat nearby. He quietly backed away. Guerra gladly crawled into the back of Grout's truck, dubbed "the cage."

Migrants deported by the United States often return to the San José church. Enrique sees some of them. A tall man arrives at the church one evening with a vacant, dull look in his eyes. He hasn't eaten in five days. His brown shirt hangs in pieces on his body, torn to shreds by the cactus. His arms are cut up and bleeding, pinpricked with thistles and thorns. He is caked in mud. The bottoms of both feet are covered by gargantuan yellow blisters. His toes are swollen like sausages. The nails have turned black. He stumbles forward on his heels, barely able to walk. He's done seventy miles in the past six days, killing five rattlers along the way. He begs for a glass of water and a shower.

Everything Enrique hears makes him terrified of snakes and scorpions. In the Texas desert, snakes come out to hunt at night, when it is cooler. That is when migrants are on the move. They fumble forward in the dark, afraid to use a flashlight. Some rely, instead, on superstitions: Take a pregnant woman with you, and the snakes will sleep as you pass by. Put three peppercorns under your tongue for good luck. There are copperhead snakes, coral snakes, cottonmouth snakes, and the blue indigo snake, so long and fast it can kill a rattlesnake. There is a bumper crop this year, and the drought has made them more aggressive.

Many times, when Enrique falls asleep, he has the same nightmare: A snake has bitten him in the mouth. He cannot call out for help.

El Hongo listens. Finally, he decides against going alone. "Why should I die doing this?" he asks himself. Somehow he will call his mother and ask her to hire a smuggler.

Nine rings of coyotes are said to operate in Nuevo Laredo. Each ring has at least fifty smugglers. But Enrique knows he cannot trust just anyone. Back home in Honduras, most smugglers are honest; they must uphold their reputations if they want business. Here they can rob, rape, or abandon their clients with impunity. Some take them straight to river bandits and get a cut. Only one smuggler in ten, says a nun at the Parroquia de San José, is trustworthy. Many migrants at the church return with smuggler horror stories.

Enrique has spent a lot of time around El Tiríndaro. Enrique has seen him take a number of men and boys across the river, always at night, usually one or two at a time, paddling furiously in their inner tubes. They always disappear into the United States. When El Tiríndaro takes them over, Enrique notices, they are never caught and sent back. El Tiríndaro has studied the movements of the Border Patrol so long, says fellow *patero* Juan Barajas Soto, that he knows what each agent does every eight hours, during the shift change.

Enrique makes a decision: When he calls his mother, he will ask her to hire El Tiríndaro. "I know," he says to himself, "that he won't strand me."

On May 18, he awakens to find that someone has stolen his right shoe. Shoes are almost as important as food and his mother's telephone number. He can think of every pair that has helped him come north. On this trip alone, there were seven. Blue shoes, white shoes, leather work boots, Nike sneakers. He has bought, borrowed, or traded for them. All have fallen apart or been stolen. But never only one.

He spots a sneaker floating near the riverbank. He snags it. It is for a left foot. Now he has two left shoes. Bucket in hand, he hobbles back to the taco stand, begging along the way. People give him a peso or two. He washes a few cars, and it starts to rain. Astonishingly, he has put together 20 pesos in all.

That is enough to trade in his 30-peso phone card for one worth 50 pesos.

He will use the 50-peso card to call his old boss at the tire store. If the boss reaches his aunt and uncle, if they know his mother's number, if his aunt or uncle will call him back . . .

PADRE LEO'S HELP

It is May 19. There is only one way his plan will work. Father Leonardo López Guajardo at the Parroquia de San José is known to let migrants phone from the church if they have cards. Each day, he serves as their telephone assistant. In flip-flops, he pads to the door every fifteen minutes or so and summons someone for a return call. Enrique will have to trust the priest to find him if his aunt and uncle call back. He has already sensed what people in Nuevo Laredo know: when it comes to migrants, Padre Leo's heart is bigger than his collections.

The priest rarely uses his office. Most afternoons and evenings he sits by the door, behind a small wooden desk, in a room that doubles as a food pantry. The room is lined with shelves stocked with cans and boxes of food—donations to help feed migrants. There is a pile of overripe fruits and vegetables on the floor. Flies buzz around it. It stinks of rotting tomatoes and onions. Liquid has seeped from the decomposing vegetables and pooled on the floor. Here, one by one, he attends to a stream of migrants. Padre Leo takes down the migrants' information, then gives them a meal card or arranges to pick up money wired by relatives in the United States.

In Nuevo Laredo, Padre Leo is not a typical priest. When he was a boy, even his mother questioned whether he was priest material. So did his teachers at the seminary, who deemed him too playful and impatient with pomp and procedure; they delayed his ordination. It took him eleven years to graduate.

Other priests in town wear nice watches and rings and act important. Padre Leo is so disheveled that visitors sometimes mistake him for one of the poor, dirty migrants sitting outside. His clothes are always rumpled. He wears the same pants for days, stained and dirty from hauling boxes of ripe vegetables. His favorite pair has frayed cuffs and a small tear in the rear. He forgets to zip them up. The men in the congregation try to help. They point at his fly. *"Ah, ah. Sí, sí, sí,"* the priest says, hastily pulling the zipper into place.

Padre Leo emerges one night from his bedroom to say Mass. His flannel shirt is inside out and buttoned incorrectly. The church's other priest looks exasperated. "Where's your belt?" he asks. Leo shuffles back to his bedroom to take another stab at dressing himself. The only time he looks neat is when he visits his family; his mother sends him back to Nuevo Laredo perfumed with cologne and in a newly pressed shirt and pants.

Priests in town favor the latest-model Grand Marquis. Padre Leo rides everywhere on a rickety blue bicycle. People call him *el Papa en la bici*. He rides when it is cold, hot, raining. When he goes to other churches to say Mass, he carries his white floor-length robe in a small bag across the handlebars. In the evenings, Enrique watches the priest return to the church on his bicycle, loaded down with bags of donated bread.

During Mass, he doesn't read from the Bible much. He conveys his message through jokes or by spinning a lesson out of a popular movie or song. He does not stand at the altar; he paces up and down the church aisle's pink floors in his white robe, which he wears with broken-down tennis shoes. As he paces, he mops copious quantities of sweat from his balding head with a large white towel. A microphone in his left hand, the towel in his right, he preaches.

Like most in his church, secretary Alma Delia Jiménez Rentería says she has learned more from what the priest practices than what he preaches. In 1997, when she was new in her job at the church, the future mayor of the city, Horacio Garza, came to visit Padre Leo. A foul-smelling migrant with badly swollen feet also needed to talk to the priest. Alma asked the migrant to wait and started to usher in the future mayor. The priest stopped her. "No. Let the mayor wait. Let the person who is most in need see me first," he said. Says Alma, "He isn't a padre who tells you what to do. He shows you through his actions, through his example. He doesn't pray with rosary or Bible. He loves God by doing good toward others. That's how he teaches you to love God."

He is impatient to get things done, tackling too many things at once. He rarely sits down for a meal, living off a chunk of chocolate in one hand, a bit of bread in the other. He scoops some rice or beans out of buckets of food left in the pantry or eats from a can of food he plucks off the shelves.

He cannot sit or stand still. Often, in midconfession, his mind wanders to the next thing he must do for migrants. "*Disculpe, ahorita vuelvo.* Pardon me, I'll be right back," he tells people, usually just as they are opening up.

He is unfailingly polite, even formal, but he can be awkward, even curt, around people. When someone gives the church money, he responds with a simple "*A. Bien.*" When he walks down the street, he is so distracted he often fails to say hello when he passes a church member. It took the arrival of two nuns in 1998 to bring some order and rules to the padre's operations.

He is humble and lives modestly. He gives his salary to the church to help it pay staff salaries. When someone gave him a nice truck, he sold it to pay church utility bills. His car, which he rarely drives to save gas and help the environment, is a tiny Mazda purchased for $400. The driver's door won't open from the outside, the vinyl dash is shredded, and the front seat has a huge hole in it.

His focus is one instilled by mentors at the seminary: "Either we are with the poor, or we are not. God teaches us to most help the poor. Any other interpretation is unacceptable." To Padre Leo, the people most in need in Nuevo Laredo are migrants. They go for days without food, for months without resting their heads on a pillow; they are defenseless against an onslaught of abuses. He vowed to restore a bit of their dignity. "He saw that these people are the most vulnerable, the most disliked by the local population. So he gave himself to them," says a church volunteer, Pedro Leyva.

He tells church members that they, too, were once migrants. Saint Joseph was a migrant. The Bible was written by migrants. Running off a migrant, he says, is like turning against yourself. A person must be more than spiritual, he tells them. They must act. "Some people read the Bible and fall asleep," says Padre Leo. "For me, it was a jolt. The worst thing as a Christian is to go through life asleep."

People knew he was special from the day he arrived. A bus and caravan of cars—sixty people—journeyed with him from his old church in Anáhuac to Nuevo Laredo to say farewell through tears. The priest knocked on every door in the neighborhood. "Good afternoon, my name is Leonardo. I'm the new priest. I'm here to serve you," he said. In a country where the church is conservative, Padre Leo announced in a newspaper article shortly after arriving, "Jesus wasn't killed for doing miracles. It was because he defended the poor and opposed the rulers and the injustice committed by the powerful."

Padre Leo gave up the two-bedroom priest's apartment attached to the church so that female migrants would have a place to sleep. He settled into a tiny room off the pantry, into which a narrow bed and chest of drawers just fit. His bathroom: the church's public restroom.

To help the migrants look more presentable, he brings a haircutter to the church. A doctor treats their illnesses for free. If they need blood, Padre Leo is the first to donate.

To clothe the migrants, he circumvents Mexican Customs, which inspects cars and confiscates used clothing coming into the country, in what Padre Leo believes is an attempt to protect Mexican clothing manufacturers. People crossing the border checkpoint on foot or on a bike are less likely to be inspected. Twice a week at dusk, Padre Leo grabs a large black duffel bag and pedals his bike over a bridge that spans the Rio Grande into Laredo, Texas. There, he buys used clothes for 20 cents a pound. With one strap hooked around each arm, he carries the bag stuffed with clothes across his back and balances another bag across the handlebars. In the gathering dark, he pedals back.

If the church stash is low or lacks a needed size, he gives away the few shoes and clothes he owns. Sometimes he slips the shoes off his feet and hands them to a migrant. "Padre, I don't have a shirt," a migrant says. The priest runs to his closet and pulls one out. These clothes are usually the shirts, pants, shoes, and jackets the members of the church's eight study groups have given the priest for his birthday, to tide him over for the year. "You give it to him, he admires it, then he gives it away," says Pedro Leyva.

To feed migrants, often more than a hundred each night, he collects food three days a week from stores in Nuevo Laredo. On Mondays and Wednesdays, he drives the church van to Laredo. At a Catholic orphanage, he hauls out leftover boxes of honeydew melon, oranges, and bread. Then he goes to a house at the end of a cul-de-sac. Rosalinda Zapata's husband works at the H.E.B. supermarket. Her hallway is lined with boxes of recently expired crackers, salsa, and potato chips. Padre Leo heads back to Mexico with the food.

As he crosses the long bridge over the Rio Grande, he begins to pray. At the Mexican side of the bridge, one in ten cars gets a red light and is pulled over for a random inspection. "God, please give me a green light. *Please.* I promise I'll be good." He tells God he doesn't want to haul contraband, but it's the only way to help the migrants. The light flashes green. He smiles and steps on the gas. Back at the church, he shows off his haul. *"Excelente! Qué bueno fue el arriesgue!* Excellent! The risk was so worth it!" He is as gleeful as a child who has gotten away with something forbidden. He is happiest when the pantry is full and there is plenty to give away.

He is the migrants' strongest advocate in Nuevo Laredo. Each September, he leads a silent procession of people who place a cross on a fence overlooking the Rio Grande, one for each migrant who has recently died trying to cross into the United States. He finds friends who can help identify migrants who drown in the river, so their families can be contacted and their bodies shipped home.

In November, after saying Mass in the middle of the cemetery for the Day of the Dead, he leads a crowd over to a common grave in the corner of the cemetery. He leads a prayer for dead migrants who are buried here. "This is a sad place, God. We want to remember the migrants who passed this way."

To be their champion, he has gone against the initial wishes of many in his church and faced threats from the authorities, much like Priest Salamón Lemus Lemus in Veracruz, where one in two congregants quit the church in protest at letting migrants use the parish as a dormitory. Half of Padre Leo's church members at first opposed the priest's mission to help migrants, says one church volunteer, Patricia Alemán Peña. Some thought the priest was crazy to attract what they saw as bums and delinquents to their neighborhood and objected to helping migrants at all. "This was a good neighborhood—until you brought *your* people," they complained.

Others urged him to give them a taco, but for God's sake not to allow illegals into the church. What if among the Central Americans there were dangerous criminals fleeing prosecution in their own countries? Why not let a church with more resources take on this task? Why, others asked, should all their tithes go to helping strangers, to the extent of building a room to feed them supper? Meanwhile, their church, one of the poorest of the city, was falling apart. The pews were decrepit, the bills were once so in arrears the electricity was nearly turned off, and the padre hadn't installed air-conditioning, despite summer temperatures that reach 120 degrees. A church survey showed that many didn't attend church because of the migrants. Only a tenth of the neighborhood's residents come to the Parroquia de San José. In other neighborhoods, a quarter attend Mass.

Neighbors confronted the priest. Migrants would loiter, drink, and smoke around the church. "They feel like peeing, and they just let loose!" and urinate on her front gate, says a woman who lives next to the church. Another neighbor says a migrant hugged and tried to kiss one of her twin daughters. The migrants sleep around the church, get into fights, and defecate on her doorstep. She has to scrub the sidewalk with bleach to get rid of the stench.

Many priests and the bishop admire and support Padre Leo. Others oppose him. Priests, they say, should stick to doing Mass, weddings, and baptisms. The social role of helping the poor and migrants belongs to politicians. Some snicker that he's a clown, laugh about his appearance, dismiss his humility as an act.

Once, the local director of *la migra* threatened to lock up the priest for several years on smuggling charges if he didn't bar migrants from entering his church. Leo promised to behave—and then ignored the warning.

Now three quarters of the people in his parish agree with his work. "We should say thanks that we don't have to go through this—but maybe with a bit of bread, a smile, you can lessen their load," says Peña. Without the church's help, she says, the migrants would be even more desperate, and the impact on the city would be worse. Like many others at the church, she volunteers to help cook dinner for the migrants each day. "There is no one like this man. He is too humble. Too humble," she says of her priest. "Padre Leo has taught me to give to others without expecting anything in return."

In late afternoon, Enrique reaches his old boss on the church telephone with his request. Two hours later, the padre bellows Enrique's name. As always, word spreads through the courtyard like wildfire: someone named Enrique has a phone call.

"Are you all right?" asks Uncle Carlos.

"Yes, I'm okay. I want to call my mom. I've lost the phone number."

Somehow, his boss has neglected to tell them this. Do they have it with them? Aunt Rosa Amalia fumbles in her purse. She finds the number. Uncle Carlos reads it, digit by digit, into the phone.

Ten digits. Carefully, Enrique writes them down, one after another, on a shred of paper. Just as Uncle Carlos finishes, the phone dies. Uncle Carlos calls again. But Enrique is already gone. He cannot wait.

When he talks to his mom, he wants to be alone; he might cry. He runs to an out-of-the-way pay phone to call her. Collect.

He is nervous. Maybe she is sharing a place with unrelated immigrants, and they have blocked the telephone to collect calls. Or she might refuse to pay. It has been eleven years. She does not even know him. She told him, harshly, not to come north, but he disobeyed her. Each of the few times they talked, she urged him to study. This, after all, was why she left—to send money for school. But he has dropped out of school.

Heart in his throat, he stands on the edge of a small park

two blocks from the camp. Next to the grass is a Telmex phone box on a pole.

It is 7 P.M. and dangerous. Police patrol the park. Enrique, a slight youngster with two left shoes, pulls the shred of paper from his jeans. They are worn and torn; he is too tattered to be in this neighborhood. He reaches for the receiver. His T-shirt is blazing white, sure to attract attention.

Slowly, carefully, he unfolds his prized possession: her phone number. He listens in wonderment as his mother answers. She accepts the charges.

"*¿Mami?*"

At the other end, Lourdes's hands begin to tremble. Then her arms and knees. "*Hola, mi hijo.* Hello, my son. Where *are* you?"

"I'm in Nuevo Laredo. *¿Adónde está?* Where are you?"

"I was so worried." Her voice breaks, but she forces herself not to cry, lest she cause him to break down, too. "North Carolina." She explains where that is. Enrique's foreboding eases. "How are you coming? Get a coyote." She sounds worried. She knows of a good smuggler in Piedras Negras.

"No, no," he says. "I have someone here." Enrique trusts El Tiríndaro, but he costs $1,200.

She will get the money together. "Be careful," she says.

The conversation is awkward. His mother is a stranger. This is probably expensive; he knows that collect calls to the United States from back home in Honduras cost several dollars a minute.

But he can feel her love. He places the receiver in its cradle and sighs.

At the other end, his mother finally cries.

A Dark River, Perhaps a New Life

At 1 A.M. on May 21, 2000, Enrique waits on the edge of the water.

"If you get caught, I don't know you," says El Tiríndaro. He is stern.

Enrique nods. So do two other migrants, a Mexican brother and sister, waiting with him. They strip to their underwear.

Enrique has seen smugglers ask migrants to grab hold of a long rope to cross the river. Others lock arms and form a human chain. El Tiríndaro's strategy is more risky. He uses a black inner tube, which is bulky and easy for Border Patrol agents to spot.

Across the Rio Grande stands a fifty-foot pole equipped with U.S. Border Patrol cameras. In daylight, Enrique has counted four sport-utility vehicles near the pole, each with agents. Now, in the darkness, he cannot see any.

He leaves it up to El Tiríndaro, who has spent hours at this spot studying everything that moves on the other side.

Enrique tears up a small piece of paper and scatters it on the riverbank. It is his mother's phone number. He has memorized it. Now the agents cannot use it to locate and deport her. In all, Enrique has spent four months trying to find her.

El Tiríndaro holds an inner tube. The Mexicans climb on. He paddles them to an island in midstream. He returns for Enrique with the tube.

He steadies it in the water.

Carefully, Enrique climbs aboard. Up to three migrants have drowned in a single day along this stretch of river. The Río Bravo, as it is called here, is swollen with rain, a torrent of water coursing toward the Gulf of Mexico. Two nights ago, it killed a youngster he knew, a tall, skinny migrant with a cleft upper lip. A whirlpool pulled him under. The year is not yet half over. Already, fifty-four people have been pulled, lifeless, from the river at or near Nuevo Laredo. Enrique cannot swim, and he is afraid.

El Tiríndaro places a plastic garbage bag on Enrique's lap. It contains dry clothing for the four of them. Then El Tiríndaro paddles and starts to push. A swift current grabs the tube and sweeps it into the river. Wind whips off Enrique's cap. Drizzle coats his face. He dips in a hand. The water is cold. He scans the murky water for the green snakes that sometimes skim across the waves.

All at once, he sees a flash of white—one of the SUVs, probably with a dog in back, inching along a trail above the river.

Silence. No bullhorn barks, "Turn back."

The inner tube lurches, sloshes, and bounces along. Enrique grips the valve stem. The sky is overcast, and the river is dark. In the distance, bits of light dance on the surface.

At last, he sees the island, overgrown with willows and reeds. He seizes the limb of a willow. It tears off. With both hands, he lays hold of a larger branch, and the inner tube swings onto the silt and grass. They have crossed the southern channel. On the other side of the island flows the northern channel, even more frightening because it is closer to the United States.

El Tiríndaro circles the island on foot and looks across the water. The white SUV reappears, less than a hundred yards away. It is moving slowly along the dirt trail, high on the riverbank.

Its roof lights flash red and blue on the water, creating a psychedelic sheen. Agents turn to aim a spotlight straight at the island.

Enrique and the Mexicans dive to the ground face-first. If the agents spot them and lie in wait, it could spell doom for Enrique. He is closer to his mother than ever. Authorities can deport the Mexicans back across the river, but they can send him all the way to Honduras.

Worse, he could sit in a Texas jail cell for months before the United States processed the paperwork to deport him, most likely the juvenile prison in Liberty, Texas, forty-six miles northeast of Houston, where many minors who are captured in Texas trying to enter the United States alone and illegally are sent to await deportation.

Immigrant children arrive at the jail shackled. They are strip-searched and asked to "squat and cough"—an exercise to determine if they are harboring any contraband items in certain cavities of their bodies. They file through eight locked metal doors to arrive at the E pod, where immigrant children as young as twelve are held. They are housed, at times, in the same pod with accused rapists and other felons.

Children in the E pod spend most of their time inside windowless cells that measure seven and a half by ten feet. Migrant children say the jail, operated by Corrections Corporation of America, doesn't feed them enough. Without cash to buy from the jail's commissary, they go hungry and lose weight. They see sunlight one hour a day, when they are allowed into an outdoor area surrounded by a fence topped with concertina wire.

They have little information about when they might be brought before an immigration judge or deported. The guards know little, and most do not speak Spanish.

Locked up day after day, month after month, the children grow desperate. They run circles around their tiny cells. They read the instructions on the shampoo label over and over. Some become fearful they will go crazy in the jail. They begin to talk to themselves. One boy gets so depressed he stops eating for days and bangs his knuckles against the concrete wall until they are raw. A few of the children become suicidal and try to hang themselves.

If he was lucky, Enrique would spend no more than two or three months locked up before being sent back to Honduras. It would mean starting out for the ninth time.

For half an hour on the river's island, everyone lies stone still. Crickets sing, and water rushes around the rocks. Finally, the agents seem to give up. El Tiríndaro waits and watches. He makes certain, then returns.

Enrique whispers: Take the others first. El Tiríndaro loads the Mexicans onto the tube. Their weight sinks it almost out of sight. Slowly, they lumber across the water.

Minutes later, El Tiríndaro returns. "Get over here," he says to Enrique. "Climb up." He has other instructions: Don't rustle the garbage bag holding the clothes. Don't step on twigs. Don't paddle; it makes noise.

El Tiríndaro slips into the water behind the tube and kicks his legs beneath the surface. It takes only a minute or two. He and Enrique reach a spot where the river slows, and Enrique grabs another branch. They pull ashore and touch soft, slippery mud. In his underwear, Enrique stands for the first time on U.S. soil.

NEARLY FROZEN

As El Tiríndaro hides the inner tube, he spots the Border Patrol. He and the three migrants hurry along the edge of the Rio Grande to a tributary called Zacate Creek. "Get in," El Tiríndaro says.

Enrique walks into the creek. It is cold. He bends his knees and lowers himself to his chin. His broken teeth chatter so hard they hurt; he cups a hand over his mouth, trying to stop them. For an hour and a half, they stand in Zacate Creek in silence. Effluent spills into the water from a three-foot-wide pipe close by. It is connected to a sewage treatment plant on the edge of Laredo, Texas. Enrique can smell it.

El Tiríndaro walks ahead, scouting as he goes. At his command, Enrique and the others climb out of the water. Enrique is numb. He falls to the ground, nearly frozen. "Dress quickly," El Tiríndaro says.

Enrique steps out of his wet undershorts and tosses them away. They are his last possession from home. He puts on dry jeans, a dry shirt, and his two left shoes.

El Tiríndaro offers everyone a piece of bread and a soda.

The others, hidden in a thicket of bushes, eat and drink. Enrique is too nervous. Being on the outskirts of Laredo means they are near homes. If dogs bark, the Border Patrol will suspect intruders.

"This is the hard part," El Tiríndaro says. He runs. Enrique races behind him. The Mexicans follow, up a steep embankment, along a well-worn dirt path, past mesquite bushes and behind some tamarind trees, until they are next to a large, round, flat tank. It is part of the sewage plant.

Beyond is an open space. El Tiríndaro glances nervously to the right and left. Nothing. "Follow me," he says.

Now he runs faster. Numbness washes out of Enrique's legs. It disappears in a wave of fear. They sprint next to a fence, then along a narrow path on a cliff above the creek. They dash down another embankment, into the dry upstream channel of Zacate Creek, under a pipe, then a pedestrian bridge, across the channel, up the opposite embankment, and out onto a two-lane residential street.

Two cars pass. Winded, the four scuttle into bushes. Half a block ahead, a car flashes its headlights.

PUFFS OF CLOUDS

It is a red Chevrolet Blazer with tinted windows. "Let's go," El Tiríndaro says.

As they reach it, locks click open. Enrique and the others scramble inside. In front sit a Latino driver and a woman, part of El Tiríndaro's smuggling network. Enrique has met them before, on the other side of the river.

It is 4 A.M. Enrique is exhausted. He climbs onto pillows in back. They are like puffs of clouds, and he feels immense relief.

He smiles and says to himself, "Now that I'm in this car, no one can get me out." The engine starts, and the driver passes back a pack of beer. He asks Enrique to put it into a cooler. The driver pops a top.

For a moment, Enrique worries: What if the driver has too many? The Blazer heads toward Dallas.

Border Patrol agents pay attention to Blazers, other SUVs, and vans. Some smugglers favor windowless vans. They strip out the backseats and stack the migrants like cordwood, one on top of the other. Headlights tilted up mean there are people in the back, weighing down the vehicle, says Alexander D. Hernandez, a supervisor in Cotulla, Texas. Weaving means the load is heavy and causing sway. When the agents notice, they pull alongside and shine a flashlight into the eyes of the passengers. If the riders do not look over but seem frozen in their seats, they are likely to be illegal immigrants.

Enrique sleeps until El Tiríndaro shakes him. They are out of Laredo and half a mile south of a Border Patrol checkpoint. "Get up!" El Tiríndaro says. Enrique can tell he has been drinking. Five beers are gone. The Blazer stops. Enrique and the two Mexicans, with El Tiríndaro leading, climb a wire fence and walk east, away from the freeway. Then they turn north, parallel to it. Enrique can see the checkpoint at a distance.

Every car must stop. "U.S. citizens?" agents ask. Often, they check for documents.

Enrique and his group walk ten minutes more, then turn west, back toward the freeway. They crouch next to a billboard. Overhead, the stars are receding, and he can see the first light of dawn.

The Blazer pulls up. Enrique sinks back into the pillows. He thinks: I have crossed the last big hurdle. Suddenly he is overwhelmed. Never has he felt so happy. He stares at the ceiling and drifts into a deep, blissful sleep.

Four hundred miles later, the Blazer pulls into a gas station on the outskirts of Dallas. Enrique awakens. El Tiríndaro is gone. He has left without saying good-bye. From conversations in Mexico, Enrique knows that El Tiríndaro gets $100 a client. Enrique's mother, Lourdes, has promised $1,200. The driver is the boss; he gets most of the money. The *patero* is on his way back to Mexico.

Along with fuel, the driver buys more beer, and the Blazer rolls into Dallas about noon. America looks beautiful. The buildings are huge. The freeways have traffic exchanges with double and triple decks. They are nothing like the dirt streets at home. Everything is clean.

The driver drops off the Mexicans and takes Enrique to a large house. Inside are bags of clothing, in various sizes and American styles, to outfit clients so they no longer stand out. They telephone his mother.

LOURDES

Lourdes, now thirty-five years old, has come to love North Carolina. People are polite. There are plenty of jobs for immigrants, and it seems to be safe. She can leave her car unlocked, as well as her house. Her daughter Diana quickly masters English, something she hadn't done surrounded by Spanish speakers in California.

Lourdes is always thinking about the two children she left in Honduras. When she walks by stores that sell things they might like, she thinks of Enrique and Belky. When she meets a child Enrique's age, she tells herself, "*Así debe estar mi muchachito.* My little boy must look this big now."

A small gray album holds treasures and painful memories: pictures of Belky, her daughter back home. At seven, Belky wears a white First Communion dress and long white gloves; at nine, a yellow cheerleader's skirt; at fifteen, for her *quinceañera*, a pink taffeta dress with lace sleeves and white satin shoes. Belky leans over a two-layer cake topped with white frosting and a pink angel. Lourdes spent $700 to make the party special. She promised Belky she would try to make it back to Honduras for the big event somehow. "I wanted to go. I wanted to go . . . ," Lourdes says. At eighteen, Belky wears a blue gown and mortarboard for her high school graduation.

There are pictures of Enrique, too: at eight in a tank top, with four piglets at his feet; at thirteen in the photograph at Belky's *quinceañera*, the serious-looking little brother. She most treasures a photo of her son in a pink shirt. It is the only one she has where he is smiling.

She has often worried from afar about her boy. In 1999, a sister in Honduras disclosed the truth about Enrique: "He's getting in trouble. He's changed." He was smoking marijuana. The news made Lourdes sick. Her stomach tightened into a knot for a week. Now she is more worried than ever.

Lourdes has not slept. All night, since Enrique's last call from a pay phone across the Rio Grande, she has been having visions of him dead, floating on the river, his body wet and swollen. She told her boyfriend, "My greatest fear is never to see him again."

She has spent part of the night in her kitchen, praying before a tall candle adorned with the image of San Judas Tadeo. This saint tackles difficult situations, matters of life and death. Lourdes lit the candle days ago, when Enrique made his first phone call from Nuevo Laredo. Each time Lourdes walks past the candle, she prays: "God has granted to you the privilege of aiding humankind in the most desperate cases. O, come to my aid that I may praise the mercies of God! All my life I will be your grateful client until I can thank you in Heaven."

Now a female smuggler is on the phone. The woman says: We have your son in Texas, but $1,200 is not enough. $1,700.

Lourdes grows suspicious. Maybe Enrique is dead, and the smugglers are trying to cash in. "Put him on the line," she says.

He's out shopping for food, the smuggler replies.

Lourdes will not be put off.

He's asleep, the smuggler says.

How can he be both? Lourdes demands to talk to him.

Finally, the smuggler gives the phone to Enrique.

"*¿Sos tú?*" his mother asks anxiously. "Is it you?"

"*Sí, mami,* it's me."

Still, his mother is not sure. She does not recognize his voice. She has heard it only half a dozen times in eleven years.

"*¿Sos tú?*" she asks again. Then twice more. She grasps for something, anything, that she can ask this boy—a question that no one but Enrique can answer. She remembers what he told her about his shoes when he called on the pay phone.

"What kind of shoes do you have on?" she asks.

"Two left shoes," Enrique says.

Fear drains from his mother like a wave back into the sea. It *is* Enrique. She feels pure happiness.

WAITING

She takes $500 she has saved, borrows $1,200 from her boyfriend, and wires it to Dallas.

In the house with the clothing, the smugglers wait. From the bags, Enrique puts on clean pants, a shirt, and a new pair of shoes. The smugglers take him to a restaurant. He eats chicken smothered in cream sauce. Clean, sated, in his mother's adopted country, he is happy.

They go to Western Union. But there is no money under his mother's name, not even a message.

How could she do this? At worst, Enrique figures, he can break away. Run. But the smugglers call again.

She says she has sent the money through a female immigrant who lives with her, because the woman gets a Western Union discount. The money should be there under the woman's name.

It is.

Enrique has no time to celebrate. The smugglers take him to a gas station, where they meet another man in the network. He puts Enrique with four immigrant men being routed to Orlando, Florida. They stay overnight in Houston, and at midday, Enrique leaves Texas in a green van.

Five days later, Lourdes's boyfriend gets time off from work to drive to Orlando, where Enrique has been staying with other immigrants and waiting for him to arrive. Her boyfriend is handsome, with broad shoulders, graying temples, and a mustache. Enrique recognizes him from a video his uncle Carlos brought back from a visit.

"Are you Lourdes's son?" the boyfriend asks.

Enrique nods.

"Let's go." They say little in the car, and Enrique falls asleep.

By 8 A.M. on May 28, Enrique is in North Carolina. He awakens to tires crossing highway seams: *Click-click. Click-click.* "Are we lost?" he asks. "Are you sure we aren't lost? Do you know where we are going?"

"We're almost there."

They are moving fast through pines and elms, past billboards and fields, yellow lilies and purple lilacs. The road is freshly paved. It goes over a bridge and passes cattle pastures with large rolls of hay. On both sides are wealthy subdivisions. Then railroad tracks. Finally, at the end of a short gravel street, some house trailers. One is beige. Built in the 1950s, it has white metal awnings and is framed in tall green trees.

At 10 A.M., after more than 12,000 miles, 122 days, and seven futile attempts to get to his mother, Enrique, eleven years older than when she left him behind, bounds from the backseat of the car and up five faded redwood steps, and swings open the white door of the mobile home.

To the left, beyond a tiny living room with dark wooden beams, sits a girl with shoulder-length black hair and curly bangs. She is at the kitchen table eating breakfast. He remembers a picture of her. Her name is Diana. She is nine now.

Enrique leans over and kisses the girl on the cheek.

"Are you my brother?"

He nods. "Where's my mother? Where's my mother?"

She motions past the kitchen to the far end of the trailer.

Enrique runs. His feet zigzag down two narrow, brown-paneled hallways. He opens a door. Inside, the room is cluttered, dark. On a queen-size bed, under a window draped with lace curtains, his mother is asleep. He jumps squarely onto the bed next to her. He gives her a hug. Then a kiss.

"You're here, *mi hijo*."

"I'm here," he says.

A TWIST

The Odyssey, an epic poem about a hero's journey home from war, ends with reunion and peace. *The Grapes of Wrath,* the classic novel about the Dust Bowl and the migration of Oklahoma farmers to California, ends with death and a glimmer of renewed life.

Enrique's journey is not fiction, and its conclusion is more complex and less dramatic. But it ends with a twist worthy of O. Henry.

Children like Enrique dream of finding their mothers and living happily ever after. For weeks, perhaps months, these children and their mothers cling to romanticized notions of how they should feel toward each other.

Then reality intrudes. The children show resentment because they were left behind. They remember broken promises to return and accuse their mothers of lying. They complain that their mothers work too hard to give them the attention they have been missing. In extreme cases, they find love and esteem elsewhere, by getting pregnant, marrying early, or joining gangs.

Some are surprised to discover entire new families in the United States—a stepfather, stepbrothers, and stepsisters. Jealousies grow. Stepchildren call the new arrivals *mojados,* or wetbacks, and, to gain power over their new siblings, threaten to summon U.S. immigration authorities.

The mothers, for their part, demand respect for their sacrifice: leaving their children for the children's sake. Some have been lonely and worked hard to support themselves, to pay off their own smuggling debts and save money to send home. When their children say, "You abandoned me," they respond by hauling out tall stacks of money transfer receipts.

They think their children are ungrateful and bristle at the independence they show—the same independence that helped the children survive their journeys north. In time, mothers and children discover they hardly know each other.

At first, neither Enrique nor Lourdes cries. He kisses her again. She holds him tightly. He has played this out in his mind a thousand times. It is just as he thought it would be.

All day they talk. He tells her about his travels: the clubbing on top of a train, leaping off to save his life, the hunger, thirst, and fear. He has lost 28 pounds and is down to 107. She cooks rice, beans, and fried pork. He sits at the table and eats. The boy she last saw when he was in kindergarten is taller than she is. He has her nose, her round face, her eyes, her curly hair. Lourdes has three children, but Enrique is special. He is her only son.

"Look, Mom, look what I put here." He pulls up his shirt. She sees a tattoo.

EnriqueLourdes, it says across his chest.

His mother winces. Tattoos, she says, are for delinquents, for people in jail. "I'm going to tell you, son, I don't like this." She pauses. "But at least if you had to get a tattoo, you remembered me."

"I've always remembered you."

He tells her about Honduras, how he stole his aunt's jewelry to pay drug debts, how he sold the shoes and clothes she sent to buy glue, how he wanted to get away from drugs, how he ached to be with her. Finally, Lourdes cries.

She asks about Belky, her daughter in Honduras; her own mother; and the deaths of two of her brothers. Then she stops. She feels too guilty to go on.

The trailer is awash in guilt. Eight people live here. Several have left their children behind. All they have is pictures. Lourdes's boyfriend has two sons in Honduras. He has not seen them in five years.

One of the boyfriend's cousins left behind a wife and son, two months old. He has not seen them in two years.

Another cousin and her husband left behind a four-year-old daughter. The husband has never seen the daughter; his wife was pregnant when he left. She calls every two weeks and vows to return to Honduras in a year if she hasn't been able to bring their daughter north. "The most important thing is love. Not losing that," she says. Three pictures of the little girl, in a pink shirt and pigtails, stand as a constant reminder near a television in a corner.

Enrique likes the people in the trailer, especially his mother's boyfriend; he could be a better father than his own dad, who abandoned him ten years ago to start another family.

In Honduras, Enrique's grandmother walks next door to talk to Enrique's girlfriend, María Isabel.

She has news: Enrique made it.

María Isabel wails, "He's not coming back!" She locks herself in her bedroom and cries for two hours.

For the next few months, María Isabel spends hours at a time silently sitting on a rock in front of her aunt Gloria's house. At night, Gloria hears María Isabel sobbing.

Gloria's daughter tries to console María Isabel. At least now, the daughter tells her, she's sure Enrique is alive. "Cheer up," she says. "He's there. He'll send money. If he'd stayed, you would have both died of hunger." But María Isabel, normally always giggling, is serious and sad.

Belky, too, is depressed. She stops talking. In the morning, she cries before facing each new day. She longs to be with her mother. Maybe, she tells herself, she should have gone with her brother, taken the risk. Now both Enrique and Diana are with her mother. "Now I'm the only one left here," she tells her aunt Rosa Amalia.

Three days after Enrique arrives, Lourdes's boyfriend helps

him find work as a painter. He earns $7 an hour. Within a week, he is promoted to sander, making $9.50. With his first pay-check, he offers to pick up $50 of the food bill. He buys Diana a gift: a pair of pink sandals for $5.97. He sends money to Belky and to his girlfriend in Honduras.

Lourdes brags to her friends, "This is my son. Look at him! He's so big. It's a miracle he's here."

Whenever he leaves the house, she hugs him. When she comes home from work, they sit on the couch, watching her fa-vorite soap opera, with her hand resting on his arm. Each Sun-day, they go shopping together to buy enough food to last the week. Lourdes cooks for Enrique, and he begins to put on weight.

Over time, though, they realize they are strangers. Neither knows the other's likes or dislikes. At a grocery store, Lourdes reaches for bottles of Coke. Enrique says he does not drink Coke—only Sprite.

He plans to work and make money. She wants him to study English, learn a profession.

At first he is quiet and shy. That begins to change. He goes to a pool hall without asking permission. She becomes upset. Occasionally, he uses profanities. She tells him not to.

"*¡No, mami!*" he says. "No one is going to change me."

"Well, you'll have to change! If not, we'll have problems. I want a son who, when I say to do something, he says 'Okay.' "

"You can't tell me what to do!"

The clash culminates several weeks after Enrique arrives, when María Isabel telephones collect and her call is rejected because some of the immigrants in the trailer do not know who she is.

That was right, Lourdes says; they cannot afford collect calls from just anyone.

Enrique flares and begins to pack. Enrique says, "Who are you to me? I don't even know you!"

Lourdes is enraged. She grabs him by his arm and pulls him into the privacy of her bedroom. "You will respect me!" she yells. "I am your mother." Lourdes blames Enrique's grandmother María: she spoiled the boy and let him run amok. Lourdes is determined to impose discipline on her son. She walks up behind him and spanks him hard on his buttocks, several times.

"You have no right to hit me! You didn't raise me." He tells her that only his grandmother María, who raised him, has that right. Lourdes disagrees. "I sent money. I supported you. That is raising you!"

Enrique locks himself in the bathroom and sobs. He throws about anything he can find—toothpaste, shampoo, a perfume bottle. Diana rushes into the bedroom, crying. Enrique storms out of the house. Lourdes's boyfriend and his cousin try to calm her. They cruise the streets, trying to find Enrique.

Enrique hides behind a small Baptist church two miles away. He sleeps in the graveyard behind the church, between the headstones.

Lourdes stays up most of the night. What, she worries, will be her future with Enrique?

The next afternoon, however, their love prevails. Enrique returns home and apologizes to his mother. He tells her he loves her. He comforts her with a little white lie. He tells her he spent the night safely sleeping in her car.

They share hugs and kisses. That night, they watch soap operas together on the living room sofa. As they sit side by side, Lourdes can feel her son's love.

Enrique and his mother are conciliatory at last. More than that, they might be joined by María Isabel.

One day, Enrique phones Honduras. María Isabel is pregnant, as he suspected before he left. On November 2, 2000, she gives birth to their daughter.

She and Enrique name the baby Katerin Jasmín. The baby looks like him. She has his mouth, his nose, his eyes. An aunt urges María Isabel to go to the United States, alone. The aunt promises to take care of the baby.

"If I have the opportunity, I'll go," María Isabel says. "I'll leave my baby behind."

Enrique agrees. "We'll have to leave the baby behind."

SEVEN

The Girl Left Behind

Enrique knows he does not hate his mother. But with each passing day, his resentment grows. After months with his mother, he can no longer contain it. He tells Lourdes she didn't care enough about her children to stay with them in Honduras. Did she think sending money could substitute for having his mother at his side? Or quell the loneliness he felt being moved from one relative to the next? "Money doesn't solve anything," he tells her.

He berates Lourdes for leaving him with a father she knew was irresponsible. Why didn't she put him with her own family, who cared for his sister Belky? Why didn't she send enough money, thus forcing him to sell spices from the age of ten? Why did she send Belky so much more, to cover tuition at a private school her aunt sent her to?

"Belky always got more from you," he says. If he was destitute, he had no one nearby who could help. "How could I ask you for anything?" he asks Lourdes. "I would go a year without talking to you."

He tells her he wanted to study, he just didn't want to have to beg his mother for the money. "Belky is going to be a professional. Look at me," he says.

Enrique tells Lourdes her biggest mistake was getting pregnant a year after arriving in the United States. "You shouldn't have gotten pregnant until you knew your existing kids were okay," he says.

Why did she continually promise to return for Christmas and then never show up? Once she knew he was in trouble sniffing glue, he asks her, how could she stay away? "You left me, abandoned me," he tells her. "You forgot about me."

Nothing, he tells her, was gained by their long separation. "People come here to prosper. You have nothing here. What have you accomplished?" If she had stayed in Honduras, he would have turned out better. "I wouldn't be this way if I had had two parents."

A true mother, he tells Lourdes, isn't the person who carries you in her womb. It is someone who raises and nurtures you. "My mother is my grandmother María," he tells her. He warns Lourdes that she has no right to give him advice. "You long ago lost the right to tell me what to do," he says.

Then Enrique lands the most hurtful blow. He tells Lourdes he plans to leave her and return to Honduras in two years. "I'm not going to do the same as you—stay here all my life."

Lourdes expected Enrique to love her like the five-year-old who clung to her in Honduras. She cries herself to sleep at night. She has been a good person, a good mother. Why is God punishing her?

She must show Enrique he is terribly mistaken. "What about the money I sent you?" she says. "I have witnesses!" Whenever he asked for something specific—a television, a soccer ball—she sent it. Belky got more money only because her aunt lobbied Lourdes for funds for Belky's school tuition. Lourdes lived through extreme poverty and humiliating circumstances to send as much as possible to her children. For the first time, she tells Enrique about the struggles she, too, endured during their years apart: "I killed myself trying to help you."

She's not like some mothers she knows who leave Honduras and forget their children, never call, never write. That's a mother a child can resent, even hate. I called, I wrote, she says.

Blame your father, Lourdes says. He promised to take care of you while I was away. *He* abandoned you. Your father's family had equal responsibility to provide your needs. Instead, she says angrily, your grandmother María sent you to sell spices in the market, where you learned about drugs.

"You are what you are because you didn't want to study," Lourdes says. "It's not my fault. I wanted you to study. You preferred to be on drugs." One night, as he sits down to dinner, Lourdes tells her son that if she had sent more money, he would have blown it on drugs. He sold the bed she bought him for drug money. Enrique, silent, pushes away from the table without touching his food.

He should thank her for giving him life, Lourdes says. That alone gives her the right to give him advice and discipline.

Lourdes thinks of how her own mother couldn't provide enough food for her children, how she could hate her, too. When she was eight years old, Lourdes sought out odd jobs. A neighbor gave her clothes to wash in the river twice a week. When she was nine, her mother dispatched Lourdes and Rosa

Amalia, then ten, to work for a former neighbor as live-in maids. With no money, Lourdes quit elementary school. When she was fourteen, her mother sent her to live with her eldest brother, Marco, in southern Honduras. "My mother is sacred to me. I thank her for the little she did for us," Lourdes says.

Enrique is harboring "a silly resentment," she tells him. She didn't forget him. Why can't she get him to reason? He's an ungrateful brat. Lourdes gives her son a dark prediction: "God is going to punish you," she says. Someday, she tells him, your daughter will treat you the way you now treat me.

Enrique drinks more and more beer. Their fights are often sparked by Lourdes's advice: Don't drink and drive. Control your vices. Be more frugal. You can't spend $1,000 as if it were $10.

"*Mira, hijo* . . . Look, son . . . ," she begins.

Enrique cuts her off. "All you do is yap, yap, yap! You keep sticking your nose into things that are none of your business!" he tells her. She treats him as if he were still the infant she left behind. Didn't he fend for himself growing up? Didn't he hop freight trains across Mexico?

"Shut up. Leave me in peace!" he yells. Friends worry. They hear hatred in his voice.

Enrique loves to contradict his mother, to set her off, even when he knows she is right. He talks over her. He leaves his clothes and shoes strewn in the living room, empty beer cans on the front lawn. He tells Lourdes he's going out, then refuses to tell her where.

Enrique makes Lourdes mad—and guilty.

She cooks his dinners. She packs his lunch. She washes his clothes at the Laundromat. She drops off his car and insurance payments for him. She lends Enrique $20 here and there—

more if he needs it. Would he have turned out different, she asks herself repeatedly, if she hadn't left him?

For Enrique, alcohol is an escape from the fights. Almost all of the men on his paint crew, depressed to be away from home, are big drinkers. Unlike in Honduras, in the United States beer is cheap. Some sip Budweiser on the job, stashing the cans in an empty paint bucket when the supervisor stops by. Most swing by a store to pick up a twelve-pack at the end of the workday.

At home, four men drink. One can chug twelve beers as Enrique drives him home from work. Enrique sucks down ten beers on weeknights, often with friends in front of the house. He goes to bed at midnight or 1 A.M., getting up at 6 A.M. for work. On Saturday, the drinking begins at 4 P.M. Enrique and a housemate can down forty-eight beers together. Sometimes they drink until dawn. They head to work without sleeping.

Enrique is breaking a promise he made to leave his addictions behind once he crossed into the United States. But he feels abnormal, as if he were crawling out of his skin, if he isn't high.

At least he's not sniffing glue.

Going out to drink gets him out of the trailer, where nine people live and Enrique must sleep on the living room sofa.

It also gets him away from Lourdes.

From Thursday through Sunday, in the evenings, he goes to a local bar, a gray stucco building with plywood over the windows and a gravel parking lot. Inside, under a dark, low-slung ceiling, there are four pool tables, a long bar, and a jukebox that plays Latino music.

He frequents a discotheque with a $7 entry fee. There are iron bars over the door. Inside, the walls are painted black. Next to the dance floor a DJ plays *norteña* and *ranchera* music. Green and red lights cast a glow over the crowd. Eight women work as *ficheras*—Latinas who will sit and talk to men willing to buy them $10 beers. Six beers buys two hours of companionship, $5 a dance. A few *ficheras* provide sex for more.

Enrique and his friends splurge at a topless bar. Women dance on a platform. Men tuck dollar bills into their bikini bottoms. Twenty dollars buys an invitation to a smaller room, where a dancer brushes her breasts against the men's faces. A lap dance is more. Enrique usually spends $150 each visit. One night he invites his friends to this bar, which charges $15 each to get in, and he pays for everything. He blows $300.

When he has money for drinks and marijuana, Enrique is calm and quiet. Otherwise, he gets testy. Sometimes Enrique doesn't have enough money to pay Lourdes his share of the bills. He isn't sending as much money to his daughter as he could.

Lourdes tries to scare Enrique straight, playing on his ignorance of the United States. "If you keep this up," she warns, "I'll have you locked up." She tells him that parents can do that in the United States, even if children haven't committed a crime. Enrique soon learns that Lourdes is lying.

Four months after Enrique arrives in the United States, his work hours get cut. He decides to accompany a painter on his crew to find temporary jobs in South Carolina, Georgia, and Virginia.

Even on the road, living out of motel rooms, Enrique maintains one ritual. Each Sunday, he telephones his girlfriend, María Isabel, in Honduras.

She waits for his call at the home of one of Lourdes's cousins. When she answers the telephone, she is so overcome with emotion she cannot speak. Enrique talks for one or two hours. María Isabel cries and cries.

"María Isabel, say something, anything," Enrique pleads.

"I miss you. I love you. Don't forget me," she says.

He sends her $100 or more a month. He vows he will be back in Honduras within two years.

Eventually, María Isabel tells him of some of the problems she, too, is having. Enrique's family constantly criticizes her. "Don't pay attention to them," he tells her. It is not that easy, she says. María Isabel lives across the street from Enrique's grandmother, sister, and three aunts. When she was eight months pregnant, one of Enrique's uncles insinuated that the baby didn't belong to Enrique.

Lourdes prepares for Enrique's return and their first Christmas together again. She has grown to dread the holiday. Year after year, she promised Enrique and Belky she would see them for Christmas. Each time she let them down. Each Christmas she cried and became more hard-hearted. She wished that Christmas would never arrive.

This year, paying Enrique's smuggler has left her strapped for money. She puts up a small plastic Christmas tree. She crowds it with ornaments.

"What an ugly tree," Enrique says. "You put so many things on it that it looks like a piñata!" In Honduras, his aunt had a real tree. She set up a Nativity scene with hay inside her house. There were fireworks. The whole family gathered at midnight for a special meal.

On Christmas Eve, Lourdes goes to bed early. Enrique goes out drinking with friends. He comes home late and drunk. The next morning, Lourdes gives her son a shirt. Enrique doesn't have a gift for his mother.

New Year's Eve is better. Lourdes has never celebrated New Year's Eve in the United States. It brings back too many memories of Honduras, where she would run home from a party at midnight to hug her mother.

This year, she goes to a party with Enrique. At midnight, she kisses her son. Enrique hugs her back, hard. "Happy New Year. I love you," he tells his mother. For the first time in all her years in the United States, Lourdes doesn't cry on New Year's Eve.

HONDURAS

Criticism of María Isabel by Enrique's family grows. Gloria's grandchildren play next door. They return and repeat everything they've overheard Enrique's family say about María Isabel.

Jasmín, they say, is dirty and ill cared for. The girl loves to build little houses out of mud behind Gloria's house. María Isabel changes her clothes several times a day. Still, in Gloria's disheveled home, where the back door is left open to the muddy yard, her efforts are futile.

Enrique's sister says that Jasmín is barefoot, badly dressed, her hair uncombed. She is skinny and pale and often has a cough. Why, Enrique's family asks, did María Isabel stop breast-feeding her after six months? If Enrique sends money, why doesn't María Isabel take Jasmín to a good private doctor, not the public clinic?

María Isabel cooks, cleans, and goes out on errands and purchases for Gloria's store. She walks Gloria's grandchild to kindergarten. She helps care for the four children in the house while Gloria tends to customers in her little grocery store.

Belky understands María Isabel's dilemma. She, too, has always lived as a guest in someone else's home, feeling pressure to make herself useful.

Still, concerned about Jasmín, Belky hounds María Isabel: "Why is the girl all dirty? You need to take better care of her."

Sometimes María Isabel doesn't respond. Other times, she bristles: "No, I take care of my girl." They have no right to criticize. One of Enrique's aunts has a son who is just as skinny as Jasmín. Should she have to explain that her breasts stopped giving milk? If the women next door are so concerned about Enrique's interests, why did some of them treat him like a dog, she wonders, when he lived in their home?

The women next door have another reproach: María Isabel is misspending the hard-earned money, $100 to $150 a month, that Enrique diligently sends his daughter.

María Isabel spends most of the money on Jasmín. She also gives $15 a month to Gloria. She stocks Gloria's refrigerator with fruit, milk, and chicken. She gives Gloria's daughters pocket change. She sends $10 across town to her mother to help her buy heart and asthma medicine.

To the women next door, María Isabel is showering money on her family that rightfully belongs to Enrique's child. They know exactly how much she gets. María Isabel's money comes in a joint wire that Enrique and Lourdes send to one of Lourdes's relatives.

Enrique's aunt Mirian vigilantly watches when María Isabel goes shopping, whom she goes with, how many bags they have when they return.

Mirian, a hairstylist, hears that María Isabel has bought hair dye for herself and Gloria's daughters. Mirian is livid; she is so broke she can barely buy used clothes for her three children. When she visits Gloria's house, she sees a can of Jasmín's powdered milk spilled on the floor. Gloria's grandchildren are racing around with fistfuls of white powder in their hands.

Another day, Mirian scolds María Isabel for paying $150 for a chest of drawers to store Jasmín's clothes. "You were a fool to buy such an expensive piece of furniture." My cousin could have gotten you a better one for a third of the price, Mirian tells her.

María Isabel seethes. She says nothing.

She is grateful for what Enrique sends. Still, most of the money pays for diapers, clothes, medicine, and food for his daughter. Powdered milk alone costs $20 a month.

María Isabel has spent most of her life deprived of decent clothing. Can't she buy a dress or splurge $2.50 to get her hair dyed? She cannot live with her aunt Gloria, who is in financial distress, without helping.

Mirian, a single mother, is desperate for money. Since the birth of her third child, she has cleaned a sister's house for $35 a month and food. As each of her children begins elementary school, Mirian's costs rise. They need books, supplies, and $1.50 per day for lunch at school.

"Enrique doesn't send me a dime!" she moans. His only wire has been $20 on her birthday. She remembers changing Enrique's diapers as a baby, and how later, when he was a teen, she looked out for him. When Enrique was a glue sniffer living in his grandmother's home, she cooked his meals. Now, when she is in dire need, all of Enrique's money flows to the girl next door.

She isn't spying on María Isabel, Mirian tells her family. She's just protecting Enrique's infant by demanding that María Isabel be a better mom. Does Enrique know, Mirian angrily asks her sisters, that María Isabel sends money across town to her mother?

When Jasmín turns eight months old, Mirian mails Enrique

a letter: Your daughter isn't being well cared for, she writes. María Isabel is misspending your money. I've seen some of the clothes you sent Jasmín strewn in the dirt behind Gloria's house. Enrique recalls that when he visited Gloria's house, the children there were dirty. He asks Mirian to keep an eye on Jasmín.

On the phone, he also chides María Isabel: "If you don't take good care of that girl, I will come to Honduras and take her away from you!"

For a moment, María Isabel is silent. Then her voice turns stiff. "No one takes my daughter away from me."

Gloria is fed up with the digs at María Isabel, how her actions are scrutinized, how Enrique's family tries to control her. "Stop bothering María Isabel. You are driving me nuts. Stop criticizing her," she tells the women next door.

Gloria's grandson Allan plays rough with Jasmín, who is smaller. He picks her up by the waist and throws her to the ground. He bites her and pulls her hair. When Jasmín is nine months old, Allan plops her inside Gloria's green wheelbarrow. From the porch of her grandmother's home, Belky screams, "Allan, leave the girl alone!"

Allan is already pushing the wheelbarrow. It tips.

Jasmín tumbles to the ground. She wails. María Isabel is out on an errand. "Gloria! Allan has thrown the girl off the wheelbarrow!" Belky yells.

Gloria snaps. She shouts across the dirt street that divides their homes: "You think this child is an assassin? All you do is talk shit. You stick your noses in everything!" She curses. She tells them to mind their own business.

Then she offers up Jasmín. "Here she is. Take her! You can raise her. Let Enrique send money to you," she says. "If the dollars are causing you to make all these allegations, keep the damn dollars!"

For months, the families don't cross the street or speak. But Gloria's grandchildren do. They hear the women next door say they think María Isabel is having an affair. When she's out doing errands for Gloria, they say, she's really seeing a boyfriend. María Isabel is enraged; they are sullying one of the few things she has—her honor. Whenever María Isabel sets off on an errand, one of Enrique's aunts steps outside and inquires across the street, "¿*Adónde vas?* Where are you off to?"

Jasmín will soon turn one year old.

Lourdes and Enrique send $400 and instructions: they want a joint birthday party for Jasmín and Mirian's one-year-old daughter. That way, Lourdes figures, there will be a video to send north of everyone together.

María Isabel feels she is being forced to have her daughter's celebration with women who have maligned her as a bad mother. She has barely stepped into their home since Jasmín's birth.

On Jasmín's birthday, María Isabel dresses her in the red dress and white shoes Enrique and Lourdes sent for the party. She sends Jasmín next door. María Isabel stays behind, sobbing.

Gloria finally tells María Isabel that she should go next door long enough to be in the video for Enrique. Jasmín and the other children have already taken turns whacking her piñata. María Isabel arrives as Jasmín is blowing out candles on her Winnie-the-Pooh cake. She balances Jasmín on her hip, nervously adjusting her daughter's party hat. "Happy birthday to you!" the children sing in English. María Isabel does not sing. She wipes away tears. A half hour after arriving, she retreats to Gloria's.

Enrique has a short lull in work; he stops sending money. María Isabel finds a job sanding chairs at a small furniture factory for $35 a week.

UNITED STATES

A year after Enrique's arrival, Lourdes's boyfriend smuggles his fourteen-year-old son into the United States. The boy was eight years old when his father left Honduras. That's when the boy started drinking and getting into fights. His father hopes that bringing him to the United States will straighten out the teenager. Instead, he finds new troubles. Teachers constantly call his father in to discuss his behavior. After six months, he drops out of school.

Enrique blames the boy's father for his aggressiveness and penchant to fight. As a boy, Enrique says, he never had a father to protect him. "If his father had been with him, he wouldn't be that way," Enrique says. "He wouldn't be in trouble." The teen and Enrique share a room and drink together. Lourdes fears that the boy is reinforcing Enrique's sense of abandonment.

Enrique drinks more and more. His eyes are red from smoking marijuana. After work he eats, showers, and goes out to play pool and drink late into the night.

Enrique calls María Isabel less often—every two weeks, then every month. He tells her he wants to bring her to the United States in a year.

But he hasn't saved any money for a smuggler.

Enrique has never returned to his low: sniffing glue. Now, a few days before Christmas, twenty-two months after he left Honduras, beer and marijuana are no longer enough. He ends the workday by pouring a little paint thinner into an empty Pepsi can. He brings it home. He does the same the next night. The thinner doesn't give him as good a high as Honduran glue, but it's handy.

Over the holidays, his family and others who share the trailer move into a newer, three-bedroom duplex. It has a big kitchen and a living room with three sofas draped in lilac floral slipcovers. There is enough space to hang a painting of the Virgin of Guadalupe, a wooden carving of the map of Honduras, and a small American flag. Still, the home is crowded. There is little room for Enrique to hide his growing habit.

Twice in two weeks Lourdes has seen her son hold a smelly handkerchief over his nose. She never steps inside Enrique's bedroom. One morning, concerned that he hasn't gotten up for work, she walks in. She smells something funny, like paint.

"What are you using?" she demands.

"Nothing. *Nothing!*"

She asks about the smell. Enrique yells at her. Lourdes senses that he is hiding something.

For a few days, Enrique stays cooped up in his bedroom, listening to reggaeton music. He has been sniffing thinner for two weeks. One night, he decides to go out. He walks through the living room, toward the front door.

He is hiding something under his arm. "What do you have there? Show me," Lourdes says from the living room sofa.

"None of your business."

Enrique tries to brush past her. Lourdes jumps up and grabs Enrique by the shirt. She smells paint thinner. She's asked friends some questions. Now she knows what the smell means.

Enrique shakes himself loose.

Lourdes's words tumble out. She doesn't care that her

boyfriend and three of his relatives are in the living room, listening.

"You're broken, ruined. A drug addict! Why did you even come here? To finish screwing yourself up?"

Enrique curses.

"You're a disgrace. Get your act together! Instead of seeing you this way, I wish God would take you from me!" Lourdes says. If you keep sniffing thinner, Lourdes tells him, you have to move out. She must think of her daughter.

Enrique does not respond. He peels out of the gravel driveway in his car.

Lourdes is despondent. She worries that he will kill himself driving recklessly. For the first time in her life, Lourdes feels as though she wants to die. Maybe if she were gone, she tells herself, Enrique would know what it is truly like not to have a mother.

That night, Enrique realizes that his body cannot withstand the thinner. Each time he inhales it, the left side of his head, where he took the worst of the beating on top of the train, aches badly. His left eyelid, which still droops slightly from the assault, pulses and twitches. He has excruciating pain when he turns his head.

He stops sniffing.

He's not doing it because his mother wants him to. He is doing it for himself. He focuses on his old habit, drinking.

One morning at 2 A.M., Enrique is caught doing 55 miles per hour in a 35-mile-per-hour zone. He gets tickets for speeding and having an open container of beer in his car. The sticker on his license plate is expired. Police give him a breath test. They impound the car and take him to jail, where he spends the night. Lourdes sends her boyfriend to bail him out. Enrique's license is revoked for a week.

Many of the men in his paint crew drive drunk. Nearly four times as many Hispanic drivers as non-Hispanic drivers in North Carolina have been charged with driving while impaired. Enrique's workmates tell him not to worry. The government, they say, just wants you to pay a lot of money and tell a judge you are very sorry. The real problems, they tell him, begin with your third arrest.

Enrique pays an attorney and the government $1,000. He tells a judge he is very sorry.

HONDURAS

Life in Gloria's house has turned tense.

María Isabel moved in because it was less crowded than her mother's hut. Now twelve people crowd Gloria's two-bedroom house. María Isabel shares a bedroom with five others.

Gloria's store has gone bust. The only other one in the house with a job is Gloria's husband, who makes $125 a month. Her salary plus what Enrique sends isn't enough for María Isabel to support two households, Gloria's and her mother's.

She has to get away from Enrique's sister and aunts. Slowly, she has come to hate them. "I can't take it anymore," she tells Gloria.

She'll return to her mother's primitive hut, she decides. Her mother and younger sister will help provide Jasmín, now one and a half years old, with better care. She arranges for Enrique to send money for his daughter directly to herself instead of through his family. She does not give Enrique's family next door an address where she can be reached.

María Isabel's mother, Eva, lives in a hut perched on a mountainside in a neighborhood called Los Tubos, eight square blocks named after an aboveground water pipe that carries water from holding tanks on top of the mountain to Tegucigalpa below.

On top of the mountain, Tegucigalpa's highest, shrouded in wisps of clouds by day, bathed in an orange glow of lights by night, stands a towering statue of Jesus. The gray statue stretches out both arms. They reach down toward the residents of the city below.

The road up to Eva's is so steep that many cars can't get up it. Then there is a rutted dirt road, followed by a narrow mud and clay trail that zigzags upward. María Isabel must use the roots of a large rubber tree to step up to her mother's tiny wooden hut, which clings to the hillside. Nine people sleep inside. There has been one improvement since she left six years before: a relative built a small cinder-block house next door. It has a bathroom, which María Isabel's family can use.

Most children in Los Tubos don't go on to junior high because reaching the nearest school requires bus fare. Men work as bricklayers; women clean houses in wealthy neighborhoods.

Still, as one of the city's oldest neighborhoods, it is a small step above where Gloria's and Enrique's families live. Water, which flowed through the tap every two weeks in Gloria's house, is available here every other day. Many wooden huts have been upgraded to small brick or cinder-block homes, some two or even three stories high. Their windows have glass panes instead of wooden shutters. Almost everyone has a refrigerator.

Most in Los Tubos are longtime residents, but María Isabel's family are relative newcomers. They bought a lot in 1980 as homes were being built farther and farther up the hill. Above María Isabel's hut, there are mostly lush green slopes where it is too steep to build even the smallest place.

María Isabel's family, among the poorest in Los Tubos, eats twice a day. They have no refrigerator. They cook on two small burners. All that has kept disaster away has been María Isabel's oldest sister, who sends money from Texas, where she lives.

Still, María Isabel's life gets better.

Six days a week, at 11 A.M., María Isabel sets out for her new job at a children's clothing store at the Mall Multiplaza downtown.

From the back of the store, salesgirls ask María Isabel for a certain shoe and size. She fetches it. She shoves the box through a small opening in the wall. The light-filled mall, where Tegucigalpa's well-heeled citizens shop, has beige marble floors, potted indoor palms, air-conditioning, and glass elevators.

She gets home at 10 P.M. The job pays $120 a month.

Jasmín puts on weight. Both María Isabel's mother and her younger sister care for her while María Isabel works.

Jasmín plays with her six dolls, giving them baths in an outdoor concrete trough the family uses to hold water. She brushes the dolls' hair. Afterward, she runs inside. "I bathed the baby," she announces to her grandmother, a wiry, muscular woman with salt-and-pepper hair.

She chases her grandmother's black-and-white chicks, making them scurry across the kitchen floor. She plays dress up with a five-year-old girl next door, or *agua de limón*, where they lock hands and swing each other around in circles.

When Jasmín gets hungry, Eva scrambles her eggs with black beans. She changes her whenever she gets dirty. In the afternoon, Jasmín goes to her grandmother and demands money: *"Quiero pisto!"*

Eva hands her a little change. Jasmín crawls down a steep flight of stairs to a tiny bodega below. She peers through the black iron bars on the door and points. "Those, I want those!" Jasmín says. The store owner hands her a small bag of hot pork rinds. Jasmín makes her way back up the steep slope.

Each day, the girl reminds María Isabel more and more of her father. Like Enrique, she stands slightly knock-kneed, her pelvis thrust out, her bottom tucked under. She has his deep, raspy voice. She has the same temperament as Enrique and Lourdes: she is testy, a stubborn fighter who stands her ground.

When she turns two, María Isabel takes Jasmín to talk to her father on the telephone. Jasmín loves to accompany her mother downtown on Sundays to the Axdi-Cell Internet, where they can dial Enrique more cheaply. María Isabel knows his number by heart.

She sits before the gray computer, and Jasmín stands between her legs. "Mom, pass the phone," Jasmín demands, reaching for the computer headset. "I love you, Enrique," she says. Then: "When are you coming here?" Jasmín returns to her grandmother's and proudly announces, "I spoke with my daddy, Enrique."

Often, the things Jasmín tells her father are lines that María Isabel prods her to say. It doesn't matter, says her grandmother. "They are strangers," says Eva. "But they are blood."

Eva often shows Jasmín the eight photos Enrique has sent of himself.

Jasmín knows her father sends her things. When Enrique's aunt Rosa Amalia asks her where she got the beautiful gold-and-emerald earrings she wears, Jasmín touches them. "They are from my daddy, Enrique!" She adds, "He says he loves me a lot."

Eva tells Jasmín that someday she will go see her father in

an airplane. Jasmín figures her father must have left on an airplane, too. Several times a day, when she hears one in the sky, she stops what she is doing and races outside. She looks up, her eyes bright. She thrusts both arms up and waves madly. *"¡Adiós, papi Enrique!"* she yells.

UNITED STATES

Enrique has been living with his mother for nearly two and a half years. One evening Lourdes and her boyfriend are watching a soap opera on the living room television. Enrique and a friend are playing cards down the hallway on the kitchen table. Enrique is wound up tight. He's working at a company that pushes everyone to paint excessively fast.

Enrique and his friend throw the cards down hard on the kitchen table. Each time they slap a card down, they yell.

Lourdes walks into the kitchen. She looks cross. "What are you doing?" she demands.

"If you don't want noise, you should live alone."

"You're an ignoramus," she answers.

Enrique likes to goad his mother by making noise. At dinner, he burps loudly and doesn't excuse himself. He bangs his spoon on the kitchen table. He slams doors. He plays music at high volume. He yells. He thinks it is incredibly funny to see her get mad.

Lourdes goes back to the television. Enrique and his friend slap the cards down harder and harder. Lourdes stomps into the kitchen. Her boyfriend knows trouble is near. He soon follows.

"Be quiet!" she orders.

Enrique answers badly.

"You must respect me. Don't forget, I am your mother. I gave birth to you."

"I don't love you as if you were my mother. I love my grandmother."

"I gave birth to you."

"That's not my fault!"

Lourdes grabs Enrique's shirt around the shoulders. Enrique pushes his chair back and bolts up. Lourdes slaps him on the mouth, hard. Enrique grabs her two hands, near her neck, to prevent further blows. Lourdes assumes that he is trying to grab her throat. "Let go of me!" she screams.

Lourdes's boyfriend pulls them apart. Then he ushers Enrique outside. Enrique is crying.

By the next day, all has returned to normal. Once, Enrique would have apologized. Today, there are no words of regret.

With others, Enrique is openly affectionate, especially with his half sister, Diana. He gives her money, drives her to the store, plays piggyback with her, caresses her cheek. He teaches her to dance. They play rhymes together. Unlike Diana, who can be selfish, Enrique is generous. "I have a secret to tell you: I love you," he tells her.

Still, with his third New Year in the United States, Enrique resolves to change. He can no longer wallow in what happened in the past. He must live in the present—and for the future. He's not hurting Lourdes as much as he is hurting himself.

Drinking so much alcohol makes his stomach ache constantly. He's tired of going to work after spending all night out drinking. He wants to look better when María Isabel comes to the United States.

Most important, he has to be more responsible for Jasmín. He can't have her grow up worrying about money as he did. He wants her to study. He can no longer blow hundreds of dollars in a single night of partying or thousands on troubles with the police. That has been a huge waste of money.

If he doesn't change, he will repeat his mother's mistake; time will slip by, and Jasmín will grow up without him. He must save $50,000 as quickly as possible to buy a house and start a business in Honduras.

Enrique starts working seven days a week. Bit by bit, he cuts back on beer and marijuana. He used to go out three or more times a week; now, it's just once or twice a month to play pool. He drinks a few beers, then switches to Pepsi. When friends call on his cell phone, beckoning him to party, he tells them he's not interested anymore.

He stops playing his music loud and slamming doors. When he burps, he excuses himself. He eats dinner with Lourdes. On Saturday nights, they watch the Spanish-language variety show *Sábado Gigante* together, as they did when he first arrived.

He tells friends he'll quit beer and drugs altogether when María Isabel is at his side. He hopes to bring her next year, get married.

He cuts his hair really short and loses weight. He wishes he could fix all the lingering effects of his beating on the train: the scars on his forehead and his knees, the bump under the skin by his left eye, the pain in his teeth anytime he eats anything hot or cold. Maybe he can at least get caps put on his broken teeth.

HONDURAS

Lourdes's sister Mirian is in trouble. She is out of work.

Her sister Ana Lucía offers her $50 a month to take care of her youngest child. The money falls short. Only another sister,

Rosa Amalia, holds hunger at bay: each Saturday, she brings Enrique's grandmother milk, cheese, butter, rice, sugar, beans, and vegetables.

Mirian can no longer buy construction paper for her children's projects at school. Many mornings, she doesn't have money for the school's midday meal. Those days, she keeps the children home. Sometimes they are absent from school three days in a row. Each of her three children owns one pair of shoes, purchased on a layaway plan.

She owes the grocery store up the block so much money, it cuts off her line of credit. She worries that her children are eating too much of the food her sister brings over for Enrique's grandmother. When Mirian walks her children down the block, they beg her to buy them a soda or an ice cream cone. She cannot.

"I can't stand this situation anymore," Mirian tells Belky. She wants to go to the United States. She'll go just long enough to save money to fix up her mother's house and add on a room for her own beauty parlor. She'll go for a few years and return before her children miss her much. They won't feel abandoned.

Lourdes is alarmed when she hears that Mirian wants to set out for the north on her own. No way, Lourdes tells her. Lourdes's boyfriend now pays the rent, and Lourdes has recently landed a better-paying factory job. Somehow, Lourdes and her boyfriend will come up with the money for a smuggler.

One morning, three years after Enrique left Honduras, Mirian sits her three children down to say good-bye.

"I'm going to the States. You will stay with your grandma." She tells them she is going to work and send them money, clothes, and toys. She cries. So does her oldest, nine-year-old Michelle. Junior, seven, asks when she is coming back. She cannot say.

"But are you coming back?" he presses.

"Yes."

Mirian steps off the same porch Lourdes left from fourteen years before.

Her youngest child is two and a half years old. She still breast-feeds. The girl, used to sleeping with her mother, cries for Mirian that night. Belky takes her into her bed.

For the first time, Belky understands her own mother's choice to leave her as a young child. She has watched Mirian's plight. She has seen her grapple with the gut-wrenching decision to leave. She agrees with Mirian's decision.

Meanwhile, María Isabel's life has just gotten much better. A relative who lives in the cinder-block house next door moves out. María Isabel and her family move in temporarily. They raze their old wood hut. María Isabel's brother begins to construct a cinder-block home of their own.

The relative's home isn't a vast improvement. The tin roof is held down with large rocks. A torn sheet offers privacy in the bathroom, which has no door. Occasionally, a mouse climbs up the gray walls.

Still, it has two small bedrooms. Now María Isabel shares a full-size bed with only her mother, sister, and Jasmín. In the hallway, which doubles as a living room and kitchen, Eva celebrates how far they've come. She proudly hangs four elementary school diplomas her children have earned, including María Isabel's.

María Isabel's relationship with Enrique is coming unglued. Enrique used to send her money monthly. But in the year and a half since María Isabel has returned to live with her mother, Enrique has wired money only four times, usually between $150 and $180.

Enrique is struggling financially. Fed up with the cramped

conditions in his mother's apartment and their constant fights, yearning for some scrap of privacy, he has moved out and rented a bedroom in a trailer. Rent on his share of the trailer and utilities is $280. The payments on his used pickup truck and insurance run $580 a month, plus $200 in gas. His cell phone is $50 a month, and he gives his mother $200 a month for lunch and dinner, which he has at her house each night. Fixed costs eat up more than half of the $2,400 to $2,600 a month he makes. He's had to pay two police tickets. Sometimes, when work is slow, Lourdes has to loan him money for his truck payment.

María Isabel knows none of this. She wonders if Enrique sends his daughter less money because he is spending it on another girlfriend. Enrique swears that there is no one else.

Gloria warns María Isabel: I know you adore Enrique, but don't grow old waiting for him. If he doesn't send for you or return to Honduras soon, find someone else before you lose your looks.

María Isabel has heard that Enrique drinks too much beer. "It's hard to stay away from those drugs," she says. Before, when Enrique told her he was clean, she could ferret out the truth for herself. Now that he is far away, all she has is his word.

Right after Enrique left, she felt desperate to be with him again. Over time, she has adapted to his absence. She has not dated anyone else, she says. When a neighbor in the brick house up the hill calls down that Enrique is on the line, María Isabel sprints over. Still, when she gets on the telephone, she cries less. She has matured, changed. Now her life revolves around her daughter.

"I love him," she says, "but not like before."

Equally troubling: Enrique calls less frequently. Since she moved into her mother's hut, Enrique has rung at the neighbor's house only five times.

She feels snubbed. It feels as though the phone calls have become a one-way street. She stops calling Enrique as well. Both are stuck in their pride. He hasn't hired a smuggler because she hasn't asked for one; she hasn't said yes to coming because he hasn't hired a smuggler. They are drifting apart.

She has tired of spending Sunday morning, her sole day off, downtown at the storefront Internet store dialing Enrique. The manager types the number into one of the gray computers; $3 buys fifteen minutes.

"Hello, my beautiful girl," he coos at María Isabel.

"Hello, how are you?"

He asks how Jasmín is. "I love you. Do you have another boyfriend there?" he asks. "No," María Isabel answers. Enrique wishes she could be more affectionate on the telephone. María Isabel knows he wants her to say she loves him, but she can't; she has always been painfully shy. She feels inhibited in the Internet store.

When she first moved back into Eva's, María Isabel went to call Enrique every other week. Now they go two months without speaking. She brushes it off as a scheduling problem. Or she rationalizes, "I call him when he calls me."

Enrique no longer talks of returning to Honduras. He tells her he likes the comforts of the United States. He hints that he wants her to come north soon. Yet the more attached María Isabel becomes to Jasmín, the more she resists leaving her.

UNITED STATES

After a few weeks, Mirian reaches the United States and settles in with Lourdes. She buys fake identification papers and quickly lands a restaurant job making biscuits. She nets $245 a week.

She tells Lourdes that she will be there three years, no more. She doesn't buy any furniture. She won't let herself adjust to the comforts of life in the United States such as hot water. She takes cold showers. She constantly reminds herself of the things she dislikes about the United States: children live confined indoors. Diana spends her afternoons and evenings chatting with friends on the Internet or watching television. In Honduras, Mirian's children play outside and come indoors only when they get hungry.

U.S. immigration agents raid Wal-Marts around the country for illegal immigrants. Mirian frets about being deported. She doesn't like the way people from North Carolina look at her in public sometimes. As if she were inferior, different. On her days off, she stays in.

In Honduras, each Sunday after church, Enrique's family takes Mirian's children to the airport, where they call their mother from a computer telephone.

"Study a lot. Don't fight. Be good to your grandma," Mirian tells them. Junior tells her he often feels like crying. He tells her he cannot sleep well at night. Quick-minded and chatty, he also tells Mirian about his excellent report card. Then he asks her to send him a bicycle.

Mirian says she's sending Nike shoes and Spider-Man, Hulk, Batman, and Barbie dolls. "I've bought beautiful things to send you."

Mirian's youngest is frightened when she hears her mother's voice on the telephone. For the first month, she pushes the telephone away. She hears her cousins call Mirian "Auntie" on the telephone. When she finally talks to her mother, she starts calling her mother "Auntie," too.

"I'm not your aunt. I'm your mother," Mirian corrects her.

"No, you're my auntie," the girl insists.

Enrique shares the trailer with two Mexican couples. They have four young children. They are a constant reminder of Jasmín.

Inside his bedroom, Enrique tapes two pictures of his daughter to his armoire mirror, one of her in a blue-and-white dress, another in a red-and-white dress. Two more framed pictures of her are on the shelf by his bed.

He didn't like school. He worries: Will she be the same?

Enrique loves sweets; whenever he buys some, he thinks of buying candy for Jasmín. Nearly every day, he sees things she might like. He tells himself he would buy them for her if she were there. He talks about her constantly to his friends.

His happiest moments are when photographs arrive. Or when María Isabel puts Jasmín on the line. *"Te quiero, papi,"* Jasmín says. "I love you, Daddy." He knows María Isabel prompts Jasmín to say nice things to him. He doesn't care. In the end, she'll understand what's what.

"I'm your daddy. Do you love your daddy?" Enrique asks.

"Yes, I love you."

She asks him to send things. *"Papi,* I want a piñata! One with candy inside!"

"I think she'll love me when she sees me," he tells himself.

He pictures how their lives together will be. Everyone in Lourdes's house eats dinner at different hours, whenever they get home from work. *His* family will eat dinner together.

HONDURAS

As Jasmín turns three, she is inseparable from her mother. At night, they sleep in the same bed. In the morning, before she readies herself for work, María Isabel bathes her daughter with buckets of water and plaits her hair into two braids.

When María Isabel heads off to work, Jasmín is in tears. *"Mami! Mami!"* she cries.

Barefoot, she scrambles down the ravine after her mother. Her grandmother dashes after her and grabs her.

"Ya vuelvo. I'll be right back," María Isabel calls up the hill as she walks away.

At night, when María Isabel climbs back up the hill, Jasmín runs to her. She sits on her lap, her hands draped around her mother's neck. They rub noses. They play patty-cake. María Isabel asks Jasmín to count to ten. With each number, she hoists her girl up in the air, then down. "Oh, you're getting so heavy!" Jasmín grabs her mother's hair, her ears. She squeals with delight.

"What did you do today?" María Isabel asks. "Did you take a nap today?" In a sweet, squeaky voice, Jasmín answers each of her mother's questions.

On María Isabel's day off, Jasmín is always at her side. María Isabel takes her daughter by the hand. They go downtown or to visit Gloria. She walks her down the sidewalk by Pizza Hut, crowded with carts piled with potatoes, plantains, and avocados. It is where Lourdes once sold gum and candy from a little box with Enrique at her side.

She carries Jasmín in her arms to the city's central plaza, where children beg with outstretched arms. She takes her into the cathedral, up to the gilded altar. She prays. She asks that Jasmín not get sick, that Enrique stay away from drugs. Then she takes Jasmín for a scoop of ice cream.

Today, Sunday, she readies Jasmín for a friend's birthday party. She dresses her in a pink-and-white outfit and the gold hoop earrings, bracelet, and pendant of Jesus her father sent.

As they walk across the heart of Tegucigalpa, Jasmín is a chatterbox. At the party, at the corrugated tin shack of María Isabel's cousin, Jasmín eats chicken, tries to blow up a red balloon, and borrows a pink bike with training wheels. But after a short while, she climbs into her mother's lap. María Isabel bounces her on her knees. Jasmín strokes her mother's hair and whispers into her ear. María Isabel straightens Jasmín's braids. She rocks her in her arms. Jasmín kisses her mother lightly. Jasmín finds a bougainvillea branch blooming with red flowers and brings it to her mother.

When it is Jasmín's turn to swat at the pink, dog-shaped piñata with a wooden stick, María Isabel cheers her on: "Hit it hard, hard!"

She helps her get a piece of cake, then lines her up for her bag of party favors. She shows her how to blow a whistle, one of the gifts.

At dusk they take a bus home, Jasmín in María Isabel's arms. Lights twinkle on the hills of Tegucigalpa. María Isabel undresses Jasmín and slips on her white nightgown. Jasmín dumps her bag of party favors on the floor, eager to see what is inside. There are two butterfly hairpins. María Isabel puts them in Jasmín's hair. Jasmín dances to the music from the family's small television, twizzling her hips, her hands in the air.

At 7:30 P.M., María Isabel climbs into bed with her daughter. Jasmín holds a bottle of milk with her left hand. With the right hand, she rubs her mother's belly. It is a ritual. She cannot fall asleep without stroking her mother's belly. Slowly, as she sucks on the milk, Jasmín loses her grip on the bottle. Her eyes flutter. María Isabel rolls her over and rubs Jasmín's back until the girl falls asleep.

She can no longer imagine leaving her daughter. She has to tell Enrique.

At most, she might leave Jasmín when she is old enough to understand what is happening. "She would have to be at least five years old for me to leave her. Then, at least, I could try to explain it to her," María Isabel tells her family. Not a day before, she says firmly. It is the same age Enrique was when his mother left.

Some of her friends tell her she would be a fool not to follow Enrique to the United States. She is young and can find work now, but women over the age of twenty-five or twenty-eight are no longer considered for many jobs in Honduras, something made clear in newspaper employment ads.

One factory, S. J. Mariol, hires only women ages eighteen to twenty-five, says Leydi Karina López, head of human resources at the company. In the large brick building in Tegucigalpa, young women sit in rows behind sewing machines, furiously stitching medical scrubs for export to the United States. One woman sews a triangle at the bottom of the neck. She does it 2,520 times a day, forty-four hours a week, for $110 a month.

"We look at the work, and it requires a lot of energy and dedication. At thirty, they might have back problems or eye problems or arthritis. We want to avoid that," López says. Without high productivity, she says, the work will move to lower-wage countries such as China.

The children's store María Isabel works at won't hire women older than twenty-three. Middle-aged women have three options, says Argentina "Norma" Valeriano, María Isabel's neighbor: washing and ironing clothes, cleaning houses, or making tortillas at home, jobs that pay $50 to $90 a month. A family needs $350 a month minimum, says a social worker, Francis Jeanett Gómez Irias, with the Instituto Hondureño de la Niñez y la Familia.

In 1998, Hurricane Mitch caused many Honduran businesses to go under. Unemployment and subemployment combined now affect 43 percent of Hondurans. Government jobs go to people in certain families or with good connections, says Norma. Most of María Isabel's neighbors, including twenty-five on her block, have no work, she adds. They survive only because someone in the family has gone north and sends back money. The children of single mothers suffer most, she says.

María Isabel wouldn't be the first in her family to go to the United States and leave children behind. Her aunt, Eva's sister Tina, left four children in Honduras to go to Los Angeles in the early 1980s. María Isabel's eldest sister, Olga, went to Houston in 1990. She left José, one and a half years old, and Dennis Alexander, three, with her mother, Eva. For eight years, Olga sent Eva $50 or $100 a month to help her raise the boys. In 1998, Eva's other sister, Laura, left two children behind.

Eventually, the three women were able to bring their children to the United States, some legally, others with smugglers.

When María Isabel sees couples walking down the street with their children, it saddens her. If she went to the United States, would it allow Jasmín to have both her parents at her side more quickly? Jasmín, she knows, needs her father.

Jasmín has taken to calling the only man in Eva's house, her twenty-seven-year-old uncle Miguel, *papi*. With Enrique, Jasmín has to be coached to talk. With Miguel, words of affection come naturally.

One evening, Jasmín returns from a friend's birthday party. She runs to Miguel with a bag full of candy, a party treat. *"Papi!"* Jasmín says, handing him pieces of the candy. *"Papi, tenga.* Here, Daddy." She doesn't normally share her candy; with Miguel, she is generous. She gives him a full report of the day: how she hit the piñata, ate rice and cake, drank soda, how people took pictures. Jasmín runs and flops on his bed. Miguel chases her, tickling her ribs.

Many afternoons, when María Isabel is away at work, Jasmín eludes her grandmother and wanders next door, where Miguel is constructing the family's new house. She climbs the ladder to the second floor. There, she serves as Miguel's little assistant. As he lays floor tiles, Miguel points to the sponge; Jasmín brings it. He points to a flat spatula. She brings that, too. "Pass me the hammer," he says in his gentle voice.

When Miguel heads down the hill at dusk to play soccer, he says, "*Me voy, Jasmín.* I'm off, Jasmín." She quickly answers, "*Vamos, papi!* Let's go, Daddy!"

Enrique senses that his daughter has begun to identify someone else as her father. Late in the year, as Christmas approaches, he promises her he'll come visit.

María Isabel sees even more reasons to stay in Honduras with her daughter. A yearlong government advertising campaign has highlighted the dangers of the journey. Newspapers carry a stream of accounts of people injured or killed during the trek north.

María Isabel's sister Irma tried to make it to the United States but ran out of money in Mexico and had to turn back. So did one of her brothers. María Isabel asks one of her sisters about her trip. She tells her she was often hungry. María Isabel asks if she was raped. The sister doesn't answer.

What if she doesn't make it? What would become of her daughter?

She'd have to live illegally in the United States, always fearful of being caught and deported. There is racism; she would be treated as inferior. Her mother emphasizes that the United

States is a cold place, where neighbors barely know one another.

She doesn't want to miss all the important moments in Jasmín's life. She thinks about everything Enrique has already missed. Soon, Jasmín will attend her first day of kindergarten.

María Isabel has heard how mothers who leave lose the love of their children.

Rosa Amalia, who raised Enrique's sister Belky, has seen the effects of these separations. She advises María Isabel to wait until Jasmín is older, when Enrique might be able to bring them both together.

María Isabel devises a plan to stay. If she doesn't have any more children and she works hard, she can give her daughter a shot at a good education. "It's not impossible. With one child, I can give her what she wants," María Isabel says.

"I'm not leaving without Jasmín," she tells Gloria.

Belky has secretly been seeing a new boyfriend, Yovani. Eventually, Yovani goes to Rosa Amalia, who has raised Belky, to *pedir la llegada*—ask for permission to date. Rosa Amalia agrees after Yovani vows chastity. Rosa Amalia wants Belky to stop living in limbo, always fixating on reunifying with her mother. She hopes she will finish her studies in business administration and eventually form her own family in Honduras.

Belky begins to think that if she doesn't see her mother soon, she will never see her. "I just want to give her a hug. A bunch of hugs. I just want to be by her side—even if it's for a short while," she says.

One night Yovani proposes as they sit outside her cinderblock hut. Yovani is not handsome. He lives with his mother, a tamale maker, in a tiny wooden shack. But he is kind, drinks rarely, and buys her little presents. He treats her like a queen.

She loves him. Belky asks Lourdes to provide a few thousand dollars to build a tiny house on land beside her grandmother's home—land reserved for the house Lourdes was to build upon her return. When she marries, her mother won't be there. Her aunt and uncle will walk her down the aisle.

UNITED STATES

Lourdes works on a cleaning crew, then on a factory assembly line. It is hard living with so many people jammed into her apartment, especially because the men don't help. When she arrives home, the kitchen trash is full, the floors are dirty, and she must cook and clean for everyone.

Although the men come home at different hours, Lourdes waits up to serve each of them dinner. On her day off, she takes the men's laundry—six baskets—to the Laundromat. On Sunday, she buys $300 in groceries, enough to last the clan a week. Having seven people split the cost of the three-bedroom apartment, which costs $800 a month, allows Lourdes to send money back to her daughter and mother in Honduras. To Lourdes, it seems as though every relative in Honduras who has money troubles thinks they can ask her for help.

One night, Enrique and a friend start talking about gangs in Honduras. Lourdes says that Honduras is a horrible, lawless place. Enrique chafes at such talk, especially from Lourdes. It is your country, he says. "Mom, I don't know why you hate your country so much."

"I'll never go back," she says.

The discussion devolves into another big fight. For the third time since he arrived, Enrique accuses Lourdes of abandoning

him in Honduras. He tells her his true mother is his grandmother María. Enrique has hung a picture of the Last Supper
above the headboard of his bed. It reminds him of her. His
grandmother had several pictures of the Last Supper hanging
in her hut. He misses the beans and spaghetti she made for him.
He misses going to church with her as a child.

Lourdes believes that Enrique's comments reveal a fear: If
he goes back to Central America, his mother will not follow
him. They will once again live apart.

Lourdes's boyfriend tries to find a way to alleviate the sadness he sees in Lourdes.

"*Mira*, honey," he says, "*tome la distancia*. Look, honey, put
some distance between you." It's no use arguing and fighting
with Enrique, he tells her. It's a fight you will not win. You're
both equally stubborn. Neither of you likes to be contradicted
or told he is wrong. You have to control your anger when Enrique baits you.

If Enrique does something she doesn't like, Lourdes ignores
it. She still cooks his dinner but no longer serves him his plate of
food. She stops doing his laundry. They no longer routinely go
out to dinner on Saturday night or grocery shopping on Sunday.

With the new year, Lourdes, her boyfriend, and their relatives decide to leave North Carolina. The paint firm where
most of the men work is in financial trouble and has cut back
on everyone's hours. Jobs are scarce.

They move to Florida, where a cousin of Lourdes's boyfriend gets everyone painting jobs. Lourdes and her sister
Mirian start as hotel maids for $6.50 an hour. Each cleans
sixteen to eighteen rooms per shift. Eight people cram into
a small two-bedroom apartment. Enrique sleeps on the living room sofa. He hates it. He misses his friends in North

Carolina. He has to get up before dawn to be painting by 6:30 A.M.

Lourdes's sister Mirian toys with the idea of bringing her children to the United States but quickly dismisses it as too dangerous. She switches to a job washing dishes for $9 an hour. She focuses on saving enough to return to her children in what she hopes will be another two years. She needs to save $10,000 to $15,000 to add a beauty salon to her mother's house and send her three children to school. So far, she has banked $1,200.

Enrique constantly nags Mirian to go back. "Why are you going to abandon your kids?" he asks her. After fights with his mother, Enrique always has a warning for his aunt Mirian. "This will happen to you, because you left your children when they were young. You think that filling our bellies is the same thing as love."

As Enrique mulls over returning to North Carolina, he becomes more loving with his mother. He hugs and kisses her often. Finally, he decides to go.

Lourdes begs him to stay. She tells him she will not follow him back to North Carolina. She has a life now in Florida with her de facto husband, daughter, and sister. "You've never acknowledged me as a real mother. I have to work at my life with my husband now," she tells Enrique.

Enrique quietly packs and leaves.

Lourdes wants to enjoy her life more and worry about Enrique less. She and her boyfriend go out Saturday nights to a buffet dinner. Lourdes relishes moments with her daughter Diana. She teases Diana when she flubs a phrase in Spanish. Diana helps teach her mother English in a southern drawl.

Lourdes and her boyfriend can finally afford their own

apartment. She'd like to open a paint store with him someday, maybe buy a double-wide trailer. Mostly, she prays for an amnesty for immigrants so she can become legal and bring her daughter Belky to the United States.

"God, give me my papers. I want to be with my daughter," she says. "I ask God to give me this before I die." She begins to sob. "Is that so much to ask of God? I don't ask God for riches. Or other things."

In North Carolina, Enrique focuses on working, on saving money, on cutting down even more on drinking and drugs. He'll need $5,000 for a smuggler to bring his girlfriend north.

Enrique gently tries to convince María Isabel to commit to the move. "María Isabel, you know I am very good to you. I give you everything," he tells her on the telephone. He loves her. He misses her serene, calm nature, how much she would cry and giggle, how simple she is. He misses walking her home from school holding her hand.

If they live apart too long, Enrique fears, María Isabel will find someone else. "If you find someone who loves you as much as I do, go with him," Enrique says. "I left you. I understand."

In truth, he desperately wants to hear her protest such talk, to know if she is interested in anyone else. She tells him she loves him for life. Why doesn't she tell him she wants to come be with him? He is reaching his breaking point. He resolves to call her and ask point-blank: Are you coming or not?

He knows María Isabel has been stalling, that she is anxious about leaving Jasmín. He's been stalling, too: he wants to learn English and get his vices totally under control before bringing her to the United States. Yet the sooner María Isabel comes, the easier it will be for both of them to save money and return to Honduras. The sooner he will see his daughter. He is resolved to be with her by the time she is five, six at the latest.

If not, Jasmín won't embrace him as her father. "She'll see me as a stranger," he says. He'll go back to Honduras when she is six, even if it is for a brief visit and he has to make his way back through Mexico illegally again.

"I need to see her. To be with her."

As time passes, Enrique sees other things with equal clarity. He knows now that his mother will never offer an apology for leaving him. He tries to put the love he has always felt for Lourdes above the resentment he has harbored all these years. He gives his mother his first gift: $100 for her birthday. She uses it to buy a dress and a bottle of lotion.

Enrique and Lourdes start to call each other two or three times a week to talk. Enrique has long called his mother *señora*. Now, he says, *"Ma."* With each call, he is more loving.

"Tan bonita mi mami, la quiero mucho. My beautiful mother, I love you so much," he says.

Lourdes teases, *"¡Mentiroso viejo!* You old liar!"

He even begins to make plans to move from North Carolina to Florida. He does not want to live apart from his mother anymore.

Lourdes is sure that God is answering one of her prayers: that Enrique straighten up, stop drinking, and no longer feel so bitter toward her. "It's like a miracle," she says. It is as if all the hurt he felt inside had to come out and now he is ready to move on. She feels the same warmth and love from Enrique as when he first arrived on her doorstep in North Carolina.

"He always wanted to be with me," she says.

María Isabel and Jasmín in Tegucigalpa, 2003

THE GIRL LEFT BEHIND

It is spring 2004. Enrique has been gone for four years. Enrique and María Isabel have not spoken for more than four months, since last Christmas. Enrique calls his sister Belky. Go find María Isabel, he tells her. Tell her she must call me.

María Isabel dials from the Internet store.

"Why don't you call me?" he asks. She answers curtly that she doesn't have anything to talk about.

"Are you ready to come?" he asks.

María Isabel tells herself he is joking. When he was sniffing glue in Honduras, he often said things he didn't really mean. Even if he's serious, she can't leave until Jasmín is at least five years old. She promised.

You must make a decision, Enrique says. Now. If not, he vows, he will remake his life, find someone else.

"I don't want to leave," she tells him.

Enrique cajoles. I've changed, he tells her. I drink, but just a little now. I don't use glue. "I'm not the same person."

She doesn't budge.

If you come, he tells her, it will be the best thing for Jasmín. Together, we'll provide her a better life. We'll both be able to return to her sooner.

Now she is listening. "I'll think about it," she says.

Her answer fills Enrique with hope. He starts calling María Isabel constantly. I need you, he says. You're the mother of my child. You're the only one I want to marry.

Day and night, María Isabel turns it over in her mind. If she stays and marries, her husband would never treat Jasmín as if she were his own.

María Isabel decides: In the long run, leaving will help Jasmín. Eventually, she will be with her real mother and father, everyone together. She strikes a deal with Enrique: Jasmín will live with Belky but spend weekends with her mother. "I will do it for my daughter," she says.

A few days later, word reaches María Isabel from a smuggler. He will call next week, probably on Tuesday or Wednesday. She must be ready.

María Isabel hauls all of Jasmín's clothing and dolls over to the cinder-block hut where Belky lives behind her grandmother's home. She waits next door at Gloria's for the smuggler to call Rosa Amalia, who has just gotten hooked up to phone service. She hugs her daughter over and over. She cries and cries.

Jasmín asks, "Why are you crying so much, Mommy?"

María Isabel tells Jasmín her arm hurts. She tells her a cavity in her mouth aches.

"Don't cry, *mami*," Jasmín says. Saddened by her mother's tears, Jasmín cries, too.

"Why are you crying?" Rosa Amalia asks the girl.

"Because my *mami* is crying. My *mami* cries all the time."

María Isabel hasn't told her daughter she is leaving. She can't. Still, Jasmín is bright.

A neighbor asks María Isabel, "Are you leaving already?"

Jasmín asks, "Where is my mother going?"

She asks her mother why she has moved all her clothes from her grandmother Eva's to Belky's hut across town. Why, she asks her mother, has María Isabel packed a white backpack with her own clothes?

"I'm going out," María Isabel says. "I'll be right back."

"Where are you going?"

"I'm going downtown."

"Are you coming back?"

"Yes."

Jasmín believes her, and this time she does come back.

Sometimes when Jasmín asks if her mother is coming back, María Isabel is silent. She does not answer.

She doesn't like lying to Jasmín. But María Isabel is sure her daughter is too young, at three and a half, to understand the truth. She can't handle a scene, demands by Jasmín to take her with her. She doesn't want to see her daughter cry. This is easier, better, María Isabel tells herself.

Wednesday. The smuggler calls at 1 P.M. María Isabel must be across town, at Tegucigalpa's main bus station, at 3:30 P.M. The smuggler says he will be wearing a red shirt and blue jeans. What will María Isabel have on? A black blouse and blue jeans, Enrique's family tells him.

María Isabel heads back to Belky's hut with Jasmín. She holds her in her arms and gives her a last bottle of milk.

María Isabel heads over to Enrique's grandmother's. "I'm leaving now. Good-bye," she says.

"God bless you," the grandmother says. The family will pray for her during her journey north, she tells her.

Next door, at Gloria's, María Isabel hugs her mother and sister. Enrique's aunt Rosa Amalia takes Jasmín back to Belky's hut, hoping to prevent a scene. Jasmín will have none of it. She's overheard some of the good-byes, that Rosa Amalia is driving María Isabel to the bus terminal.

"I'm coming! I'm coming to drop off my mother," she tells Rosa Amalia, who relents.

Jasmín runs to the car and gets in. María Isabel takes the backpack, which contains a change of clothes and one picture of her daughter. Belky and her boyfriend climb in, too.

At the bus terminal, Rosa Amalia won't let Jasmín get out

of the car. Only passengers are allowed beyond the waiting room. María Isabel is relieved. She tells herself that it is all right, that Jasmín doesn't really understand what is happening.

María Isabel does not say good-bye to her daughter. She does not hug her. She gets out of the car and walks briskly into the bus terminal. She does not look back. She never tells her she is going to the United States.

Rosa Amalia lifts Jasmín onto the hood of her car. As the bus pulls out of the terminal, she tells the girl to say good-bye. Jasmín waves with both hands and calls out, *"Adiós, mami. Adiós, mami. Adiós, mami. Adiós, mami. Adiós, mami."*

AFTERWORD

Women, Children, and
the Immigration Debate

An estimated 1.7 million children live illegally in the United States, most from Mexico and Central America. Like Enrique, almost all have spent time away from a parent before following him or her to the United States. One in four children in the nation's schools is an immigrant or the child of an immigrant—a group whose numbers, between 1990 and 2000, grew seven times faster than that of children with both parents born in the United States.

Children leaving Central America to find their mothers in the United States now face a tougher, more treacherous journey than ever before. Anti-gang crackdowns in El Salvador, Honduras, and Guatemala have pushed many gangsters north into Chiapas, where they prey on migrants aboard the trains. Gangsters who once used border cities in Guatemala as their homes have moved their bases into Chiapas. Freight trains pull in to the station in Tonalá, in northern Chiapas, with dead migrants atop the boxcars. In 2004, fed up with rampant violence, more than 5,000 Tapachula residents marched in the streets demanding that Mexico establish a death penalty for gangsters.

Since Enrique's journey, the number of police agencies targeting migrants in Chiapas has grown from five to eight. To elude the additional officers, migrants take ever greater risks to get on and off moving trains. The result: the number of migrants arriving at Tapachula's general hospital with train injuries has more than doubled.

The train is no longer stopped by *la migra* at La Arrocera, the checkpoint where migrants had to outrun bandits lying in wait. In 2003, when La Arrocera became too dangerous even for *migra* agents, the train stop was moved to Los Toros, Chiapas. There, reinforced by three other police agencies and the army, sixty to eighty officers swarm the train, using ladders to reach atop the cars, catching four of five migrants. Just south of the checkpoint, in Tres Hermanos, a new crop of bandits has emerged. Migrants who try to avoid the authorities by walking the tracks are robbed, injured, and even killed by local thugs.

To the north, in Nuevo Laredo, along the Rio Grande where Enrique camped, a battle for control of the border rages among rival Mexican drug cartels. The body of El Tiríndaro, the smuggler who crossed Enrique into Texas, was found in February 2002 near the road to the Nuevo Laredo airport. He had been blindfolded, tortured, and shot in the head, execution style. El Tiríndaro, identified as Diego Cruz Ponce, was one of fifty-seven murders in Nuevo Laredo that year, and the violence has escalated since then. In 2005, the new police chief, who vowed to bring law and order to the city, was gunned down hours after taking office.

Across the length of Mexico, people who help migrants are troubled to see more pregnant women and parents with young children aboard freight trains. Some parents are carrying babies in their arms.

Despite the increased danger, more migrants are making the attempt. Between 2001 and 2004, the number of Central American migrants detained and deported each year by Mexico nearly doubled, to more than two hundred thousand. Most come from Guatemala, El Salvador, and Honduras and are trying to reach the United States. In Tapachula alone, up to seventeen buses full of detained migrants are sent south each day. Some of the buses are designated just for children who have been traveling alone through Chiapas. During the same period, the number of Central American children detained by the U.S. Border Patrol while entering the country illegally and without either parent nearly doubled.

Throughout Latin America, even in traditional societies such as Mexico, where most legal and illegal migrants to the United States come from, divorce and separation are increasingly common. That promises to produce more single mothers who feel forced to make the same choice Lourdes made long ago: leave their children and head north.

The growing influx of women and children will fuel questions already raging about immigration: Is it good for the migrants themselves, for the countries they come from, and for the United States and its citizens?

For immigrants, the material benefits of coming to the United States are clear. The money Lourdes sent Enrique allowed him to eat and dress better and attend school longer. Once he arrived in the United States, Enrique drove his own truck and could make a decent living if he worked hard. Enrique loves how clean the streets are compared to those in Honduras, how most people respect and obey the laws. His aunt Mirian notes that the United States is less class-driven than Honduras. Here, people don't look down on her if she dresses humbly. Lourdes enjoys taking showers with indoor plumbing, as well as the relative safety of her neighborhood, where she can wear a gold necklace without worry. She has the freedom to get in her car and go anywhere she wants.

Enrique acknowledges drawbacks. He must live in the shadows, knowing he can be deported at any time. He faces racism. When he goes into a restaurant and can't order well in English, he gets dirty stares. "They look at you as if you are a flea," he says. Salespeople in stores often attend to Anglo customers first. Even Mexicans look down on Central Americans, whom many view as inferior. Enrique's aunt Mirian says her restaurant employers pay her less than they pay her Anglo colleagues—and assign immigrants the hardest tasks.

Life in America, Enrique and others say, is too hurried. In Honduras, people work half a day Saturday and rest Sunday. Here, Enrique paints seven days a week in an endless struggle to pay bills. "Here," he says, "life is a race."

For most immigrants who come to the United States, the biggest downside is the toll parent-child separations exact on families. The family conflicts are most visible in the nation's schools, where teachers and administrators from New York to Los Angeles struggle daily to mend the damage caused by the years apart for parents and children.

NEWCOMER TRAUMAS

Life inside Los Angeles's Newcomer School, a transitional school for newly arrived immigrant students, shows both how common and devastating these separations are for the immigrants themselves.

Each day, the school's soft-spoken counselor, Gabriel Murillo, finds the small wooden box outside his office full of "request to see the counselor" slips. More than half of the 430 high school students will ask to see him by year's end. The reason? *Problemas familiares,* they write: family problems. Most have recently reunited with a parent, usually a mother. On average, they have not seen the parent in a decade.

Hour after hour, parent-child meetings play out with a scary similarity, Murillo says. Idealized notions each had of the other quickly shatter. Some children felt resentful before coming north; others have deeply buried anger that emerges after months with their mothers.

Inside Murillo's office, children usually fire the first salvo: "I know you don't love me. That's why you left me there." Some mothers, to avoid traumatic farewells, told their children they were going out to the market or to see their children's teachers, and instead left for the United States. The children say their mothers lied to them from the start. They prayed their mothers would get caught by the U.S. Border Patrol and sent back. They demand that their mothers admit their mistakes and apologize for leaving them.

Mothers endured pain leaving their children and struggled to work hard and send back money, and they demand respect for their sacrifice. They are certain the separations were worth what was gained.

But their children say they would have preferred being together, even if it meant going hungry. "I didn't want money. I wanted you there." They tell their mothers they would never leave their own children. They tell them they are worse than animals. Even an animal doesn't desert her litter.

Murillo fights what is usually a losing battle. "It's a huge emotional scar. For some, the damage continues for the rest of their lives. It is irreparable," he says. Some eventually improve their relationships with their mothers, but it takes years.

Mothers expect to finally have the perfect family when their children arrive. Instead, they face rejection and constant fights. Eventually, they realize the choice they made may have cost them the love of their children. Children who thought they would find love and an end to loneliness discover that they feel more distant than ever from their mothers, even though they are now with them.

Some children are resentful because they were abused or neglected by their caretakers or bullied by others back home. One in twenty girls at the school admits to being molested by a male relative. They blame their mothers for not being there to protect them.

Others are angry because they had to leave behind a grandmother who became the person who loved and nurtured them most—a real mother. They worry that their departure means the loss of the grandparents' only source of income. They know they may never see their grandparents again.

Actions by both mothers and children make matters worse. Children act out, doing everything possible to push their mothers away. It is their way of testing whether their mothers really love them, whether they can trust them, whether their mothers will abandon them again.

Mothers, beset by guilt, don't discipline their children or set rules. To pay off their debts to the smugglers, they often work overtime, and after so much time apart, children feel their mothers are ignoring them again. Some mothers continue to work as live-in nannies or housekeepers after their children arrive. They place their children in an apartment with relatives or friends, calling at night, visiting on weekends.

The conflicts Murillo sees are most acute when the child was the last to be brought north because the mother couldn't afford to bring everyone at once. Such children come to believe that the mother favored the children she brought north first.

The clashes are also severe when the mother has a new husband or has given birth to additional children in the United States. Some mothers, fearful of how children left behind would react, have hidden these new families from them. Newly arrived children try to create conflicts between their mothers and the new husbands, hoping to drum them out. Children born in the United States, jealous that their mothers are showering the newcomers with attention, tell lies about the new children, hoping to get them in trouble and shipped back.

Some mothers, Murillo says, do many things right. They leave children with relatives who constantly emphasize that the parents left to help their children. They keep in constant contact during the separation. They are open and honest about their lives in the United States. They never promise anything, especially a visit or reunion, until they are positive they can deliver. Even in these cases, Murillo says, the reunions are rocky. He has dealt with students who tried to stab their mothers, who asked to have guardianship transferred to someone else, who turned suicidal.

One mother says: "I think it's like the Bible says. People will move around. But not find peace."

Many reunified children, not finding the love they had hoped for with their mothers, search for love elsewhere, Murillo says. Some boys find a family in the local gangs and end up selling drugs. A girl might find unconditional love by getting pregnant, having a baby, and moving in with the father. Gangs and pregnancy are much more common among reunited children than among those born here, says Zenaida Gabriel, a case manager at Sunrise Community Counseling Center, where some Newcomer students go for help.

Newcomer School psychologist Laura Lopez estimates that only 70 of 430 students will complete high school. Indeed, immigration expert Jeffrey Passell says nearly half of all Central American children who arrive in the United States after the age of ten don't graduate from high school.

A Harvard University study found that immigrant children in U.S. schools who spent time separated from parents are often depressed, act up, have trouble trusting anyone, and don't respond to the authority of parents they weren't raised with. Los Angeles Unified School District psychologist Bradley Pilon believes only one in ten immigrant students ultimately accepts his or her parent and puts the rancor he or she feels toward the parent in perspective.

Murillo's conclusion: "The parents say: I had to do it. But that's not enough for these children. All of them feel the resentment." Special education teacher Marga Rodriguez adds, "This isn't worth it. In the end, you lose your kids." But she admits she doesn't know what it's like not to have anything to feed your hungry children.

Oscar Escalada Hernández, director of the Casa YMCA shelter for immigrant children in Tijuana, Mexico, agrees. "In the end, it is a mess," he says. "The effect of immigration has been family disintegration. People are leaving behind the most important value: family unity."

The survivors, like Enrique, try to block out problems with their mothers and focus on what is good for them and their futures. They work to ensure that the love they feel for their mothers overcomes the rancor they also feel inside.

LANDS LEFT BEHIND

The exodus of immigrants has been bittersweet for the countries they leave as well. It has provided an escape valve for countries with enormous economic problems, such as Mexico and Honduras. The outflow of workers has kept unemployment from climbing even higher.

Immigrants also send huge amounts of money from the United States to their families back home—typically one in ten dollars they make. This brings $30 billion a year to Latin America alone. The cash flow makes up a whopping 15 percent of El Salvador's gross domestic product and is Mexico's second largest contributor to the economy, after oil. Recipients use money sent back by immigrants for food, clothing, and medical expenses and to educate children. Grandparents who get money to care for children left behind would be destitute without the payments.

Immigrants who return to their home countries also bring skills acquired while living in a more technologically advanced country, says Norberto Girón of the International Organization for Migration in Honduras. They bring lower levels of tolerance for corruption and stronger demands for democratic processes, says Honduran immigration expert Maureen Zamora.

Immigrants' desire to communicate with families back home in Honduras has resulted in improved telephone and Internet services.

But the separation of children and parents has had lasting negative consequences. Huge groups of parentless children have fueled rampant growth in juvenile delinquency and gangs in Honduras, says Glenda Gallardo, principal economist with the United Nations Development Program. "If your mom leaves you, if she disappears, it marks you in a way for life," she says.

The Mara Salvatrucha, 18th Street, and Mao Mao gangs control whole neighborhoods, where they impose a "war tax" on taxis, bicycles, or buses passing through. A disproportionate number of the 36,000 gangsters in Honduras come from families in which the mother has migrated north, says Zamora. Grandparents, guided by guilt that the child they are raising isn't with his mother, go light on discipline. They also worry that if the child complains and gets moved to another relative, the money the mother sends may go elsewhere as well.

A public advertising campaign launched in 2002 is one sign Honduras is facing damage caused by family separations. The advertisements run on television and radio, and are plastered on billboards at the Tegucigalpa bus station, where Hondurans head north. "Father, mother," reads an advertisement with a young girl on a swing. "Your children need you. Stay here. In Honduras there are opportunities to get ahead. Discover them!"

"We are seeing a disintegration of the family," warns Norberto Girón, the Honduran migration official. "Keeping the family together—even if they are poor—is more important than leaving and improving their economic conditions."

IMMIGRANT NATION

Each year, the United States legally admits nearly a million people, more than twice as many as in the 1970s. Another 700,000 arrive illegally, up from 200,000 to 300,000 a year in the 1980s and early 1990s. Today, 36 million residents of the United States were born in another country; nearly a third of those live in the United States illegally. The number of immigrants coming into the country in recent years is the highest ever recorded. And while the proportion of the population that is foreign-born, at 12 percent, is still lower than the all-time high of 15 percent in 1890, it has risen from 5 percent in 1970.

More than six in ten residents of Miami and four in ten of Los Angeles are from another country. Some Mexicans and Mexican Americans have jokingly dubbed the influx *la reconquista*—the reconquest of lands once held by Mexico.

Enrique and Lourdes disagree about the impact of this on the United States. Enrique says that were he an American citizen, he would want to curtail illegal immigration. Like most on his paint crew, he explains, he gets paid cash under the table and contributes no taxes on what he earns. He uses publicly provided services, including emergency medical care. And he sends a portion of his income to Honduras, rather than spending it in his community.

Lourdes disagrees. Yes, she says, her daughter was born at a public hospital, and she received welfare for a time. Still, she pays taxes and is entitled to those services. To her, immigrant labor is the engine that helps drive the American economy. Immigrants like herself, she says, work hard at jobs no American wants to do, at least not for minimum wage with no health benefits or paid vacation time. Immigrants' willingness to do certain backbreaking jobs at low wages provides goods and services to all Americans at reasonable prices, she says.

Many Americans understand that being born in the United States, with all the opportunities that entails, is a matter of sheer serendipity. They are happy to share a bounty few countries possess. They want the United States to provide desperate people a shot at a better life.

Others believe that the wave of immigrants from Latin America is blowback, of sorts, for U.S. policies. In recent decades, the United States has supported, and sometimes even helped install, repressive regimes in Latin America. These regimes, they note, propped up economic elites who resisted reforms and perpetuated unequal political and economic systems. This fueled poverty, civil wars, and the resulting economic crisis that is now pushing so many to migrate to the United States.

Employers in the United States see other benefits. Enrique's former boss in North Carolina argues that he must pay native-born workers more than immigrants—yet they work slower, balk at putting in overtime, and don't want to do the hardest jobs. Enrique says native-born painters take a lot of breaks and demand to be paid extra for overtime hours. One of Enrique's co-workers in North Carolina agrees, adding, "Americans say: If they fire me, I can get a better job." The co-worker says that being in the country illegally motivates him to do good work and keep his employment stable. His family in Honduras, he knows, depends on the money he sends. It would be tough to get another job because he is in the country illegally and doesn't speak English.

Many experts say immigrants help the economy grow and prevent businesses that rely on cheap labor from being forced to close or go abroad. In some low-education occupations, according to a 1997 study by the National Research Council that is considered among the most comprehensive assessments of the effects of immigration, a quarter to a half of all hours nationwide are worked by immigrant women. Immigrant production of goods and services, the NRC found, added a modest but significant $1.1 billion to $9.5 billion to the nation's $7 trillion economy.

American households benefit, too. Immigrants lower the cost of nearly 5 percent of all goods and services that people in U.S. households buy, according to the NRC. That means cheaper food and clothing. Because of immigrants, certain services—child care, gardening, car washing—are within reach of more Americans. Immigrant women who work as nannies and caregivers provide something invaluable: kindness and nurturing, often at the expense of their own children, says Kristine M. Zentgraf, a sociology professor at California State University at Long Beach.

Immigrants' biggest contribution, others say, is how their presence brings new blood, new ideas, and new ways of looking at things that drive creativity and spur advances. A disproportionate number of the nation's high achievers, the NRC study noted, such as Nobel laureates, are immigrants. Indeed, it is often the most motivated people who are immigrants. Who else would leave everything they know, cross Mexico on top of freight trains, and come to a place where they have to start from scratch?

BENEFIT AND BURDEN

Some opposition to immigration is racism, a resistance to change, a discomfort with having people around who don't speak the same language or have similar customs. Yet some of the negative consequences of immigration are real, and are becoming increasingly evident as more women and children arrive.

Overall, the NRC said, immigrants use more government services than the native-born. They have more children, and therefore more youngsters in public schools. This is especially true for immigrants from Latin America, whose households are nearly twice as large as those of the native-born. It will cost the government two and a half times as much per household to educate their children, the study found.

Immigrants are poorer, have lower incomes, and qualify for more state and local services and assistance. Immigrant women receive publicly funded prenatal and obstetric care. Their U.S.-born children are entitled to welfare, food stamps, and Medicaid. Compared to native households, immigrant families from Latin America are nearly three times as likely to receive government welfare payments.

Because immigrants earn less money and are less likely to own property, they pay lower taxes. Some immigrants receive their salaries in cash and pay no taxes at all. In all, immigrants and their native-born children pay a third less tax per capita than others in the United States, the NRC study found. Households headed by immigrants from Latin America pay half of what natives pay in state and federal taxes.

The fiscal burden to taxpayers is greatest in immigrant-heavy states such as California, where an estimated one in four illegal immigrants live, and where half of all children have immigrant parents. Local and state governments shoulder the biggest cost generated by immigrants: public education. An average nonimmigrant household in California paid $1,178 more in state and local taxes than the value of the services they received. Conversely, immigrant households paid $3,463 less than the value of the services they received, the NRC found.

The crush of immigrants has hastened the deterioration of many public services, namely schools, hospitals, and state jails and prisons. Classrooms are crowded. Hospital emergency rooms have been forced to close, in part because so many poor, uninsured, nonpaying patients, including immigrants, are provided with free mandated care. In Los Angeles County, jails have had to release prisoners early because of overcrowding caused, in part, by criminal immigrants. A 2001 University of Arizona study found that in the twenty-eight southwestern border counties of Arizona, California, New Mexico, and Texas, the cost of arresting, prosecuting, and jailing illegal immigrants who commit crimes amounted to as much as $125 million per year. The Center for Immigration Studies, which seeks reduced immigration levels, found that in 2002, nationwide, households headed by illegal immigrants used $26.3 billion in government services and paid $16 billion in taxes.

Those hardest hit by the influx of immigrants are disadvantaged native-born minorities who don't have a high school degree—namely, African Americans and previous waves of Latino immigrants. They must compete for the same low-end jobs immigrants take.

Wages for high school dropouts, who make up one in fourteen native workers, have dropped in recent years. Between 1980 and 2000, a Harvard University study found, the influx of immigrant workers to the United States cut wages for native workers with no high school diploma by 7.4 percent, or $1,800 on an average salary of $25,000.

Sometimes, whole industries switch from native to immigrant workers. In 1993, I looked at efforts to unionize Latino janitors in Los Angeles. Previously, the jobs had been largely held by African Americans, who had succeeded in obtaining increased wages and health benefits. Cleaning companies busted their union, then brought in Latino immigrant workers at half the wages and no benefits.

In 1996, I went to an ordinary block of two-bedroom homes in East Los Angeles to understand why nearly a third of California Latinos had supported Proposition 187, a voter initiative to bar illegal immigrants from schools, hospitals, and most public assistance. The measure passed and was later struck down by the courts.

For residents of the block, support for Prop 187 wasn't a nativist reaction or scapegoating in tight economic times. They said ill feelings toward illegal immigrants were grounded in how the newcomers had affected their neighborhood and their lives. For them, the influx had meant not cut-rate nannies and gardeners, but heightened job competition, depressed wages, overcrowded government services, and a reduced quality of life.

The newcomers who moved into the neighborhood were poor. Residents estimated that the block's population had tripled since 1970; up to seventeen immigrants were jammed into one small stucco house. Some lived in garages without plumbing, using lawns to relieve themselves. The second- and third-generation Latinos on the block felt it was their working-class neighborhoods that bore the brunt of a wave of impoverished, unskilled workers. Immigrants were arriving at an unsettling pace, crowding them out of jobs and lowering wages. Immigrants weren't just taking jobs natives didn't covet; they competed for work as painters, mechanics, and construction workers.

In the 1980s, the RAND Corporation, a Santa Monica think tank, found that the benefits of immigration outweighed the costs. By 1997, they had reversed course. The economy wasn't producing new jobs for high school dropouts, an increasing proportion of whom—roughly half—were unemployed. RAND said some native adults had become unemployed because of immigrant competition. They recommended the country slash legal immigration to 1970s levels.

Some immigration experts question whether it makes sense to allow so many immigrants with low levels of education from poor, underdeveloped countries when the United States needs to compete globally in industries requiring high levels of education, creativity, and know-how. Mexican immigrants arrive with an average of five to nine years of education.

Others experts focus on how adding more than a million immigrants a year to the United States' population affects overcrowding of parks, freeways, and the environment. Immigration accounted for more than half of the 33 million new U.S. residents in the 1990s. With nearly 300 million people, the United States has almost five times as many residents as when Ellis Island welcomed new arrivals.

In Los Angeles County, the surge in immigrants helped cause the poverty rate to nearly double, to 25 percent, between 1980 and 1997. The effect, at least in the short term: a sea of poor and working-class neighborhoods amid islands of affluence.

SCHIZOPHRENIC POLICIES

In the end, any calculus of the benefits and burdens of immigration depends on who you are. People who own businesses and commercial interests that use cheap immigrant labor benefit the most from immigrants like Enrique and Lourdes. They get a ready supply of compliant low-cost workers. Other winners are couples who hire immigrants to care for their children and drive them to school, tend to their lawns, clean their houses, and wash their cars.

High school dropouts have the most to lose. So do residents of immigrant-heavy states such as California, where an estimated third of illegal immigrants live, because services immigrants use disproportionately, such as public schools, are funded with local and state taxes.

Polls show Americans in recent years have hardened their views of immigrants, particularly those who are in the country illegally. A growing proportion—two thirds, compared with half in the mid-1970s—thinks the government should reduce immigration from current levels.

Many immigration observers believe U.S. officials have pursued a purposefully schizophrenic immigration policy. The government has added Border Patrol agents along the nation's southwestern border and walled off seventy-six miles of that divide. Politicians talk tough about catching illegal immigrants. Meanwhile, critics say, efforts to enforce many of the nation's immigration laws are weak to nonexistent.

Labor-intensive industries—agriculture, construction, food processing, restaurants, domestic help agencies—want cheap immigrant labor to bolster their bottom lines. Whenever immigration authorities make even cursory attempts to enforce a 1986 law that allows employers to be fined up to $10,000 for each illegal immigrant they hire, businesses—onion farmers in Georgia, meatpacking firms in the Midwest—bitterly complain. Fines on businesses and raids by immigration enforcement agents have gone from sporadic to virtually nil. Similarly, a pilot project allowing some employers to check the immigration status of job applicants via telephone has never expanded nationally and remains voluntary.

In essence, politicians have put a lock on the front door while swinging the back door wide open. A crackdown on the U.S.-Mexico border, begun in 1993, was designed to shift immigrant traffic to more remote parts of the border, where Border Patrol agents have a tactical advantage. Since the buildup began, the number of agents patrolling the border and the amount of money spent on enforcement have both tripled, according to a 2002 study by the Public Policy Institute of California (PPIC). Yet there is no evidence, the PPIC concluded, that the strategy has worked. In fact, the number of immigrants in the United States illegally has grown more quickly since the border buildup began.

Many outcomes of the new strategy have been unintended—and negative, the PPIC says. More illegal immigrants now use smugglers (89 percent, compared to 70 percent before). Immigrants, particularly those from Mexico, once returned home after brief work stints in the United States. Today, the increasing difficulty and cost of crossing means more come and stay. The new strategy has also resulted in more than three hundred deaths each year, as migrants are forced to cross in areas that are less populated, more isolated, and more geographically hostile.

Some priests in Mexico whose churches are located near the rails are so sure the flow of Central American migrants will be neverending that they have recently built their own migrant shelters. As long as the grinding poverty such as Enrique's mother lived in exists, priests in these churches believe, people will try to get to the United States, even if they must take enormous risks to get there.

In the United States, many immigration experts have concluded that the only effective strategy for change is to bolster the economies of immigrant-sending countries. Hondurans point out a few things that would help bring that about. Forgiving foreign debt would allow more of their country's resources to go into development. Implementing U.S. trade policies that give a strong preference to goods from immigrant-sending countries would help spur growth in certain industries, such as textiles, that employ women in Honduras. Others believe the United States, notoriously stingy among industrialized nations in per capita gifts of foreign aid, should boost donations. Individuals, Hondurans note, can support nongovernmental organizations that encourage job-creating small businesses or improve the availability of education in Honduras, where 12 percent of children never attend a school.

Most immigrants would rather stay in their home countries with their extended families. Who wants to leave home and everything he or she knows for something foreign, not knowing if he or she will ever return? Not many.

What would ensure that more women can stay home—with their children, where they want to be? María Isabel's mother, Eva, says, simply, "What would it take to keep people from leaving? There would have to be jobs. Jobs that pay okay. That's all."

NOTES

The reporting for this book spanned five years. During that time, I spent a total of six months, in 2000 and in 2003, in Honduras, Guatemala, Mexico, and North Carolina. The initial travel was done for a newspaper series for the *Los Angeles Times*. Subsequent travel and interviews would expand the series into this book.

I found Enrique in Nuevo Laredo, Mexico, in May 2000. I spent two weeks with him there and rejoined him at the end of his journey in North Carolina. Then, based on extensive interviews with him in Mexico and during three visits to North Carolina, I retraced each step he had taken, beginning at his home in Honduras.

Between May and September 2000, I spent three months working my way north through Mexico just as Enrique had, riding the tops of seven freight trains and interviewing people

Enrique had encountered, along with dozens of other children and adults making the same journey. I walked around immigration checkpoints and hitchhiked with truckers, exactly as Enrique had. To retrace Enrique's steps, I traversed thirteen of Mexico's thirty-one states.

Though I witnessed a part of Enrique's journey, much of his travel and life come from the recollections of Enrique and his mother. Enrique recalled his travel experiences largely within weeks of when they occurred. The recalled scenes and conversations were corroborated, whenever possible, by one or more individuals present.

I conducted hundreds of interviews in the United States, Honduras, Mexico, and Guatemala with immigrants, immigrant rights advocates, shelter workers, academics, medical workers, government officials, police officers, and priests and nuns who minister to migrants. At four INS detention centers in California and Texas and in two shelters for child migrants in Tijuana and Mexicali, Mexico, I interviewed youngsters who had made their way north on top of freight trains. I conducted interviews from Los Angeles and also consulted academic studies and books about immigration.

In 2003, I retraced Enrique's journey for a second time. I spent time in Honduras with Enrique's family; his girlfriend, María Isabel; and their daughter, Jasmín. I witnessed some of the scenes depicted of María Isabel's life with her daughter. I again traveled through Honduras and Guatemala and retraced the rail route, starting in Tapachula, Chiapas, Mexico. To obtain additional details on the journey and people who help migrants along the rails, I spent time in five regions of Mexico.

I spent two weeks with Olga Sánchez Martínez, a shelter worker in Tapachula, Mexico, and a week with Father Leonardo

López Guajardo at the Parroquia de San José in Nuevo Laredo, Mexico. I made a fourth trip to North Carolina to interview Enrique, Lourdes, and others in their family. In 2004, during a visit by Lourdes to Long Beach, California, I accompanied her to places where she once lived and worked. Between 2000 and 2005, I conducted regular interviews with Enrique and Lourdes by telephone.

The decision to use only the first names of Enrique and Lourdes is a continuation of a decision made by the *Los Angeles Times* that I supported. The newspaper has a strong preference for naming the subjects of its articles in full. It did so with two members of Enrique's family and a friend. But the *Times* decided to identify Enrique and his mother, father, and two sisters by publishing only their first names and to withhold the maternal or paternal name, or both, of six relatives as well as some details of Enrique's employment. A database review by *Times* researcher Nona Yates showed that publishing their full names would make Enrique readily identifiable to authorities. In 1998, the Raleigh, North Carolina, *News and Observer* profiled an illegal immigrant whom it fully identified by name and workplace. Authorities arrested the subject of the profile, four co-workers, and a customer for being undocumented immigrants. The *Times*'s decision was intended to allow Enrique and his family to live their lives as they would have had they not provided information for this story. For the same reason, I have decided in this book to identify Enrique's girlfriend by her first name and to withhold the maternal or paternal name, or both, of her relatives.

The following is an accounting of where information in this book comes from. It is an extensive but by no means complete list of who helped make Enrique's story possible. Throughout the book, people's ages and titles are for the time when Enrique made his journey.

PROLOGUE

Information about the number of legal and illegal immigrants comes from the U.S. Department of Homeland Security's Office of Immigration Statistics and demographer Jeffrey S. Passel, a senior research associate at the Pew Hispanic Center. Passell estimated that between 2000 and 2004, 700,000 illegal immigrants arrived each year. Information about the initial wave of immigrants who were single mothers and came to the United States is from Pierrette Hondagneu-Sotelo, a sociology professor at the University of Southern California, and Wayne Cornelius, director of the Center for Comparative Immigration Studies at the University of California, San Diego. Hondagneu-Sotelo also provided the estimated growth in U.S. domestic worker jobs in the 1980s.

The University of Southern California study that discusses how many live-in nannies have left children behind is "I'm Here but I'm There: The Meanings of Latina Transnational Motherhood," published in 1997. The Harvard University study that details the percentage of immigrant children separated from a parent during the process of immigration is "Children of Immigration," published in 2001.

1. THE BOY LEFT BEHIND

Much of the account of Enrique's and Lourdes's lives in Honduras, Lourdes's departure from Honduras, their lives apart, and Enrique's departure to find his mother are drawn from Enrique, Lourdes, and family members. These include Enrique's sister Belky; his aunts Mirian, Rosa Amalia, and Ana Lucía; his uncle Carlos Orlando Turcios Ramos; his maternal grandmother, Águeda Amalia Valladares, and paternal grandmother, María Marcos; his mother's cousin María Edelmira Sánchez Mejía; his father, Luis, and stepmother, Suyapa Álvarez; his girlfriend, María Isabel, and her aunt Gloria; Enrique's cousins Tania Ninoska Turcios and Karla Roxana Turcios; as well as Enrique's friend and fellow drug user José del Carmen Bustamante.

The estimate that a total of at least 48,000 children enter the United States from Central America and Mexico each year, illegally and without either parent, comes from 2001. It was reached by adding the following numbers: The U.S. Immigration and Naturalization Service said it had detained 2,401 Central American children. The INS had no figure for Mexican children, but Mexico's Ministry of Foreign Affairs said the INS had detained 12,019 of them. Scholars, including Robert Bach, former INS executive associate commissioner for policy, planning, and programs, estimated that about 33,600 children are not caught. For 2000, the total was 59,000.

The reasons children travel to the United States and information that many come in search of their mothers come from Roy de la Cerda, Jr., the lead counselor at International Educational Services Inc., an INS-contracted detention shelter for unaccompanied minors in Los Fresnos, Texas. His information was corroborated by Aldo Pumariega, principal at the Bellagio Road Newcomer School; Bradley Pilon, a psychologist who counsels immigrant students in the Los Angeles Unified School District; and Rafael Martínez, director of Casa YMCA, a migrant shelter in Piedras Negras, Mexico.

The estimate that half of Central American child migrants ride trains without smugglers is from Haydee Sanchez, executive director of Youth Empowerment Services, a nonprofit Los Angeles group that helps immigrants; Olga Cantarero, a coordinator for the nonprofit Casa de Proyecto Libertad in Harlingen, Texas, which provides legal help to INS child detainees; and Roy de la Cerda.

Details about travel through Mexico come from migrant children in Mexico and the United States and from children in INS detention facilities in Texas and California. Included are my observations as I traveled with children on Mexican freight trains. The University of Houston study about violence to children is titled "Potentially Traumatic Events Among Unaccompanied Migrant Children from Central America," published in 1997.

Accounts of encounters with children as young as seven on the rails come from Pedro Mendoza García, a railroad security guard at a depot near Nuevo Laredo.

The remarks of a nine-year-old boy searching for his mother who was in San Francisco are from Haydee Sanchez in Los Angeles.

The typical age of children on this journey comes from INS data and migrant shelter workers in Mexico.

The description of how children recall their mothers is from interviews with several of them, including Ermis Galeano, sixteen, and Mery Gabriela Posas Izaguirre, fifteen, questioned in Mexico on their way to find their mothers in the United States.

Lourdes elaborated on her description of being abandoned in 1989 at a downtown Los Angeles bus station by her smuggler by returning to the station with me in 2004. During the 2004 trip, further details of Lourdes's life in Long Beach were obtained as Lourdes took me to places where she had once lived and worked, including a Long Beach bar. Several of Lourdes's Long Beach friends were also interviewed and corroborated how they and Lourdes had been scammed by a woman claiming she could help them become legal residents.

For the account of Enrique's life with his paternal grandmother, I visited the home of the grandmother and the home of Enrique's father, as well as the market where Enrique sold spices.

Santos's return to Honduras comes from Lourdes and her family members in Honduras, who said they had witnessed his behavior. Santos himself couldn't be located.

The smugglers' fees for bringing Central American children to the United States come from immigrant women and Robert Foss, legal director of the Central American Resource Center in Los Angeles.

The description of the Tegucigalpa dump and its scavengers is from my observations and interviews with children at the dump. I also witnessed children hauling sawdust and firewood. I spent time at the school in El Infiernito where children arrive without shoes.

Lourdes's life in North Carolina comes from Lourdes, her boyfriend, her daughter Diana, and their friends and relatives.

The description of María Isabel's childhood, her move to her aunt Gloria's house, and her devotion to Enrique is from Gloria, María Isabel, her sister Rosario, her brother Miguel, her mother, Eva, and from time I spent at Gloria's and Eva's homes in Tegucigalpa.

The account of life in El Infiernito is from my visit to the neighborhood accompanied by the teacher Jenery Adialinda Castillo. I accompanied the Tegucigalpa priest Eduardo Martín on his evening rounds to feed glue-sniffing homeless children.

Enrique's attempt to reach his mother in 1999 was corroborated by José del Carmen Bustamante, his companion on the journey.

2. SEEKING MERCY

Enrique's experiences in and around Las Anonas were written from interviews with Sirenio Gómez Fuentes; Mayor Carlos Carrasco; Carrasco's mother, Lesbia Sibaja; residents Beatriz Carrasco Gómez, Gloria Luis, and other villagers; San Pedro Tapanatepec mayor Adan Díaz Ruiz; and the mayor's driver, Ricardo Díaz Aguilar. I visited the Fuentes home, the Las Anonas church, and the mango tree where Enrique collapsed.

Manuel de Jesús Molina, who in 2000 served as assistant to the mayor of Ixtepec, a nearby town, said that Enrique's experience of being robbed by the judicial police was common in the area. The denial that judicial police rob people comes from Sixto Juárez, chief of the Agencia Federal de Investigación in Arriaga, Mexico.

The estimate of how much a wounded migrant costs the nearest hospital comes from personnel at the Hospital Civil in Arriaga, Mexico.

The account of how Mexican immigration officers shake down Central American migrants comes from retired immigration agent C. Faustino Chacón Cruz Cabrera.

The descriptions of Enrique's first six attempts are from interviews with Enrique and from my observations of other migrants along the same route. I visited the spot near Medias Aguas where Enrique had been stung by bees. I went to the Tapachula cemetery and the mausoleum where Enrique had slept. The cemetery caretaker, Miguel Ángel Pérez Hernández, and Mario Campos Gutiérrez, a supervisory agent with the government migrant rights group Grupo Beta, provided information about recent violence in the graveyard. The annual number of deportees from Mexico is from the National Migration Institute of Mexico.

The description of the violence and gangs in the Guatemalan border town of Tecún Umán comes from Father Ademar Barilli and Marvin Godínez at the Casa del Migrante shelter in Tecún Umán and from Flaudio Pérez Villagres, head of the tricycle taxi union in the town.

The beating on the train is from interviews with Enrique and residents of Las Anonas and San Pedro Tapanatepec. Robberies in which migrants are stripped and hurled from trains are commonplace, according to Grupo Beta, whose officers occasionally patrol the trains; Father Flor María Rigoni, a Catholic priest at the Albergue Belén migrant shelter in Tapachula, Chiapas; Baltasar Soriano Peraza, a caseworker at the shelter; and other migrants who have been robbed on the trains by street gangsters. Railroad personnel and Mayor Carrasco estimated how fast the trains travel in the area.

How María Isabel reacted to Enrique's departure and her decision to follow him come from María Isabel, her aunt Gloria, and her mother, Eva.

Enrique's medical condition and treatment are from Enrique and Dr. Guillermo Toledo Montes, who treated him. Mayor Díaz provided the doctor's receipt detailing Enrique's treatment. I visited the clinic and the police command post where Enrique slept.

Detailed cases of migrants' injuries at the Arriaga hospital come from my interview with the president of Arriaga's Red Cross first aid responders, Isaac Santelis de los Santos, and hospital social worker Isabel Barragan Torres. I reviewed the hospital files of all injured migrants between 1999 and 2003.

The bus ride to Guatemala is from interviews with Enrique, migrants on the bus, and my observations while riding the bus to El Carmen, Guatemala, where the trip ends. How street gangsters rob riders is from Baltasar Soriano Peraza, the caseworker at the Albergue Belén shelter; the Mexican immigration agent Fernando Armento Juan, who accompanies migrants on the bus; and migrants, including Carlos Sandoval, a Salvadoran, who said he had been accosted by gangsters with ice picks.

3. FACING THE BEAST

The crossing of the Río Suchiate is from interviews with Enrique, other migrants who made the crossing, and my observations as I crossed on a raft. Facing Chiapas, "the beast," is from Father Flor María Rigoni. The lessons about Chiapas are from Enrique, other migrants, and Father Arturo Francisco Herrera González, a Catholic priest who helps migrants at the Parroquia de San Vicente Ferrer in Juchitán, Oaxaca.

The story of how Enrique slept in the Tapachula cemetery and ran for the train comes from interviews with Enrique and from my observations at the cemetery of the ritual of running for the train. I accompanied the Tapachula municipal police on a dawn raid of the cemetery, did a tour of the cemetery with its caretaker, and visited the crypt where Enrique had slept. To describe Enrique's trip to a Tapachula jail, I accompanied migrants who were captured by police and taken to the same lockup. The train's speed is from Jorge Reinoso, who in 2000 was chief of operations for the Ferrocarriles Chiapas-Mayab railroad, and from Julio César Cancino Gálvez, an officer of Grupo Beta, who is a former Tapachula train crewman. "The train ate him up" comes from Emilio Canteros Mendez, an engineer for Ferrocarriles Chiapas-Mayab, and was confirmed by migrants I met on the trains. The dangers of Chiapas were explained by Father Rigoni.

The description of how a train feels and choosing where to ride and what to carry is from Enrique and from my observations and interviews with migrants while riding on two freight trains through Chiapas. Reinoso provided information about the age and condition of tracks in Chiapas and the frequency of derailments, one of which I witnessed. Train nicknames are from migrants, Grupo Beta officers, and former crewman Julio César Cancino Gálvez.

Tales of avoiding branches and what migrants yell when they see a branch come from Enrique and from my observations on the top of a train when a migrant was knocked off. Julio César Cancino Gálvez and several train conductors explained the various reasons trains sometimes must stop.

The assertion that agents shoot at migrants at the La Arrocera checkpoint comes from C. Faustino Chacón Cruz Cabrera; Hugo Ángeles Cruz, an immigration expert at the Colegio de la Frontera Sur in Tapachula, Mexico; railroad employees who said they had witnessed such shootings, including José Agustín Tamayo Chamorro, chief of operations at Ferrosur railroad, and Emilio Canteros Mendez; and migrants who said agents had fired at them at La Arrocera, including Selvin Terraza Chan, twenty-one, José Alberto Ruiz Méndez, fifteen, and Juan Joel de Jesús Villareal, fifteen. Hernán Bonilla, twenty-seven, showed Enrique and me scars he said came from cigarette burns received from immigration agents in the area.

The *madrinas'* efforts at La Arrocera come from Elba Flores Nuñez, a former coordinator of the Centro de Derechos Humanos Tepeyac del Istmo de Tehuantepec, a rights group; Reyder Cruz Toledo, the police chief in Arriaga, Chiapas; Jorge Zarif Zetuna Curioca, a former mayor of Ixtepec; Mario Campos Gutiérrez; C. Faustino Chacón Cruz Cabrera; and a La Arrocera resident, Guillermina Gálvez López.

The dangers of La Arrocera were detailed by Enrique, other migrants, Grupo Beta officers, and the immigration agent Marco Tulio Carballo Cabrera at the nearby Hueyate immigration station. I observed migrants' anxiety as they approached the checkpoint on two train rides through La Arrocera. Migrants pleading for help when they suffered electric shock is from Guillermina Gálvez López. How migrants hide their money is from migrants I met riding on the trains. Enrique's run around La Arrocera comes from Enrique; Clemente Delporte Gómez, a former Grupo Beta Sur officer; and my observations as I walked around the checkpoint, witnessed two bandit chases, and entered the brick house where women had been raped.

The description of bandits and their activities at La Arrocera is from Julio César Cancino Gálvez, who again accompanied me to the checkpoint in 2003. I obtained additional information about bandits then from local *migra* supervisor

Widmar Borrallas López and La Arrocera railside residents Amelia López Gamboa, Jorge Alberto Hernández, Virgilio Mendes Ramírez, María del Carmen Torres García, and three men who feared giving their names. I also took a tour of the bandits' favorite bars in the nearby town of Huixtla.

The strategies for preventing rape were detailed by Grupo Beta officers and Monica Oropeza, executive director of Albergue Juvenil del Desierto, a migrant shelter for minors in Mexicali, Mexico. The 1997 University of Houston study "Potentially Traumatic Events Among Unaccompanied Migrant Children from Central America" details the dangers. The AIDS warning that girls write on their chests is from Olivia Ruiz, a cultural anthropologist at the Colegio de la Frontera Norte in Tijuana, who researches the dangers migrants face riding trains through Chiapas.

The Cuil bridge ambushes were described by Clemente Delporte Gómez and Grupo Beta Sur officer José Alfredo Ruiz Chamec.

The dislike of Central American migrants comes from migrants, professor Hugo Ángeles Cruz, and Tapachula residents, including Miguel Ángel Pérez Hernández, Guillermina Gálvez López, and Juan Pérez. While riding trains through Chiapas, I witnessed Mexican children pelting migrants with rocks.

María Isabel's foiled plan to follow Enrique to the United States comes from María Isabel; her mother, Eva; her aunt Gloria; and Gloria's daughter Gloria Elizabeth Chávez.

The account of heat on the train and how migrants stayed awake is from Enrique. I witnessed migrants doing similar things to stay cool and awake, including Reynaldo Matamorros, who strapped himself to the end of a hopper car to nap; José Rodas Orellana, who took amphetamines; and José Donald Morales Enriques, who did squats. I rode on one train where a chorus broke out at 4 A.M.

How gangsters stalk migrants is from Grupo Beta officers, Baltasar Soriano Peraza, and my observations on the trains. Information about gangsters forcing two boys to have sex together is from José Enrique Oliva Rosa and José Luis Oliva Rosa, fifteen-year-old twins who rode on a train where the incident occurred.

The assertion that the judicial police conducted shakedowns at San Ramón and threatened migrants is from Emilio Canteros Mendez, an engineer on the Ferrocarriles Chiapas-Mayab railroad. Some migrants, including Dennis Iván Contreras, twelve, told me that officers at San Ramón had made similar statements to them. The denial that judicial police engage in such robberies is from Sixto Juárez, chief of the Agencia Federal de Investigación in nearby Arriaga.

For how migrants are devoured by the train, in 2000 I interviewed Carlos Roberto Díaz Osorto in his hospital bed in Arriaga, Chiapas. I later viewed his medical file.

In 2003, I spent two weeks with Olga Sánchez Martínez. I spent time with Olga at her shelter as she dressed migrants' wounds and accompanied her to church, to a prosthesis maker, to sell used clothing, on rounds at the local hospital, on a beach outing with injured migrants, and in her efforts in the middle of the night to find a casket for someone who had just died at her shelter.

To write about Olga, I spoke with migrants living at her Shelter of Jesus the Good Shepherd, including Tránsito Encarnación Martínes Hernández, Fausto Mejillas Guerrero, Leti Isabela Mejía Yanes, Hugo Tambrís Sióp, Edwin Bertotty Baquerano, Juan Carlos Hernández, Francisco Beltrán Domínguez, Efren Morales Ramírez, Carlos López, Fredy Antonio Ávila, and Mario Castro. I interviewed Olga; her husband, Jordán Matus Vásquez; her friends; and shelter volunteers Marilú Hernández Hernández, Fernando Hernández López, Roldán Mendoza García, and Carmen Aguilar de Mendoza. At the Tapachula general hospital, I interviewed three people who had observed Olga's work: the doctors Jorge Luis Antonio Álvarez and José Luis Solórzano, and a hospital social worker, Margarita Márquez Morán.

I observed Wendy hours after the rape and interviewed several migrants who had been with her when the incident occurred.

Enrique's time in Ixtepec comes from Enrique and my observations as I retraced his steps in Ixtepec.

4. GIFTS AND FAITH

The description of the statue of Christ is from interviews with Enrique and from my observation of other migrants on a train passing the same statue. Information about religious items, Bible readings, and how migrants show their faith is from migrants Marco Antonio Euseda, Oscar Alfredo Molina, and César Gutiérrez. I heard migrant Marlon Sosa Cortez recite the prayer to the Holy Trinity as he rode on top of a train.

The assertion that Oaxacans are friendlier is from interviews with Enrique and other migrants, as well as Jorge Zarif Zetuna Curioca, the former mayor of Ixtepec; Juan Ruiz, the former police chief of Ixtepec; and train engineer Isaías Palacios.

The exchange between food throwers and Enrique comes

from Enrique and is similar to words I heard while observing food throwers in various towns and as food throwers in Encinar, Veracruz, threw bananas and crackers onto a train I was riding. In Veracruz, I interviewed food throwers in several villages. At Encinar: Ángela Andrade Cruz; Jesús González Román, his sister Magdalena González Román, and their mother, Esperanza Román González; Mariano Cortés; and Marta Santiago Flores and her son Leovardo. At Fortín de las Flores: Ciro González Ramos, his children Erika and Fabián, and a former neighbor, Leticia Rebolledo. At Cuichapa: Soledad Vásquez and her mother, María Luisa Mora Martín. At Presidio: Ramiro López Contreras and his son Rubén López Juárez. The 2000 World Bank study cited is "The Effect of IMF and World Bank Programs on Poverty." Rural malnutrition information is from Mexico's 1999 national nutrition survey, conducted by the Instituto Nacional de Salud Pública.

In 2003, I interviewed various Veracruz church members who helped migrants with food, shelter, or protection from the police, including Raquel Flores Lamora, Baltasar Bréniz Ávila, Francisca Aguirre Juárez, and María del Carmen Ortega García.

For the account of the decision to help migrants at the Parroquia María Auxiliadora in Río Blanco, Veracruz, I relied on the priest Salamón Lemus Lemus; the volunteers Luis Hernández Osorio, Gregoria Sánchez Romero, and Leopoldo Francisco Maldonado Gutiérrez; the church cook, Rosa Tlehuactle Anastacio; the church secretary, Irene Rodríguez Rivera; Father Julio César Trujillo Velásquez, the director of media affairs for the Diocese of Orizaba; and Monsignor Hipólito Reyes Larios, the Catholic bishop of Orizaba.

The beating of migrants in El Campesino El Mirador is

from María Enriqueta Reyes Márquez, who witnessed the incident, and Samuel Ramírez del Carmen of the Mendoza, Veracruz, Red Cross.

The types of train cargoes and the cost of migrant injuries are from Cuauhtemoc González Flores, chief of accident investigations for the Transportación Ferroviaria Mexicana railroad.

Enrique's robbery at the Córdoba station is from Enrique and from my observations at the shed where it happened. Other migrants gave accounts of similar robberies at Córdoba. The camaraderie with others aboard the train north of Orizaba and preparations for the cold to come are from Enrique and from my observations of other migrants at Orizaba. The description of tunnels is from Enrique and the switchman Juan Carlos Salcedo, and from observations by *Los Angeles Times* photographer Don Bartletti and me as we rode through the tunnels on top of a freight train. Information on the danger of the El Mexicano tunnel is from José Agustín Tamayo Chamorro of the Ferrosur railroad. What migrants yell as they ride through the tunnels and what they do to keep warm are from Enrique, confirmed by my observations.

In 2000, I found the Mexico City culvert where Enrique waited for a train. In 2003, I returned to interview Lechería residents Olivia Rodríguez Morales and Oscar Aereola Peregrino and Lechería station personnel director José Patricio Sánchez Arrellano, who gave me a tour and history of the station. The account of the electrical lines in Mexico City is from Enrique and Cuauhtemoc González Flores of Transportación Ferroviaria Mexicana, and from my observations at the railroad's computer center.

The number of security officers at the San Luis Potosí station is from Marcelo Rodríguez, chief of security at the station for Transportación Ferroviaria Mexicana.

Enrique's stay in San Luis Potosí making bricks comes from Enrique and interviews with brick makers, including Gregorio Ramos, José Morales Portillo, and Juan Pérez. His trip to Matehuala is from Enrique and from my observations during a bus ride on the same route.

The reluctance of truck drivers to give migrants a ride was confirmed by Modesto Reyes Santiago, a truck driver, and Faustina Olivares, owner of the No Que No diner, which is frequented by truckers. I also hitchhiked on a truck between Matehuala and Nuevo Laredo.

5 . ON THE BORDER

The description of how migrants arrived in Nuevo Laredo after having lost the phone numbers they were carrying comes from Deacon Esteban Ramírez Rodríguez of the Parroquia de Guadalupe in Reynosa, Mexico, and several migrant children stranded in Nuevo Laredo, including Ermis Galeano and Kelvin Maradiaga. Migrant twins José Enrique Oliva Rosa and José Luis Oliva Rosa told of having been kidnapped.

The reluctance to help Central Americans was depicted by Raymundo Ramos Vásquez, director of Comité de Derechos Humanos, Grupo 5 de Febrero, a human rights group in Nuevo Laredo, and Marco Antonio Valdez, a resident. The statement that Jesus was a migrant comes from Oscar Alvarado, caretaker for the Parroquia de San José's migrant shelter, and was confirmed by Enrique and other migrants.

The description of the encampment is from Enrique and

camp residents Hernán Bonilla, Miguel Olivas, Luis Moreno Guzmán, and Jorge Enrique Morales, as well as from my observations at the camp.

I observed Enrique washing cars for money.

The account of meal cards comes from Father Filiberto Luviano Mendoza at the Parroquia del Santo Niño and volunteer Leti Limón at the Parroquia de San José. Migrant Miguel Olivas described the meal-card black market.

I observed dinner for migrants at the Parroquia de San José and how migrants gathered around the map of Texas after the meal to discuss their route. Father Leonardo López Guajardo at the Parroquia de San José calculated the percentage of the church's meals that go to children. I interviewed and observed the lives of other children Enrique met in Nuevo Laredo who were also going to find their mothers, including Ermis Galeano, Mery Gabriela Posas Izaguirre, her aunt Lourdes, and Kelvin Maradiaga.

Talk of hardships and injuries during the trip north by migrants outside the Parroquia de San José comes from my observations of these conversations and from María del Tepeyac, a nun who ran the church's medical clinic.

The portrayal of El Tiríndaro, his heroin habit, and his protection of Enrique is from my observations and interviews with Enrique and the camp residents Miguel Olivas, Hernán Bonilla, and Omar Martínez Torres. In 2003, I interviewed one of El Tiríndaro's Los Osos associates, Juan Barajas Soto, when he was in the Nuevo Laredo jail, Centro de Readaptación Social No. 1, who provided additional details about El Tiríndaro, Los Osos, and Enrique's stay at the encampment. The migrant Jorge Enrique Morales gave Enrique bits of tacos and contributed to the picture of life at the camp.

Enrique's account of the Nuevo Laredo jail was corroborated by Raymundo Ramos Vásquez at the human rights group Comité de Derechos Humanos, Grupo 5 de Febrero. The account of Enrique sleeping in the abandoned house, which I visited, comes from Enrique and photographer Don Bartletti's observations.

The rendering of Mother's Day comes from Central American mothers, including Águeda Navarro, Belinda Cáceres, Orbelina Sánchez, and Lourdes Izaguirre, and from my observations as they consoled one another. A mother's prayer to live is from my observations as I watched Lourdes Izaguirre pray.

Lourdes's thoughts and actions after her son left home are from Lourdes and were confirmed by her cousin María Edelmira Sánchez Mejía, with whom Lourdes spoke at the time.

Enrique's glue-sniffing habits are from Hernán Bonilla and from my observations. Juan Barajas Soto, who was interviewed at the jail in Nuevo Laredo in 2003, recalled Enrique's hallucinogenic talks with trees at the camp and about wanting to be with his mother.

I saw Enrique shortly after he got his tattoo and watched as he struggled to obtain his second phone card. Enrique's effort to beg for money in downtown Nuevo Laredo is from Enrique and Hernán Bonilla.

The dangers of the river and checkpoints come from the migrants Miguel Olivas, Hernán Bonilla, and Fredy Ramírez; the U.S. Border Patrol supervisor Alexander D. Hernandez and officers Charles Grout and Manuel Sauceda in Cotulla, Texas; and my observations.

The description of the desert dangers is from interviews with the migrants Miguel Olivas, Gonzalo Rodríguez Toledo, Luis Moreno Guzmán, Elsa Galarza, Leonicio Alejandro

Hernández, Mario Alberto Hernández, and Manuel Gallegos; U.S. Border Patrol agents Charles Grout and Manuel Sauceda and the dog handler Ramón López; and my observations while accompanying agents for three days on the Texas border. I observed Franca running alongside the train while on patrol with Cotulla Border Patrol agents. I was on hand when the migrant Isaías Guerra was caught and described his desert ordeal. The General Accounting Office says at least 367 migrants died crossing the southwestern border into the United States in 2000.

The account of Leonardo López Guajardo's assistance to migrants comes from an interview with the priest in 2000 and with Sisters Elizabeth Rangel and María del Tepeyac. In 2003, I spent a week with the priest. I followed him to church; as he said Mass in a cemetery and to incarcerated prisoners; and as he traveled throughout Laredo, Texas, and Nuevo Laredo, Mexico, to pick up donated food, clothing, and other items. I interviewed people who donated goods to the priest, including Sister Isidra Valdez, Lydia Garza, Rosalinda Zapata, Margarita Vargas, and Eduardo Brizuela Amor. I spent time with two nuns helping him, Sisters Leonor Palacios and Juanita Montecillo.

To better understand the priest and his work with migrants, I spoke with the church secretaries Alma Delia Jiménez Rentería and María Elena Pineda de Aguilar, and the church volunteers Patricia Alemán Peña, Miguel Delgadillo Esparza, Pedro and Leti Leyva, José Guadalupe Ramírez, Horacio Gómez Luna, Rogelio Santos Aguilar, Rocío Galván García, Juana R. Cancino Gómez, and Felipa Luna Moreno. I interviewed Carlos Martín Ramírez, a doctor who treats migrants pro bono for the priest. I spoke with the church's neighbors Juana Mexicano de Acosta and Juan Acosta Hernández.

6 . A DARK RIVER,
PERHAPS A NEW LIFE

Enrique's 1 A.M. departure is drawn from interviews with Enrique and migrant Hernán Bonilla, who witnessed the departure, as well as my subsequent observation of the staging area on the south bank of the Rio Grande and my observation of other nighttime crossings and pursuits by the U.S. Border Patrol. El Tiríndaro's words to Enrique and the two Mexicans about getting caught are from Enrique. Other migrants told me that this is a standard speech from smugglers to migrants before they cross the river.

The drowning in the river is from Enrique and other migrants, including three at the Parroquia de San José. The migrants said they had watched a youngster named Ricki drown in a whirlpool two nights before.

The account of crossing to the island and then to the United States is from interviews with Enrique and from my subsequent observation of the island from Enrique's crossing site on the south bank of the river. I retraced Enrique's steps on both sides of the river and went to the spot where he had first touched U.S. soil. I retraced his run along Zacate Creek, past a sewage treatment plant, and up an embankment into a residential area on the outskirts of Laredo.

A description of the jails where migrant children are held when they are caught by U.S. authorities comes from time I spent in these facilities, including a week at Los Angeles's Los Padrinos Juvenile Detention Center and a week in the Liberty County Jail in Liberty, Texas. I also spent a week at a shelter where migrants are held in Los Fresnos, Texas, operated by International Educational Services, and a similar shelter in San Diego, California.

Corrections Corporation of America has denied allegations that the children in its custody were not adequately fed; however, the jail in Liberty, Texas, operated by Corrections Corporation of America no longer houses immigrant children. Immigrant children detained by the Border Patrol entering the country illegally are now handled by the Office of Refugee Resettlement within the U.S. Department of Health and Human Services, an agency which uses jails sparingly and favors more nurturing open shelters and foster care.

The description of how Border Patrol agents spot suspect vehicles comes from Alexander D. Hernandez, supervisory agent for the Border Patrol at Cotulla, Texas, during a patrol along the same stretch of highway in south Texas that Enrique's smugglers used. The depictions of how Enrique bypassed the Border Patrol checkpoint come, in part, from my observations during a visit to the checkpoint.

Lourdes's life in North Carolina and the description of her photos are from Lourdes, her boyfriend, and other immigrants who lived with them. She showed me the photos of her children.

The account of Enrique's calls from Dallas to his mother comes from Enrique, his mother, and her boyfriend.

The ride from Florida to North Carolina is from my observations as I retraced the North Carolina portion of the trip. Enrique's reunification and conversations come from Enrique, his sister Diana, Lourdes, and my observations as Enrique retraced his steps into the house, into the kitchen, down the hallways, and into his mother's room.

The reaction by María Isabel to Enrique's arrival in North Carolina is from Belky, her aunt Rosa Amalia, María Isabel, and her aunt Gloria.

The relationship between Enrique and his mother, including the resentment of immigrant children at having been left behind, is from Enrique, Lourdes, Diana, Lourdes's boyfriend, and his cousin, as well as Maria Olmos, principal of the Newcomer Center at Belmont High School, a school for immigrants in Los Angeles; Gabriel Murillo, a former counselor at Belmont; and Aldo Pumariega, the principal of the now closed Bellagio Road Newcomer School in Los Angeles.

The account of Enrique's job, earnings, and purchases is from my observations.

7. THE GIRL LEFT BEHIND

The accounts of life for Enrique, María Isabel, Lourdes, her sister Mirian, and others are based on my trip to Honduras and North Carolina in 2003 and interviews with Enrique, Lourdes, and members of their families in Honduras and in the United States between 2000 and 2005. I spent a week in 2003 observing the lives of María Isabel and her daughter, Jasmín, in Honduras. I spent time at each of the three homes where María Isabel had lived in Tegucigalpa. I accompanied María Isabel to her job at the children's clothing store.

The description of María Isabel's life in Honduras is from María Isabel, her sister Rosario, her brother Miguel, her mother, Eva, and her aunt Gloria. I interviewed Ángela Emérita Nuñez, the woman who first employed María Isabel and in whose house she often slept during her teen years, and Ángela's daughter, Ángela María Rivera. Suyapa Valeriano, who lives near Eva's home in Los Tubos and took phone calls from Enrique for María Isabel, also provided details.

Additional information comes from Enrique's maternal and

paternal grandmothers, his sister Belky, his aunt Rosa Amalia, his uncle Carlos, and Lourdes's cousin María Edelmira.

To better understand Los Tubos, the neighborhood where María Isabel lived with her mother, I took a tour of the area with Reina Rodríguez and María Isabel Sosa of the local health clinic, the Centro de Salud El Bosque. Oscar Orlando Ortega Almendares of the health center provided a history of the neighborhood and of María Isabel's family. I spoke with José Luis Pineda Martínez, the director of the local school María Isabel attended, the Escuela 14 de Julio. I interviewed Cydalia de Sandoval, president of the Asociación Damas de la Caridad San Vicente de Paúl, which runs a local day-care center and orphanage, and with Argentina Valeriano, owner of the neighborhood bodega, the Pulpería Norma.

The description of Honduras's economic and social conditions comes from Maureen Zamora, a migration expert in Honduras; Marta Obando at UNICEF's Honduras office; Norberto Girón with the International Organization for Migration; Glenda Gallardo, the principal economist, and Alex Cálix, the director of national development information, at the United Nations Development Program in Honduras; Francis Jeanett Gómez Irias, a social worker with the Instituto Hondureño de la Niñez y la Familia; Nubia Esther Gómez, a nurse with the program; and Leydi Karina López, the head of human resources of S. J. Mariol, a clothing factory in Tegucigalpa. I also consulted documents in the UNICEF library in Tegucigalpa.

For the depiction of Enrique's life in North Carolina with Lourdes between 2000 and 2005, I spoke with Enrique, a fellow painter and friend, Enrique's boss, Lourdes, her boyfriend, the boyfriend's son, the boyfriend's brother, Lourdes's daughter Diana, and her sister Mirian.

AFTERWORD

The number of undocumented children in the United States is from the 2005 Pew Hispanic Center study by senior research associate Jeffrey Passell entitled "Unauthorized Migrants: Numbers and Characteristics."

Chiapas's troubles with Central American gangs are from Gabriela Coutiño, a spokeswoman for the National Immigration Institute in Tapachula. The assertion that the number of migrants injured by the trains has doubled since Enrique's journey is from Grupo Beta Sur, social workers at Tapachula's general hospital, and Olga Sánchez Martínez, who runs a shelter for the injured.

Changes in where and how the train stops for Mexican authorities to grab migrants come from Coutiño; Julio César Cancino Gálvez of Grupo Beta Sur; Widmar Borrallas López, a supervisor at *la migra*'s El Hueyate Station near La Arrocera; and Tres Hermanos resident Gregorio Ralón Villareal.

The number of Central Americans detained and deported by Mexico is from the National Immigration Institute.

I spent time during 1999 and 2000 at Los Angeles's Newcomer School, where I interviewed dozens of mothers and children and attended classes and student therapy and counseling sessions.

The 1997 National Research Council study cited is entitled "The New Americans: Economic, Demographic, and Fiscal Effects of Immigration." The 2003 Harvard University study about immigrant effects on wages is "The Labor Demand Curve Is Downward Sloping: Reexamining the Impact of Immigration on the Labor Market," by George J. Borjas, professor of economics and social policy at the John F. Kennedy School of Government.

I refer to stories in the *Los Angeles Times:* "For This Union, It's War," August 19, 1993, and "Natives, Newcomers at Odds in East L.A.," March 4, 1996.

The 1997 RAND study that discusses the excessive number of immigrants is "Immigration in a Changing Economy: The California Experience," by Kevin F. McCarthy and Georges Vernez.

ACKNOWLEDGMENTS

Much of the original research for this book was done to report a newspaper series for the *Los Angeles Times*. I could not have done this book without the backing of the world-class newspaper whose editors gave me the time and resources to produce the newspaper series "Enrique's Journey," which became the foundation for this book.

I am particularly indebted to my *Los Angeles Times* editor, Rick Meyer. Rick is the best editor a reporter could hope for. He is incredibly supportive, and yet he demands that a story achieve the highest standards. His infectious enthusiasm for a good yarn makes you try to do your best work. He taught me more than any other editor I've had about how to tell a story. It is no mystery why reporters clamor to work for Rick.

I would also especially like to thank John Carroll, who believed in "Enrique's Journey" from the beginning. As the executive editor of the *Los Angeles Times,* John showed great gut instincts in how to tweak the story to make it better. He painstakingly and skillfully edited twelve drafts. John's eyes light up at the thought of rolling up his sleeves, pencil in hand, and finding ways to make each sentence, paragraph, and part of a story better. I am also indebted to John for giving me the time off to expand the series into this book.

I am thankful to the dozens of people at the *Los Angeles Times,* too many to name, who were also instrumental in making this story better and more multifaceted. These include people who worked on editing, copyediting, photography, research, graphics, design, Web presentation (including multimedia efforts), and the Spanish-language translation of the series for the Web.

At Random House, I want to thank my editor, Dan Menaker, whose input and passion for this book served to make every part of it better, and editor Stephanie Higgs and production editor Evan Camfield for the care they showed in working to make each part of the book its best.

I thank my agent, Bonnie Nadell, who gave me the initial nudge to write this book, and whose support and wise counsel helped immeasurably throughout.

Hundreds of people helped me in the process of researching and writing this book. Some, in particular, gave me an extraordinary amount of their time and effort.

First and foremost are Enrique, Lourdes, and María Isabel.

Enrique and Lourdes agreed to cooperate despite the obvious pitfalls. As illegal immigrants, they took a real risk in helping me. All they had was my assurance that I would tell their story faithfully and to the best of my abilities, and that doing so might help others understand what families like theirs go through and what the migrant journey is like. For them, this project was a leap of faith. They gave me weeks and weeks of their time over the course of five years, putting up with endless and probing questions, with little more than the hope that I would clearly and accurately convey their experiences. I cannot thank them enough.

I want to thank their families in the United States and in Honduras, who were equally open and patient with me. In the United States, I am indebted to Lourdes's boyfriend and to Diana. The book would not have been possible without the generous help in Honduras of Belky, Rosa Amalia, Mirian, Carlos Orlando Turcios Ramos, Tania Ninoska Turcios, Karla Roxana Turcios, María Edelmira Sánchez Mejía, Ana Lucía, María Marcos, Águeda Amalia Valladares, Gloria, and Eva.

Along the route, I thank Mexico's train companies—Ferrocarriles Chiapas-Mayab, Transportación Ferroviaria Mexicana, and Ferrosur—for allowing me to ride on their trains. Virginia Kice and others at the INS helped me gain access to jails and shelters where migrant children were held. At one of those shelters in Texas, International Educational Services, program coordinator Ruben Gallegos, Jr., helped me interview dozens of migrant children.

In Chiapas, Grupo Beta Sur, and specifically agent Julio César Cancino Gálvez, helped me safely access some of the most dangerous spots where migrants travel, including the train tops. Olga Sánchez Martínez and her family took me into their home and showed me true generosity. Others who gave much of their time in Chiapas were Olivia Ruiz, Hugo Ángeles Cruz, Jorge Reinoso, Gabriela Coutiño, and Sara Isela Hernández Herrera.

In Nuevo Laredo, I thank Padre Leonardo López Guajardo

and four nuns who are instrumental to his work, Elizabeth Rangel, María del Tepeyac, Leonor Palacios, and Juanita Montecillo. I also want to thank human rights activist Raymundo Ramos Vásquez.

In Texas, Border Patrol trackers Charles Grout and Manuel Sauceda gave me invaluable insights. In Los Angeles, I owe much of my understanding of how these separations hurt families to former Newcomer School counselor Gabriel Murillo.

Finally, the person I most want to thank is my husband, Bill Regensburger, who endured my long absences as I reported this book, and who has always been a loving, patient, and ardent supporter of my work.

ABOUT THE AUTHOR

SONIA NAZARIO, a projects reporter for the *Los Angeles Times,* has spent more than two decades reporting and writing about social issues. Her stories have tackled some of this country's biggest issues: hunger, drug addiction, immigration.

She has won numerous national awards. In 2003, her story of a Honduran boy's struggle to find his mother in the United States, entitled "Enrique's Journey," won more than a dozen awards, among them the Pulitzer Prize for feature writing, the George Polk Award for International Reporting, the Grand Prize of the Robert F. Kennedy Journalism Award, and the National Association of Hispanic Journalists Guillermo Martinez-Marquez Award for Overall Excellence. In 1998, she was a Pulitzer Prize finalist for a series on children of drug-addicted parents. In 1994, she won a George Polk Award for Local Reporting for a series on hunger.

Nazario grew up in Kansas and Argentina and has written extensively from Latin America and about Latinos in the United States. She began her career at *The Wall Street Journal,* where she reported from four bureaus: New York, Atlanta, Miami, and Los Angeles. In 1993, she joined the *Los Angeles Times.* She is a graduate of Williams College and has a master's degree in Latin American studies from the University of California, Berkeley. She lives in Los Angeles with her husband.

ABOUT THE TYPE

This book was set in Baskerville, a typeface which was designed by John Baskerville, an amateur printer and type-founder, and cut for him by John Handy in 1750. The type became popular again when The Lanston Monotype Corporation of London revived the classic Roman face in 1923. The Mergenthaler Linotype Company in England and the United States cut a version of Baskerville in 1931, making it one of the most widely used typefaces today.